deep focus

Engaging Culture

WILLIAM A. DYRNESS
AND ROBERT K. JOHNSTON,
SERIES EDITORS

The Engaging Culture series is designed to help Christians respond with theological discernment to our contemporary culture. Each volume explores particular cultural expressions, seeking to discover God's presence in the world and to involve readers in sympathetic dialogue and active discipleship. These books encourage neither an uninformed rejection nor an uncritical embrace of culture, but active engagement informed by theological reflection.

deep focus

FILM AND THEOLOGY IN DIALOGUE

robert k. johnston,
craig detweiler,
and kutter callaway

B

Baker Academic
a division of Baker Publishing Group
Grand Rapids, Michigan

© 2019 by Robert K. Johnston, Craig Detweiler, and Kutter Callaway

Published by Baker Academic
a division of Baker Publishing Group
PO Box 6287, Grand Rapids, MI 49516-6287
www.bakeracademic.com

Printed in the United States of America

Library of Congress Cataloging-in-Publication Data
Names: Johnston, Robert K., 1945– author.
Title: Deep focus : film and theology in dialogue / Robert K. Johnston, Craig Detweiler, and Kutter
  Callaway.
Description: Grand Rapids : Baker Publishing Group, 2019. | Series: Engaging culture | Includes
  bibliographical references and index.
Identifiers: LCCN 2018036418 | ISBN 9781540960030 (pbk. : alk. paper)
Subjects: LCSH: Motion pictures—Religious aspects—Christianity. | Motion pictures—Moral and
  ethical aspects.
Classification: LCC PN1995.9.C49 J64 2019 | DDC 791.43/6823—dc23
LC record available at https://lccn.loc.gov/2018036418

ISBN 978-1-5409-6150-1 (casebound)

19 20 21 22 23 24 25   7 6 5 4 3 2 1

green
press
INITIATIVE

#1 0393 98655

To our family, friends, colleagues,
and students
who, like the finest films,
continually prod us
to open our eyes so that we may see
and our ears so that we may hear

contents

acknowledgments

This book reflects a combined sixty years of teaching classes in film and theology by the three of us. We thank the several thousand students we have had whose collective wisdom shines forth on every page. Our book has taken on depth and texture because of the insights and questions of these students, whether at Fuller Seminary, Biola University, Regent College, California State University Fullerton, Pepperdine University, Acadia School of Theology, or the Seattle School of Theology & Psychology. We would also like to thank our many colleagues in the academy and in the film industry who have shaped our research and writing on theology and film. We are deeply indebted to this community of scholars and practitioners who not only inspire our work but also share our love of moving pictures.

Craig and Kutter would also like to offer an additional word of thanks to Rob Johnston, our mentor, colleague, and dear friend. It is not often that one gets the chance to learn from a person who literally wrote the book on a given topic, but in our case it's true. The first edition of *Reel Spirituality* was a landmark book in what was, at the time, only a nascent discipline. When the second edition hit the shelves in 2006, it quickly became the seminal text in an ever-expanding field. The doctoral research we pursued under Rob's tutelage and the subsequent books we have written simply would not have existed if it were not for Rob's pioneering work. We are both grateful and humbled to have coauthored with Rob this follow-up to *Reel Spirituality*. In a previous era, it would be customary to honor the life's work of a scholar like Rob with a Festschrift. But Rob would likely balk at the idea of an entire volume dedicated to him. In a very real sense, our contributions to this book are written in honor of Rob. Even though the book is not about him, every last page is the product of his ongoing influence in our individual lives and in the field of theology and film as a whole.

introduction

a phoropter for film

I didn't want you to enjoy the film. I wanted you to look very closely at your own soul.

—Sam Peckinpah, filmmaker

The Adjustment Bureau (2011) is a movie whose genre is hard to pin down. Matt Damon stars as David, an ambitious congressman drawn to ballet dancer Elise (Emily Blunt). Yet a mysterious bureau of men in black hats seems determined to keep them apart. Is *The Adjustment Bureau* an action/suspense thriller, like *The Bourne Ultimatum*, which this movie's writer and director, George Nolfi, also cowrote? Perhaps it is a political drama? But the plot revolves around a romance suffused with science-fiction elements (based on a short story by Philip K. Dick). Thanks to a character identified as the Chairman, it also includes evocative religious ideas that invite reflection around the theme of free will and destiny. Most cross-genre films don't work; *The Adjustment Bureau* is an exception. Nolfi has given us a movie that teenagers and adults alike enjoy—and then ponder.

When postproduction on the movie was complete, the studio was still trying to sharpen its marketing strategy and decided to reach out to the Reel Spirituality Institute at Fuller Seminary. They arranged for an initial prescreening of the movie at a nearby Cineplex with seating for close to three hundred. Nolfi was at the screening anonymously, as were the studio marketing people. Rob Johnston stood up after the movie and asked the audience two questions: How many believed that their parents had married the person God intended for them? And how many believed that their parents had freely chosen the person

1

The Adjustment Bureau (2011), © MRC II Distribution Company L.P.

they fell in love with? With each question, roughly half of the audience raised their hands, and then everyone laughed. What had been put into a story by Nolfi resonated with the stories of everyone in the theater. Somehow we are destined and yet free—at the same time.

A lively discussion followed about the film and about the audience's understanding of how destiny played out in their own lives. Is there, as Aquinas, Luther, and Calvin claimed, a secret plan, something in addition to God's revealed will that governs our lives? There is in the movie. At a second screening to a full house, a rabbi and an imam joined Johnston and Nolfi for an interreligious dialogue about David and Elise's free will, or lack thereof. How did we understand the God of Abraham, a God we all believed in, to be directing the lives of women and men? The same quandaries proved common to us all.

In an interview with the Writers Guild of America, Nolfi reflected: "Film is a way to raise larger questions in a way that people want to engage with as opposed to it smelling like spinach. Academic philosophers talk to a really small group of people who are also academics, but the question of what society values is hugely important for everything from whether or not the Egyptian army fires on its own people to whether we have health care in the United States that tries to include everybody."[1]

Universal Studios asked Reel Spirituality to prescreen the film still a third time to a large audience in Orange County, California, where Craig Detweiler and Catholic nun Rose Pacatte, FSP, joined Rob for a postscreening discussion. Based on these screenings and conversations, the studio decided to market the movie as entertainment for adults that invited viewers to look closer and to delve deeper into life's meaning and possibilities. Reflection on free will and fate became part of the marketing plan. And the strategy worked. *The Adjustment Bureau*, which cost approximately $50 million to make, grossed $128 million worldwide!

Conversation around theology and film is not like eating filet mignon or truffles—something done only by a small elite but irrelevant to the larger population. No, being engaged by a movie and invited to look closer can be a weekly event that is as near as your neighborhood movie theater, where the story's deep focus reveals life's possibilities and problems. But not everyone can clearly see. As in life, many of us are aided by wearing glasses with carefully calibrated lenses. This book provides a series of lenses to help us discern more clearly the images projected before us.

In creating the appropriate lenses for the viewing glasses we wear, ophthalmologists make use of a phoropter. Though you might not know the instrument by its name, most of us know this machine. It is that oversized piece of equipment in the eye doctor's office used to determine the prescription for glasses. The machine switches multiple lenses in front of your eyes with the goal of finding that combination that can improve your vision. A phoropter is used to fine-tune your focus, to help your vision be as clear and accurate as possible. This book seeks to function as a phoropter. By presenting a series of lenses through which to view movies—narrative, audiovisual, critical, theological, ecclesial, historical, ethical, cultural, and converging—we seek to provide you, the reader, with tools ("spectacles") to achieve a deep focus. After two introductory chapters ("Coming Attractions"), the next three chapters ("Act I") deal with how the more formal aspects of film contribute to its meaning; another three ("Act II") deal with the theological as a useful critical perspective; and the final two ("Act III") suggest how a dialogue between the formal and the substantive aspects of film can clarify meaning.

A theological lens helped bring clarity to the viewing of *The Adjustment Bureau* by its studio. Just as film theorists have sometimes used feminist theory, or psychoanalytic theory, or perhaps postcolonial theory to bring a movie's story into focus, so theology can be helpful in providing a clarity of vision that otherwise might be lacking. Many films, on closer inspection, invite their viewers to consider life on a more spiritually centered level. They invite us to explore not only life, but Life. During modernity, such transcendent possibilities for film viewing were often questioned. However, since the turn of the millennium, an increasing number of viewers and film critics have come to recognize a movie's invitation to explore ultimate questions and to pursue theological possibilities. Movies can invite personal discovery and at times even prove revelatory.

Get Out (2017), © Universal City Studios Productions LLLP

A theological lens isn't the only one that can clarify our sight. Formal, critical lenses are equally important to our understanding. *Get Out* (2017) follows the conventions of a horror movie, as filmgoers literally scream at a young African American man, Chris Washington, to get out of the rural house of the diabolical Armitage family. Filmmaker Jordan Peele described his groundbreaking box-office smash as a "social thriller." *Get Out* tapped into the cultural zeitgeist in bold ways, cutting through the patina of liberal politics surrounding race, class, and power. When asked to explain why audiences responded so positively to his cinematic provocation, Peele said, "I think people are scared to talk about race and when we suppress things— ideas, thoughts, feelings, fears—they need to get out in some way. I think 'Get Out' is a film that satisfies the need to think about, discuss and deal with race but it does it in a way that's more comfortable because it's fun."[2] *Get Out* invites robust discussions of filmmaker intention, genre reinvention, and cultural tension.

An analysis of one key scene, "The Descent of Chris into the Sunken Place," reveals so much about how cinema works. Sitting in her warm-toned house, psychologist Missy Armitage (Catherine Keener) begins to ask Chris (Daniel Kaluuya) about his past, focusing on the trauma of losing his mother. Chris is slowly hypnotized by the sound of Missy's spoon, rotating around her teacup. The camera pushes closer to Chris's tear-stained face as he recalls the feelings of helplessness that engulfed him. He flashes back to a suppressed memory of himself as a boy, sitting in front of a television, scared to confront the painful reality of losing a beloved parent. The shots alternate between Missy, the teacup, Chris's hands, and his face, riddled with shame and grief. The intercut sounds of Missy's voice, the circling spoon, and the musical score rise until

Chris is locked in place. Missy makes an ominous command: "Now, sink into the floor." The music stops. She insists, "Sink."

The scene cuts to Chris, falling to dark, bottomless depths as reality fades away. *Get Out* shifts to a fantastic, metaphorical place where Chris plunges further from the living room. There are no frames of reference in this black pit of despair. Words fail him in this limbo. More ominous musical notes rise. We are snapped back to Chris, still in Missy's house, but staring directly at the camera. Director Jordan Peele breaks the fourth wall as Missy now also stares directly into Chris's face (and at the audience). We see the horror from Chris's perspective, staring out and being stared at. *Get Out* places viewers within the highly subjective experience of being turned into a helpless, mute object. Missy announces, "Now, you're in the sunken place." Chris cries out, but his voice is not heard. He is powerless to escape—paralyzed on the surface, reaching out in a desperate cry for relief from within a private, isolated hellhole. Acting, cinematography, and sound transport us all to a sunken place of unfathomable despair.

What is the sunken place? It is a frightening place of paralysis. It is riddled with inchoate longing: the horror of being voiceless, unheard, and unable to alter our situation. It is the experience of far too many African Americans across history and even today. Journalist Ross Lincoln called the sunken place "particularly horrifying because it works as a metaphor for not only the literal history of slavery, but for cultural appropriation and the use of social niceties to enforce social hierarchies." This potent metaphor woke many to the feelings within a politically polarized America. Peele acknowledged the ways in which "we're all in the Sunken Place," tweeting, "The Sunken Place means we're marginalized. No matter how hard we scream, the system silences us."[3]

From this formal analysis of cinematic technique, we open up to a larger discussion of immensely important cultural touchstones. When we place a film like *Get Out* into deep theological focus, we may also sharpen our understanding of God and Scripture. We may read with new acuity the first verse of Psalm 22: "My God, my God, why have you forsaken me? Why are you so far from saving me, so far from my cries of anguish?" The frustrated exclamations of Job—"Though I cry, 'Violence!' I get no response; though I call for help, there is no justice" (Job 19:7)—take on new urgency. The complaints of the prophet Habakkuk—"Why do you make me look at injustice? Why do you tolerate wrongdoing?" (Hab. 1:3)—emerge as both timely and timeless when placed alongside the sunken place of *Get Out*. Both *Get Out* and the Bible are laden with people crying out and reaching up in a desperate plea for help, for relief, for justice. Applying various lenses to film and theology can spark conversations of the utmost depth, urgency, and importance.

Indeed, *Deep Focus* was itself born from a series of ongoing conversations between the three of us about the cinema and its theological significance. As this conversation emerged, we learned a great deal not only about the power of creative collaborations but also about the vital role that an interpretive community plays in both expanding and clarifying one's vision. Thus, what started as a small group project has extended far beyond the three of us to include the perceptive insights of numerous other scholars, film critics, and filmgoers, as well as the historic theological tradition of which we are each a part. Our hope is that the book sparks similar discussion and reflection among fellow film fans, small groups, college students, seminary classes, and faith communities.

Let us, then, look through the rotating lenses of the following chapters as they help us deepen our focus. We will begin with a reflection on the power of story—on why we go to the movies in the first place.

coming attractions

1

the power of film

The task I'm trying to achieve is above all to make you see.
—D. W. Griffith, filmmaker

Sister Rose Pacatte, a film educator and reviewer for the *St. Anthony Messenger*, tells of going to the movie theater to see *The Missing* (2003). Dressed in street clothes, she sat next to a young professional woman with whom she struck up a conversation. Sister Rose asked, "Why did you come to the movies today?" The woman replied, "This is the third movie I've seen today. I think my boyfriend is going to propose to me today, and I'm not sure I am ready. I always come to the movies when I have to figure out my life." "So you needed a retreat or spiritual direction," Sister Rose commented, "but you came to the movies." "That's what I and my friends always do," was the reply. "We can always find solutions in the movies."[1]

Stories like these abound, but they highlight a fairly simple fact: movies function as a primary source of power and meaning for people navigating the complexities of life in our contemporary world. Along with the church, the synagogue, the mosque, and the temple, movies often provide people stories through which they can understand the world in which we live. There are plenty of vibrant and meaningful places of worship. But as Sister Rose's story suggests, both those within and those outside the church recognize that movies are providing primary stories around which we shape our lives. Movies block out the distractions around us and encourage an attentiveness toward life. Presenting to viewers aspects of their daily realities, both intimate and profound, movies exercise our moral and religious imaginations. They allow us to try things on. From the cinematic stories we encounter, our spirits quicken.

Robert McKee, author of *Story*, wholeheartedly agrees:

> Religion, for many, has become an empty ritual that masks hypocrisy. As our faith in traditional ideologies diminishes, we turn to the source we still believe in: the art of story. The world now consumes films, novels, theater, and television in such quantities and with such ravenous hunger that the story arts have become humanity's prime source of inspiration, as it seeks to order chaos and gain insight into life. Our appetite for story is a reflection of the profound human need to grasp the patterns of living, not merely as an intellectual exercise, but within a very personal, emotional experience.[2]

In other words, we could describe a world without stories in a number of ways, but "human" would most certainly not be one of those ways. We are narrative beings through and through. Stories not only structure our world emotionally, but they also serve as the "vehicle that carries us on our search for reality, our best effort to make sense out of the anarchy of existence."[3]

In our contemporary world, cinematic stories are just as much part of our life as eating, sleeping, and interacting on social media. Box-office revenues in North America and around the world are solid despite the proliferation of online streaming services.[4] Indeed, the perceived economic threat of the streaming revolution has, in many ways, reinforced and elevated the "event-like" pleasures of theatergoing. As *Los Angeles Times* critic Mary McNamara puts it, "There ain't no home screen high enough, ain't no smartphone wide enough, no noise-cancelling headphones deep enough, to ever replace the full body and mind immersion of going to the movies. 'Going to the movies' is a personal and cultural through-line, an ever-shifting ritual by which we mark our own changing lives."[5]

With companies like Netflix, Hulu, and Amazon purchasing and producing their own slate of first-run films at increasing rates, film-going has shifted rather dramatically from the Cineplex to the home (or anywhere we carry a smartphone). The aggregate result is that more people are watching more films more often than ever before. Yet movies are more than profit margins and box-office receipts. Their broader cultural value cannot be reduced to the big data concerning Netflix traffic, social media impressions, and advertising dollars. Movies serve not simply as a commodity but as the primary storytelling medium of the twenty-first century, interpreting reality for us, providing us with a common language, and acting as a type of cultural glue.

For instance, when the planes crashed into the towers on 9/11, witnesses said the scene looked like something from a disaster movie. As they recounted the terrifying details of being at ground zero on that fateful day, numerous Manhattan residents referenced the Bruce Willis movies *Die Hard* (1988), *The Siege* (1998), and *Armageddon* (1998) as a way of making sense of the violence and chaos they had encountered.[6] Reality seemed, on that day, less real than the reels on the big screen. Their only frame of reference for this kind of terrorism was what they had already witnessed in movies. In the years that have followed, films like *United 93* (2006), *Extremely Loud & Incredibly Close* (2011), and *Zero Dark Thirty* (2012) continue to serve as constant reminders of that fateful day, prodding us neither to forget nor to overly romanticize the past. In many respects, these movies represent the primary material artifacts of our shared cultural memory.[7]

Thus, in ways both big and small, the cinema has become an important means of cultural communication, a contemporary language in need of understanding and explication—which is why certain institutions of higher education, like the University of Southern California, now encourage undergraduates to take at least one cinema/television course in order to learn how to "read and write" with media. It's also why movies are commonly used as part of the core curriculum in such disparate fields as philosophy, sociology, English, religion, and psychology. Some even believe that cinema studies is positioned to become the new MBA, a means of general preparation for careers in fields as diverse as law and the military.[8] Indeed, at the risk of overstatement, anyone who does not have some basic awareness of the power and meaning of film cannot possibly understand contemporary culture. It's just that important.

A Deep(er) Focus

The power of a movie lies first of all in what transpires within the individual viewer as she or he gazes at the screen. Like any well-told story, certain films have the capacity to provide us with a richer variety of experience than would normally be possible. Films serve as a kind of deep focus lens for the viewer, bringing clarity and insight to otherwise opaque and enigmatic realities. Producer Jerry Bruckheimer declared, "We are in the transportation business."[9]

Jerry Sittser's book *A Grace Disguised* provides a powerful example of how film stories can bring about this deep focus. Jerry is a religion professor at Whitworth College in Spokane, Washington. The book relates his response to the catastrophic loss of his wife, his mother, and one of his daughters in a car crash in 1991. A drunk driver hit the van he was driving, and only Jerry and three of his young children survived. Five years later, he wrote his book reflecting on how a person might grow through loss.

Sittser shared that among the things that helped him and his children to cope were the stories of countless others—friends, strangers who wrote to him, and even those they read about or saw on the screen. After commenting on the stories that had helped him personally, Sittser turned to reflect on the stories that were meaningful to his children, Catherine (eight years old at the time), David (seven), and John (only two). Quoting Sittser:

> The children read books and watched movies that somehow touched on the theme of loss. John asked me to read *Bambi* dozens of times after the accident. He made me pause every time we came to the section that told the story of the death of Bambi's mother. Sometimes he said nothing, and the two of us sat in a sad silence. Sometimes he cried. He talked about the similarity between Bambi's story and his own. "Bambi lost his mommy too," he said on several occasions. Then he added, "And Bambi became the Prince of the Forest." . . . Catherine found comfort in Disney's movie version of *Beauty and the Beast* because the main character, Belle, grew up without a mother and, as Catherine has observed, became an independent, intelligent, beautiful person.[10]

Here then is the power of the cinema writ large. On a deeply personal level, this animated film about a compassionate, intelligent, and liberated woman (who loves to read!) helped to redeem the life of one little girl whose mother had died.

But Disney's version of Belle didn't have to be a bookworm. In fact, she almost wasn't. Speaking in October 1998 at a seminar in Hollywood, Linda Woolverton, the screenwriter of *Beauty and the Beast*, recounted her struggle with the executives at Disney to keep Belle as a reader, someone whose main love was books. The Disney brass felt that reading was boring when portrayed on the screen. They wanted a more active hobby, something more physical in nature. Linda argued, however, that by making Belle an intelligent woman with a love for literature, the film could provide a stronger, more positive role model for young female viewers. Linda won the argument, and Catherine Sittser benefited.

That Belle might have been different, and that even the slightest change to her character might have impacted a whole generation of filmgoers like Catherine, is a reflection of the real power of film as it comes to bear on both our individual stories and the larger story of our common culture. The character of Belle was so beloved that Disney brought her back for a live-action version of *Beauty and the Beast* in 2017 (starring Emma Watson as Belle). It was one of a number of films released in 2017 featuring strong female leads and/or written and directed by women filmmakers (e.g., *Wonder Woman*, *Lady Bird*, *Mudbound*, *Disobedience*, *Girls Trip*, *The Beguiled*, *The Zookeeper's Wife*). Lamentably, Hollywood still has a long way to go when it comes to incorporating the voices of (strong) women (a topic we'll address further in upcoming chapters), but when taken together, the critical acclaim and financial success of these films underscores their power to capture the contemporary cultural imagination.

The year 2017 also happened to coincide with the twenty-fifth anniversary of director Penny Marshall's *A League of Their Own* (1992). Starring Geena Davis, Rosie O'Donnell, and Madonna as baseball players, and Tom Hanks as their begrudging manager, the movie tells the story of the first female professional baseball league, formed during World War II. At the time of its release, it was an important movie in its own right. But Geena Davis's anniversary reflection on the way it shaped not only her own sense of self but also that of the countless young girls who watched the movie over the course of its twenty-five-year history stands as a testament to the enduring power of film narratives. As Davis narrates,

> [*A League of Their Own*] was huge. It was very pivotal to my life in multiple ways. One was experiencing the reaction of young girls to the movie and so many girls and young women saying, "I took up sports because of that movie." I still have the same number of girls and women telling me they play sports because of that movie now as I did then. It's like a rite of passage to see this movie. It's got remarkable longevity. Also, just on a personal level, I had never really played any sports, and I definitely couldn't play baseball when I got cast. And so I trained really hard, and it was the first time that I was told that I had untapped athletic ability, which was an incredible compliment in my book, and so I felt like I really did, and it changed everything about my self-esteem and my self-confidence.[11]

Such is the power of film—not only for those who watch movies but for those who make them as well.

Sociocultural Power

As Geena Davis's comments suggest, movies are not only meaningful for individuals; they can also have a significant impact on the broader society. When a cartoonist named Walt Disney created the character Bambi, deer hunting nosedived in one year from a $5.7 million business to $1 million.[12] On a more trivial level, sales of Reese's Pieces candy tripled within two weeks after their use in *E. T. the Extra-Terrestrial* (1982), while Tom Cruise helped boost sales of two brands of sunglasses—first Ray-Ban, which he wore in *Risky Business* (1983), and then Oakley, whose sales increased after the company paid to have Cruise use its glasses to receive instructions in *Mission: Impossible II* (2000). Similarly, sales of pinot noir increased and became the wine of choice after being featured in *Sideways* (2004). The movie also spawned a tour of the Santa Barbara County wineries used as locations in the movie, just as Omaha, Nebraska, has its own tour of sites used in other Alexander Payne movies—*Citizen Ruth* (1996), *Election* (1999), and *About Schmidt* (2002).[13]

"Film-induced pilgrimages" of this kind don't seem to be slowing down either.[14] *Amelie* (2001) sparked tours of Paris, rejuvenating the corner of Montmartre where she "lived." *Into the Wild* (2007) continues to call sojourners to Fairbanks Bus 142 in Alaska where twenty-four-year-old Chris McCandless died in 1992. And New Zealand tourism went up significantly as a result of *The Hobbit* films (2012, 2013, 2014), *The Lord of the Rings* trilogy (2001, 2002, 2003), and *The Chronicles of Narnia: The Lion, the Witch and the Wardrobe* (2005).[15]

Beyond tourism patterns and consumer purchasing habits, though, certain films have played key roles in bringing about deeper shifts within the sociocultural imagination. *Blackfish* (2013), for example, examined the plight of killer whales held in captivity at SeaWorld. In response to the film, numerous musical acts, business partners, and sponsors cut ties with the well-known marine zoological park. Government legislation banned entertainment-driven orca captivity in response to the documentary. The company's stock value fell by 50 percent within a year of the film's release. SeaWorld is now phasing out the orca show, and there will be no more breeding of these beautiful animals in captivity. A small, independent documentary film can effect real social change. From climate change (e.g., *An Inconvenient Truth* [2006] and *An Inconvenient Sequel: Truth to Power* [2017]) to America's educational system (e.g., *Waiting for Superman* [2010]), or even the ill effects of corporate food production (*Super Size Me* [2004] and *Food, Inc.* [2008]), documentary films are uniquely positioned to raise our social consciousness and, in some cases, provoke actual change.

Film's impact on society doesn't always move in a progressive or even positive direction, though. Consider the example of smoking onscreen. In 2012, the US surgeon general released a report that illustrated a direct causal relationship between youth who watched smoking in the movies and those who started to smoke.[16] Yet, in spite of these findings, tobacco use in the top-grossing US movies increased by 80 percent from 2015 to 2016, a marked reversal from the overall decline in tobacco use in major Hollywood films between 1950 and 2006.[17] Reflecting on this unsettling recent trend, Craig Detweiler says, "The tension arises because filmmakers are often going for a particular look or feel. Smoke is very photogenic, and actors are always looking for something to do with their hands, a bit of business. . . . I think the challenge is for studios and filmmakers to put ethics ahead of aesthetics."[18] It is one thing to acknowledge the power of film to inspire and enliven; it is quite another to suggest that, because film's aesthetic power is never straightforward or simple, filmmakers bear a unique kind of social responsibility with the mass art they create.

In addition to addressing (or sometimes failing to address) any number of social concerns, film has become, increasingly, where the public learns its history. *Dances with Wolves* (1990) offers us a Lakota perspective on the Civil War. *Schindler's List* (1993) chronicles the horrors of the Holocaust. *Good Night, and Good Luck* (2005) recaptures the paranoia of the McCarthy era. *12 Years a Slave* (2013) and *The Birth of a Nation* (2016) underscore our brutal, racist roots; *Malcolm X* (1992) and *Selma* (2014) show us the civil rights struggle; *BlacKkKlansman* (2018) uses the story of a black police officer in late-1970s Colorado Springs who infiltrates the KKK and links that story with white supremacists in Charlottesville today. *The Hurt Locker* (2008) and *Lone Survivor* (2013) give us our (limited) understanding of the wars in Iraq and Afghanistan; some have argued that *MASH* (1970), though ostensibly about the Korean War, was meant to teach its contemporary viewers about the irrationality and inhumanity of the Vietnam War.

If the intent of a film like *MASH* is open to such differing interpretations, it would be difficult to harbor any illusion about director Steven Spielberg's intention in *Saving Private Ryan* (1998). Just as he hoped, it has become a primary shaper of opinion concerning World War II. Tom Hanks, the lead actor, took up the cause of veterans as a result of his experience. For some whose fathers and mothers fought in these wars but came home silent about the horrors they experienced, the film has brought new dialogue and healing. Younger people came to understand for the first time something of the sacrifices that were made during the war. Some, after seeing the film, even went so far as to reach out to veterans, who were in their seventies at the time, to thank them for what they had done.[19]

Culturally speaking, though, the power of film is not limited to merchandising, social action, or history lessons. In his provocative book *Life: The Movie* (1998), Neal Gabler views American culture itself as taking on the characteristics of a movie. Life in the West has become show business for many, where we each play a role and long for our moment of celebrity. Gabler argues that it is not politics or economics but entertainment "that is arguably the most pervasive, powerful, and ineluctable force of our time—a force so overwhelming that it has finally metastasized into life."[20] Motion picture entertainment—fun, accessible to everyone, sensuous, offering a release from order and authority—has captured the American spirit.

The conversion of life into an entertainment medium is pervasive. Gabler observes that in the late 1990s, we were coached in our roles by Martha Stewart, and our costume designer was Ralph Lauren. Since then, the effects have only been amplified. Ideas have become sound bites, reduced to 280 characters. Not only do politicians appear first on talk shows like *The Late Show with Stephen Colbert* and *The Daily Show with Trevor Noah*, but news programming that once featured "hard journalism" is now pitched almost entirely for our enjoyment; it is prime-time fare. Hard news is increasingly written using the techniques of fiction, so that it can be read at Starbucks on a smartphone app. The apotheosis of this phenomenon was the election of Donald Trump to the highest office in the land—a reality-TV star who seems perfectly comfortable running the US government in the same way he hosted NBC's *The Apprentice*. It's crass and highly controversial entertainment, but his core demographic loves every minute of it. So it is only slightly ironic that, although the network ratings for his TV appearances as president are through the roof, his approval numbers could not be worse.

Blurring the lines between the "real world" and the "reel world" even further is the fact that almost everyone today carries a highly sophisticated camera in the palm of their hands. Our incessant need to capture it all on "film" causes many to encounter life primarily through the screen of their smartphone. Whether it's a child's first steps, a friend's wedding, or something far more mundane, life itself has become a performance to be filmed, edited, and posted on social media, where the "real" event takes place. Indeed, filmed acts of violence like terrorist attacks, police shootings, and racially charged street demonstrations often take on a digital life of their own long after the actual events transpire. These cinematic displays not only shape the court of public opinion (and even the actual courtroom) but also demonstrate the ways in which our memories and firsthand experiences are now filtered predominately through a camera's lens. The clever thriller *Searching* (2018) demonstrates that our lives have become so mediated via screens that an entire film could be composed from just the digital footprints captured on our devices. This is not about life and art simply imitating one another; it is rather that the two are no longer distinguishable.

As Gabler demonstrates, movies play an increasingly significant role in defining both ourselves and our society. Or as controversial director Elia Kazan said, film is now "the language of [hu]mankind."[21] Movies broaden our exposure to the world and provide alternate interpretations of life's meaning and significance. Values and images are formed in response to life's experiences, with movies providing the data of countless new stories. Movies have become a type of lingua franca. Who doesn't know the story of *Titanic* (1997)? Think, too, of the millions of children who have seen *Toy Story 3* (2010) or *Moana* (2016). The greeting "Wakanda forever" crossed over from *Black Panther* (2018) into communities inspired by the robust vision of the technologically advanced African nation. *Crazy Rich Asians* (2018) recast the Cinderella story in a Singaporean context that became a source of profound ethnic pride for so many underrepresented filmgoers around the globe. We all long to be seen, to relate to characters and their struggles on screen. Even in the church or the synagogue, theological discussion is more likely to happen following a movie than a sermon.[22] Put differently, movies are more than entertaining diversions from what matters; they are life stories that both interpret us and are interpreted by us.

Silver Screen Sanctuaries

Even though most of us watch movies and, in some cases, are deeply affected by them, we seldom try to understand what we have seen, let alone relate it to our wider religious beliefs and practices. Film is seen as one thing, religious faith as quite another. Such a disconnect is understandable, at least on the surface. Movies are, on one level, a somewhat trivial form of entertainment, a luxury of modern life. Our spiritual faith, on the other hand, concerns our vocation and destiny; it is foundational. But such easy dichotomies crumble under closer scrutiny. Worship services also entertain (consider the pageantry and music), while movies sometimes engage us at the core of our being.

Reflecting on his experience as a young boy, director Martin Scorsese remembers going to the movie theater with his family: "The first sensation was that of entering a magical world—the soft carpet, the smell of fresh popcorn, the darkness, the sense of safety, and, above all, sanctuary—much the same in my mind as entering a church. A place of dreams. A place that excited and stretched my imagination."[23] To borrow the words of French filmmaker Eric Rohmer, the cinema was for Scorsese "the cathedral of the twentieth century."[24]

In light of these kinds of comments, it is easy to make facile comparisons between screen and sanctuary: popcorn and Coke in place of bread and wine; ticket price for tithe; high ceilings to suggest transcendence; attendees speaking in hushed tones while they expectantly await the start; a certain ritual involved with where we sit and how often we go; a sense of disappointment—even betrayal—if the event falls short of expectations. But behind all such forced analogies is the primary fact that both cinema and church provide "life-orienting images."[25] As Read Mercer Schuchardt suggests in a commentary on the website Metaphilm, "Like religion, a good movie really does answer the only three questions worth asking in life: who you are, where you come from, and what you should do."[26]

Or listen to George Miller, the producer of films as diverse as *Happy Feet* (2006) and *Mad Max: Fury Road* (2015): "I believe cinema is now the most powerful secular religion and people gather in cinemas to experience things collectively the way they once did in church. The cinema storytellers have become the new priests. They're doing a lot of the work of our religious institutions, which have so concretized the metaphors in their stories, taken so much of the poetry, mystery and mysticism out of religious belief, that people look for other places to question their spirituality."[27]

In the pages that follow, we will consider whether Christian theology, as Miller suggests, has become overly rationalized to the detriment of the life-transforming power of its original story. For now, we acknowledge that movies provide for many alternate forms of transcendence—encounters that take place outside the confines of the church but are nonetheless understood to be religiously significant.

For instance, Catherine Barsotti, our colleague at Fuller Seminary and co-editor of *Finding God in the Movies* and *God in the Movies*, points to Peter Weir's *The Year of Living Dangerously* (1982) as a deeply spiritual film that had a transformative effect on her. Barsotti describes Weir's film as a turning point in her life, a moment of conversion. Being immersed in the pain and poverty of Jakarta, seeing it both literally and figuratively through the eyes of Billy Kwan, she could not escape the question that Billy asks Guy, quoting Tolstoy (who is quoting Luke 3:10): "What then must we do?" Billy goes on to tell Guy that Tolstoy sold all he had to relieve the suffering around him. Guy is not persuaded, believing that government leaders and structures should be involved, not him. Billy himself had tried to respond personally by providing money for a young prostitute and her sick child. But when the boy dies from drinking polluted water, Billy can no longer avoid political involvement. Pounding out on his typewriter the same question, "What then must we do?," Billy decides to challenge President Sukarno to feed his people. He hangs a banner over a balcony and is killed for his action. Quoting Barsotti directly:

> "What then must we do?" I left the theater with that phrase and the agonizing eyes of the children of Jakarta burned onto the screen of my mind. In Luke 3, we first hear this question as John the Baptist is preaching repentance and calling the people to bear fruit worthy of their conversion. When the crowd doesn't get it and asks, "What then must we do?" he tells them to live ethically and generously: "Whoever has two coats must share with anyone who has none; and whoever has food must do likewise." Or to tax collectors, "Collect no more than the amount prescribed for you" (vv. 11, 13). In Luke 4, we hear Jesus echoing the same ethic and compassion as he begins his ministry with these words: "The Spirit of the Lord is upon me, because he has anointed me to bring good news to the poor. He has sent me to proclaim release to the captives and recovery of sight to the blind, to let the oppressed go free" (v. 18).
>
> A combination of people, events in my life, and the Holy Spirit had prepared me to see this film. It became a turning point, a recovery of sight. The next week I returned to my project at work, appraising a hospital, but I saw the world

differently. Within weeks I applied for a leave of absence and within months left for Mexico to work as a short-term missionary. Six months after my return, I resigned my position to start my own appraisal business in which I would work only thirty hours a week so that I could give myself to the youth of my church and community, to the financial and political struggle to build a shelter for women and children in my city, and to study in the area of cross-cultural theology and ministry. The last twenty-two years have included a variety of tasks, jobs, ministries, and people. And it seems that Billy Kwan's, Tolstoy's, and the Bible's question still rings in my ears, "What then must we do?"[28]

Weir's movie became the means by which Barsotti heard her incarnate Lord compelling her to answer this question in concrete ways. And it changed her life.

Origin Stories

The three of us (Rob, Craig, and Kutter) can each identify a number of cinematic encounters that, like Barsotti's, have not merely communicated abstract truth that we later recognized as appropriately religious or orthodox but have actually transformed our lives. As academic theologians who have each published previous work in the area of theology and film, our first-order experiences with the revelatory power of film have motivated a great deal of our scholarly research and writing. Movies have functioned for us, in various times and situations, as cautionary tales, as moments of spiritual encouragement, and even as opportunities to hear God speak. They have served as occasions for encountering the Spirit's wider revelatory presence, both redeeming and redirecting our lives.

In what follows, we offer a few examples of our own personal stories, in hopes of setting the stage for the remainder of the book, which represents our attempt to grapple theologically with the power of film in our own lives and the lives of so many others.

Craig Detweiler on Raging Bull *(1980)*[29]

Movies may have been my first love, but as I emerged from Martin Scorsese's *Raging Bull*, I was catapulted toward a different kind of obsession. Robert DeNiro's haunting portrait of boxing champ Jake LaMotta left me beaten and bruised. I watched the perils of self-immolation, as Jake destroyed his relationships with his brother, his wife, and his fans. Jake ends up alone, in jail, literally banging his head against the wall crying, "Why? Why? Why?" As a high school jock with my own independent streak, I recognized far too much of myself in Jake. As the film ended, director Martin Scorsese offered a curious counterpoint.

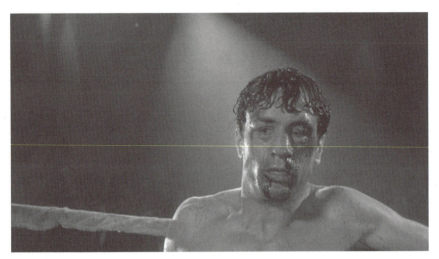

Raging Bull (1980), © United Artists Corporation

The credits read, "All I know is this, once I was blind, but now I can see." I recognized the blindness in Jake and me, but I wondered, "What does it mean to see?" A violent, profane, R-rated movie had provided the spark to a spiritual search—film forged theology.

I had no theological terms to describe this phenomenon. I did not recognize that "LaMotta is such a guilt-ridden individual that he 'atones for his sin by absorbing vicious punishment in the ring.'"[30] I was too young to understand how "the boxing ring has even been construed as 'a metaphorical re-creation of the crucifixion.'"[31] But this movie compelled me to action. I responded to a friend's invitation to attend a Young Life meeting. This wild and wacky youth ministry offered fresh and funny home theater. Students gathered in basements and living rooms for singing, games, and a moving discussion of Jesus. It was shockingly relevant, particularly as I saw the loving principles of Jesus embodied by the adult volunteers. I listened carefully and weighed the options for almost a year. As a freshman in college, at Young Life's Windy Gap camp, I committed all I knew of myself to all I'd heard and read about Jesus. It was a wondrous meeting: the beginning of a propulsive wrestling match involving my heart and soul that continues unabated to this day. Jesus continues to address my blindness and offer sustaining sight.

Kutter Callaway on Up *(2009)*[32]

On the opening weekend for Disney/Pixar's animated film *Up*, my wife and I settled into two theater seats located in the midst of a frenetically undulating sea of parents and young children. Although this was certainly not strange for a Saturday matinee screening of what is ostensibly a children's film, we became increasingly aware of the fact that not only were we surrounded by an overwhelming number of individuals whose raw energy belied their diminutive stature, but we were also apparently the only two filmgoers who had failed to arrive that day with a ready-made nuclear family of our own. As we observed numerous parents attempting to corral their children in preparation for the beginning of the movie, we were unexpectedly confronted with the sobering reality that life is so often marked by the palpable presence of an absence—a discernible lack that indelibly shapes who we are and how we see the world. More specifically, our lives were distinguished by the absence of children. After trying unsuccessfully for an extended period of time to bear children, my wife and I reveled in the joy of discovering that we had finally conceived. Yet, as the apparent randomness and absurdity of life would have it, we subsequently lost two pregnancies to miscarriage, each one further reinforcing a certain degree of helplessness and a commensurate loss of identity both as individuals and as a family.

It was this very juxtaposition—our personal experience of loss along with the presence of what seemed to be a surfeit of children—that formed the immediate context for our viewing of *Up*.

Given our personal experience and the context in which we viewed the film, the music in *Up* was nothing less than transformative for both my wife and me. The images of Carl and Ellie's miscarriage during the "married life"

Up (2009), © Disney Enterprises Inc./Pixar

montage offered us an invitation to remember our loss and, in an important sense, functioned as an embodiment of our pain. But it was the music that expressed something that even the most explicit visual or narrative reference to our pain-filled story could not contain: the redemptive power of a hard-won hope.

Needless to say, I was unable to stop the film after the married life montage in order to request that each member of the audience complete a question-naire concerning the effects of the film's music. However, it was clear from the muffled sobs and tear-stained faces of nearly every adult in the theater that our experience was certainly not unique. In a way that almost defies description, the music's ineffable presence seemed to fill the theater, uniting the individual members of the audience with both the narrative and one another. It suggested the presence of an otherwise hidden meaning in the events it accompanied—a deeper coherence that helped shape these events into a meaningful narrative. Thus, the music in this film not only afforded a series of discrete images a sense of narrative and temporal unity but also, for the briefest of moments, offered us a glimpse of meaning and purpose in the face of life's apparent meaninglessness. It was a powerful, spiritual, and perhaps even revelatory experience. And it all occurred in less than four minutes.

Rob Johnston on Becket (1964)[33]

Nominated for twelve Academy Awards and starring Richard Burton and Peter O'Toole, the film *Becket* tells the story of Henry II, the Norman king of England, and his drinking buddy, Thomas à Becket. King Henry wanted free rein to live and act as he chose, to whore and wage war and tax the citizenry as he saw fit. His one obstacle to complete license was the archbishop of Canterbury, who had his own independent authority as leader of the Church of England. The archbishop often frustrated Henry's designs. In order to solve his problem, King Henry ingeniously decided to appoint Thomas, his companion in "wine, women, and song," as the next archbishop. Brilliant, except for one problem: Thomas decided to take seriously his new vocation—his calling to be God's servant—and to serve God rather than the king. King Henry tried to persuade him to compromise and accommodate to the wishes of his old friend (and king). But Thomas remained steadfast. As a result of his faithfulness, Thomas was martyred in Canterbury Cathedral on the altar steps.

When I first saw this film as a freshman in college, I did not much identify with Thomas's martyrdom (or subsequent sainthood!). But I did hear God calling me to the Christian ministry. My struggle with accepting the call to become a minister was with my image of the pastor as needing first to be a holy

Becket (1964), © Paramount Pictures

person. My Young Life leader, who ministered to me during high school, was such a person, as was my church counselor. I knew I was no saint. In the film, however, I heard God saying to me through his Spirit, "You need not be holy. Thomas was not. You only have to be obedient to my call." And I responded like Thomas and said, "God, I will be loyal to you with all my being." Here again is the power of film. Not only can it reveal and redeem, but it can also be the occasion for God to speak to the viewer.

I told of my call into the ministry at the first conference titled "Reel Spirituality," which several of us organized in the fall of 1998 and from which the title of the book *Reel Spirituality* was taken. Fifty Hollywood screenwriters and directors and fifty leading pastors and church leaders had gathered to discuss "Storytelling as Common Ground: The Church and Hollywood." When I was finished, one of the other speakers, Father Gregory Elmer, a Benedictine monk, commented that he had heard God speak to him, calling him into the monastic life, while watching the same movie! We could even identify the different scenes in the film where God had made himself known to us.

What is noteworthy in this "coincidence" is that the two of us saw the same movie, *Becket*, yet heard God's call in unique ways. For me, the issue was obedience to the call to active service in the world, and I became a Protestant minister who teaches theology and culture. For Father Elmer, the call was to purity of heart and single-minded devotion, and he became a Catholic mystic. In the chapters to come, we will consider the importance of the viewer in understanding what makes a film work. We will also consider film as the occasion not only to know about God but to know God. However, at this point, it is enough to note that a movie's story has the power to transform a life. It certainly did mine.

A Multiplicity of Lenses

Each of these stories presents us with a similar question, which we will pursue in earnest for the rest of the book: How do we understand and make sense of the power of film, not only in our own lives as individuals, but also in the broader society and in the community of faith known as the church? We suggest that a movie's power and meaning are best understood by bringing together a number of critical perspectives and allowing these interpretive lenses to interact and ultimately converge. Given our various sensibilities and experiences, each of us needs a different set of lenses to focus our vision. For instance, people like Craig who have film degrees will naturally understand certain elements of a film's formal structures far more capably than Rob or Kutter, who are both film lovers but not filmmakers. Along similar lines, it will be much more helpful for those unfamiliar with theological reflection to focus on incorporating a theological, ecclesial, or cultural lens into their critical engagement with film.

At the end of the day, the goal is not to become an expert in any one of these critical domains. Rather, the goal is to develop an audiovisual competence—a capacity to interpret and understand the art of film in a way that is both aesthetically credible and theologically faithful. It's not simply to see better and with more clarity what can already be seen but to peer through moving images in order to see what cannot be seen on their surface. To borrow from the apostle Paul, our goal is to "fix our eyes not on what is seen, but on what is unseen, since what is seen is temporary, but what is unseen is eternal" (2 Cor. 4:18). That is the truly deep focus we are after—one that holds in view both the seen and the unseen, both the temporary and the eternal.

Discussion Questions

1. What film has evoked/invoked/inspired the strongest reaction in you personally?
2. What are the primary lenses you bring into your film-going experience?
3. Do you have a truly moving picture you point back to and reflect on as a turning point in your life?

2

the church and hollywood

a historical lens

Critics debate when the first movie was shown. Some claim its origin as October 6, 1889, when Thomas Edison and his associate William Dickson, working with film from George Eastman, projected moving pictures across a screen.[1] Edison later linked the images up to a phonograph. But Edison did not secure an international patent for his invention, a machine that by 1896 allowed a single viewer a "peep show" for thirty seconds. Soon there were a variety of rivals to Edison's Kinetograph camera and Kinetoscope machine, with such exotic names as Zoëtrope, Cinématographe, and Bioscope. All provided the lucky few with magical demonstrations of flickering pictures.

The more accepted date for the beginning of cinema, however, is December 28, 1895, when the Lumière brothers put on the first paid exhibition at the Grand Café in Paris.[2] Earlier that year, Louis and Auguste had patented their projector, which used a strip of celluloid with perforations down the center. With it, they could easily transport their moving pictures. For a time, Lumière projections were offered in special showings for the rich, but soon the cinema moved to the fairgrounds of Europe and the nickelodeons of America's cities.

Mutual Experimentation

Early movies often showed a small slice of life—a train arriving at a station, a man sneezing, a gardener being squirted with his own hose, or a staged fistfight. Some early patrons were so perplexed by these moving images that they allegedly ducked the ocean waves that crashed on the screen and jumped out of the way of the oncoming train. The novelty of seeing bold depictions of reality soon wore off, however, and filmmakers turned to recording theatrical plays and developed their own tableaus. But even this cinema tended "to show or display, to be looked at rather than looked through."[3] It was more exhibition than compelling story, something André Gaudreault and Tom Gunning have called a "cinema of attractions."[4] Many of these early "movie tableaus" had religious themes.[5] *The Horitz Passion Play* was shot in 1897 on a vacant lot in Paris; the more popular *Passion Play of Oberammergau*, a nineteen-minute movie filmed in the snow of New York City (!) but claiming to be an authentic version of the German passion play, premiered in 1898.

Some of these early religious movies were even made by evangelists. Herbert Booth, son of Salvation Army founders William and Catherine Booth, was appointed commandant for Australia at the start of the twentieth century. In order to interest people in coming to their Sunday night lectures and prayer meetings, he experimented with the use of slides and film.[6] Booth, with the help of Joseph Perry, produced a multimedia show titled *Soldiers of the Cross* (1900), which combined short films with slides, hymns, sermons, and prayers. The production used a Lumière machine to show film sequences performed by nonprofessional actors chosen from Salvation Army personnel. The shorts depicted St. Stephen being stoned to death, Christ in agony on the cross, martyrs burning at the stake, animal maulings in the Coliseum, human torches in the gardens of Nero, and Christian women jumping into vats of lime rather than forsaking their Lord. Both the secular and the religious press gave the performances high praise.

Not all movies were religious in theme, however, and not all the religious films were reverent. *The Great Train Robbery* (1903) was an instant success, partly due to the shock of seeing a man in a cowboy hat pull out his gun and fire straight into the camera. Other one-reel short subjects poked fun at clerics, showing them drinking and being involved with women. But many movies continued to portray religious life with reverence, and churches were often used as movie theaters. At least seventy movies based on biblical themes were shot prior to the First World War. Reverent and straightforward, these movies were embraced by churches and proved effective competition against other forms of amusements, drawing crowds, particularly on Sunday evenings when blue laws closed most other venues. Soon the adaptation of Lew Wallace's novel *Ben Hur* (1907), the Jesus story *From the Manger to the Cross* (1912), and the Italian religious epic *Quo Vadis* (1912) all made it to the big screen as widely successful feature films. *Quo Vadis* even opened on Broadway and went head-to-head with the traditional stage.

Almost from the start, motion pictures were spectacularly embraced by audiences. In 1902, Thomas Tally opened the Electric Theater in Los Angeles, the first theater in the United States devoted exclusively to showing motion pictures. By 1907, the American market for movies had grown so large that the gross income of the movie industry was larger than the combined receipts of vaudeville and traditional theater. *Harper's Weekly* labeled it "nickel delirium."[7] One contemporary estimate suggests that by 1911, there were ten thousand theaters in the United States showing movies to a daily audience of over four million persons.[8] Ronald Holloway calls these early years of the twentieth century "the inventive age of cinema."[9] Developing techniques as they went, many of these first-generation moviemakers also had a deep mystical sense. As the poet Vachel Lindsay wrote in 1915 concerning the new cinema: "The real death in the photoplay is the ritualistic death, the real birth is the ritualistic birth, and the cathedral mood of the motion picture which goes with these and is close to these in many of its phases, is an inexhaustible resource."[10]

Growing Criticism

In the early years, the church and Hollywood seemed to be mutually reinforcing each other's needs and values. After the First World War, the relationship shifted. Although movie-theater attendance continued to soar (from 4 million daily customers in 1911, to 8.5 million in 1916, to 12.5 million in 1920), commercialism and a reaction in the larger culture to nineteenth-century attitudes began to alter the motion picture landscape. The star system was born as Mary Pickford and Charlie Chaplin received salaries of over ten thousand dollars per week, while the median household income was around seven hundred dollars per year. One estimate suggests that during these years over 80 percent of the paying public went to a movie in order to see a particular star. Movie magazines were produced showcasing Rudolph Valentino and Greta Garbo.

Paralleling the growth of the star system was the evolution of the movie theater. Its architecture no longer resembled nineteenth-century neoclassical churches, but dream palaces, expressing the romantic and exotic. In Hollywood, two of these themed palaces, the Egyptian and the Chinese, attracted huge crowds, as did the Roxy in New York, with seating for six thousand in its "royal" hall.

Increasingly, movies became escapist fare. Gangsters and monsters, intrigue and romance, filled the screen. But instead of risking a fresh, imaginative portrayal of life, whether through fantasy or realism, movies too often reverted to formulas. Although large studios and chains of theaters had created financial health for the industry, the artistic heart of the motion picture business was being put in jeopardy, as was its cordial relationship with the church.

In 1919, as a tribute to his mother, pioneering director D. W. Griffith volunteered to film the Centenary Celebration of the Methodist Episcopal Church, where seventy-five thousand congregants would assemble. Key filmmakers were invited to address the throng, and a giant, eight-story screen allowed attendees to view film. Those in attendance were encouraged to use any means possible, including movies, to share the Christian gospel.

But the key figure with regard to the church and Hollywood during the period between World War I and the Depression was not Griffith. Producer Cecil B. DeMille recognized a growing market for the illicit amid an increasingly secular culture. Religious himself, DeMille nevertheless understood the new morality of the flapper era and gave the public what they wanted—a religious gloss over salacious scenes. After viewing one of DeMille's movies, Griffith was reportedly so upset with DeMille's tactics that he said to his star Lillian Gish, "I'll never use the Bible as a chance to undress a woman!"[11] DeMille's "bathrobe" and "bathtub" epics all had a similar shape and feel to them. Based on the rationalization that indiscretion could be presented on the screen as long as the sin was eventually corrected, his spectacles were little more than glorified melodramas that included an effective combination of debauchery and piety. But perhaps it was for this very reason that they were hits with the public.

In *The Ten Commandments* (1923), which was produced for the then astronomical figure of $1.5 million, DeMille housed his portrayals of orgies within a larger moral framework of the giving of the law. In his next film, on the life of Christ, DeMille realized that he was on even more sensitive ground, so he used Protestant, Catholic, and Jewish clergy as advisors (perhaps to co-opt the opposition!). He even had Mass celebrated on the set each morning. But DeMille also turned to the best-selling author Bruce Barton, who had written his life of Christ as if Jesus were a Madison Avenue executive. Again, the formula of biblical veneer (some of the heroic postures are held so long that they bring to mind a religious painting) and contemporary recasting is evident. Four years later, *The King of Kings* (1927) opened with DeMille's usual formula of sex and piety. This time, the movie begins with an apocryphal scene in Mary Magdalene's lavish pleasure palace. Mary is expressing anger about the loss of her boyfriend, Judas, who has forsaken her to follow a preacher from Nazareth. Leaving her guests in the middle of a party, Mary rides off on her chariot to get Judas back, only to be converted upon meeting Jesus. And so the biblical story is not only retold but rewritten.

Confrontation

The continuing excesses of DeMille's orgies finally ushered in a period of direct confrontation with churches. This was particularly true of the Roman Catholic Church, which realized the power of film to shape opinion. DeMille's *The Sign of the Cross* (1932) portrayed both pagans and Christians in Nero's Rome. Again, DeMille gave his viewers an "immoral morality play."[12] It is Nero's fiddle that sounds most loudly as the camera pauses voyeuristically to capture the pagan excesses. The movie's most famous scene shows the empress Poppea, played by Claudia Colbert, bathing in milk and saying to the Christian Dacia, "Take off your clothes, get in here, and tell me all about it." The camera shows Colbert's back and legs, while not quite exposing her breasts. But it was enough; the sensual effect accomplished its intention. So too did the scenes of torture and suffering. Many, in fact, when looking at the film today, think DeMille was almost obsessed by cruelty. The film contained such a heavy dose of sex and sadism that a growing number of leaders in both the Protestant and the Catholic Church found it offensive and said so publically.

Public opposition to Hollywood had been growing since the early 1920s. After the Chicago White Sox's game-fixing baseball scandal in 1919, several high-profile scandals involving Hollywood people caused a popular backlash. Mary Pickford, "America's Sweetheart," proved to be not quite the innocent that she portrayed on the screen as she divorced her husband to marry her lover, Douglas Fairbanks. Then, in 1922, "Fatty" Arbuckle was accused of rape and contributing to the death of an actress. Though he was never convicted, the lurid stories in the press ruined his successful career. Just as the baseball establishment had looked for a "czar" to bring back into the game a perception of morality, so the movie industry moved quickly to appoint a head of their association whose character was beyond reproach.

The industry already had a loosely rendered list of thirteen prohibitions that included proscriptions of such subjects as drunkenness, nudity, crime, gambling, and illicit love. But the vague and omnibus quality of these standards, plus the lack of any enforcement tool, made them ineffective. Faced with the growing threat of government censorship, the industry organized itself as the Motion Picture Producers and Distributors of America (MPPDA) and appointed Will Hays to develop and supervise a self-censorship program. An elder in the Presbyterian Church, postmaster general of the United States, and chairman of the Republican Party, Hays brought prestige to the office. His new production guidelines were approved in 1927. Similar to the earlier attempt, they included a ban on swearing, any suggestive nudity, ridicule of the clergy, antipatriotism, and so on. But Hays made the standards more effective than the previous effort. Through his office, over one hundred scripts were rejected between 1924 and 1930. Self-censorship seemed to be working.

With the rise in production costs and the loss of editing flexibility given the advent of sound in movies, a greater codification of the rules seemed necessary. Studios were unwilling to modify their product once it was largely finished. Martin Quigley, a Catholic film journal publisher, and Daniel Lord, a Jesuit priest who had consulted with DeMille on *The King of Kings*, were brought in. After a series of meetings with Hays and with representatives of the studios, a new Production Code was adopted in 1930.

But the start of the Depression quickly changed Hollywood's willingness to live by the Code. Faced with growing red ink, the studios turned to sensationalism—to sex and violence—to lure back the public. As James Skinner opines, "Nothing succeeds like excess."[13] Gangster films such as *Little Caesar* (1930), starring Edward G. Robinson, and *Public Enemy* (1931), with James Cagney, were thought by many to glorify crime. *Blonde Venus* (1932), starring Marlene Dietrich, took prostitution as a theme, even if the star became a hooker for the sake of her child. Neither the Hays Office nor its Production Code Administration, which was created to grant a seal of approval, could stem the tide of the sensational and seductive. It was perhaps the production of *The Sign of the Cross* (1932) that best symbolized that a voluntary system of restraint would no longer work. When Hays asked DeMille what he was going to do about a provocative dance scene in the movie, DeMille replied, "Not a damned thing." And the scene was left in the final cut. But if Hollywood would not do something itself, then the church felt it had to step into the void.

The response of the Catholic Church was the creation of the Legion of Decency. In 1933 the Vatican's apostolic delegate in the United States announced that "Catholics are called by God, the Pope, the bishops and the priests to a united and vigorous campaign for the purification of the cinema, which has become a deadly menace to morals."[14] This was followed later in the year by the appointment of an Episcopal Committee on Motion Pictures, whose charge was to come up with a plan to stem the tide of Hollywood excess. Bishops around the country were also beginning to act unilaterally. In 1934 Cardinal Dougherty of Philadelphia instructed his faithful, with regard to movies, to "stay away from all of them. . . . This is not merely a counsel but a positive command, binding all in conscience under pain of sin."[15] As a result, attendance in Philadelphia theaters quickly fell by 40 percent.

Flush with a new sense of power, the Episcopal Committee came up with the idea of a pledge of decency that it would ask Catholics to abide by. The Legion of Decency asked its members to "remain away from all motion pictures except those which do not offend decency and Christian morality."[16] Within a few months, somewhere between seven and nine million Catholics had taken the pledge. With the Legion of Decency providing the strong arm, the Production Code got a new lease on life. Joseph Breen was appointed to administer the Code, and he began working with both producers and the Legion to ensure that acceptable movies were screened. The Code's "first principle" set the tone for its twelve (!) commandments: "No picture shall be produced which will lower the moral standards of those who see it. Hence the sympathy of the audience shall never be thrown to the side of wrong-doing, evil or sin." Its eighth restriction stated, "No film or episode may throw ridicule on any religious faith."[17]

Though the Code was only advisory, the Legion gave it teeth through its threat of boycott. But, to be effective, the Legion needed a standardized system for rating what was unacceptable for viewing by members in the church. Thus, the bishops turned to the International Federation of Catholic Alumnae (IFCA), a film-reviewing group of the Catholic Church that dated back to 1924 and was located in New York City, away from the pressure of Hollywood. While this group of educated women had heretofore only rated acceptable movies by placing them in two categories—suitable for church halls and suitable for mature audiences but not for church and school settings—they now were asked to rate unsuitable movies as well. And their power in influencing the Code for well over two decades is legend.

The initial results of the Hays Office, working in conjunction with the Legion and the IFCA, were impressive. By 1936, 91 percent of the movies that the Legion reviewed were given an "A" (approved) rating, and only 13 out of 1,271 movies were labeled "C" (condemned). The stories of how various film projects were altered to avoid the wrath of the censors make interesting, if dated, reading. If producers accepted the advice of Breen in the Hays Office, then the Legion usually followed with the granting of acceptable ratings.

Again, however, larger pressures from society intervened. With the advent of World War II, two-piece swimsuits were justified on the patriotic grounds of saving fabric! Women became common in the workplace, and pinup calendars were everywhere. Standards with regard to sexuality in the movies seemed hopelessly dated. The Hays Office responded by subtly easing its Code, but the Legion of Decency remained adamant that morality would be preserved. Howard Hughes's movie *The Outlaw* (1943), publicized with pictures of Jane Russell wearing a cantilevered bra that enabled her breasts to be maximized regardless of her posture, became a focal point. When in 1940 the Production

Code Office warned Hughes that Rio (Jane Russell) was not to be leaning over in her peasant blouse in front of the screen, Hughes ignored the warning. Approval was therefore denied pending thirty-seven cuts. Hughes was not through, however, and he went to the appeals board. The result was a capitulation by the Production Code Office and the ordering of cuts of only one minute. Breen had lost most of the battle. Though the wrangling over this film would last for six more years before *The Outlaw* went to national release, and though the Legion's own censors were eventually able to extract another twenty minutes of cuts, the tide was turning.[18]

By the 1950s, the system of censorship was clearly failing. Society's standards had changed concerning what was deemed acceptable. When the Broadway play *The Moon Is Blue* was adapted for the screen by Otto Preminger in 1953, the Legion opposed its use of the words *pregnant* and *virgin* (words not then heard in American movies) as well as the movie's easy posture toward girls being seduced. Although the Legion condemned the movie with a "C" rating and Cardinal Spellman warned Catholics against attendance, *Life*, *Variety*, and *Newsweek* all gave the movie strong reviews, and the courts ensured that theaters could not ban films from being shown without better reason. Over ten thousand theaters screened the movie, and it proved a box-office success, with Catholics attending in the same proportion as the general population.

To make matters worse, the Catholic rating systems worldwide were proving to be inconsistent. For example, the International Catholic Film Office awarded Fellini's *La Strada* (1954) a major prize, only for the Legion to rate it unacceptable for the general public. On the other hand, when Fellini's *La Dolce Vita* came out in 1960, there was a papal condemnation of the film, but this was not enough to keep the Legion from dividing into two camps with regard to the acceptability of the movie. The opening scene had a large granite statue of Christ being carried over the people by helicopter for installation at St. Peter's Square. In this way, Christ was symbolized as out of touch with the people. Moreover, hedonism and immorality among the rich made up the bulk of the story. Nevertheless, the artistic strength of the movie caused the Legion ultimately to deem it acceptable for mature audiences. The era of the Code and the Legion was effectively over.

A New Rating System

In the 1960s, society's standards and Hollywood's tastes changed even more quickly. *The Pawnbroker* (1965), *Who's Afraid of Virginia Woolf?* (1966), and *Alfie* (1966) appeared and, with their flashbacks of concentration camp memories, vitriolic domestic argument, and immoral and abusive seduction, set new standards of openness in Hollywood. The Production Code was now largely ineffective, and the Legion was increasingly ignored. In one year, the Legion's listing of objectionable movies rose from 15 to 24 percent. A means of providing more nuanced ratings was clearly necessary.

The growing popularity of international films was as important to the changing context as was the Code's demise. Students were flocking to cinemas to see the "artistic" films of European and Asian directors. How could the Legion give their highest rating to *Godzilla versus Mothra* (1964) and condemn Antonioni's *Blowup* (1966)? The wide popularity of serious, subtitled films in the late '50s and early '60s—movies by Kurosawa, Bergman, Buñuel, and Fellini—together with the ineffectiveness of the Production Code caused Hollywood to scrap the old system of self-regulation.

In its place, in 1966 a variant of the current ratings system was adopted, one self-administered by the major studios without church intervention. The code was developed under the direction of Jack Valenti and the Motion Picture Association of America, beginning just prior to the release of *The Graduate* (1967) and *Bonnie and Clyde* (1967). Things had changed forever in Hollywood. Sympathy could now be thrown to the side of wrongdoing and sin. Movie critic Pauline Kael noted that by the end of the 1970s, the "old mock innocence" had too often been replaced by "the sentimentalization of defeat" and a movie culture that seemed to "thrive on moral chaos."[19]

It is understandable that in some movies, a backlash against the church and its clerics was portrayed. After all, Hollywood had not been able to present anything but pietistic glosses on Christianity for most of its existence. Michael Medved is no doubt right that some in Hollywood swung the pendulum too far.[20] But there was also plenty within the church and its clergy that invited criticism and caricature. If theologians and church-related film critics were to have any voice at all in this new situation, they would need a broader and more informed approach to a Christian understanding and interpretation of film than the traditional rhetoric of caution or even abstinence. Dialogue, not censorship, was being called for. It was in this changing context that the church began to interact theologically in a new way with Hollywood.

From Beta to Streaming

Other forces were also altering the church's relationship with Hollywood. With the advent of television after World War II, movies became a staple of most people's diet, as ubiquitous as the living room in their homes. In the process, church censorship, even for the faithful, became next to impossible. In 1979, George Atkinson helped popularize the home viewing of Hollywood films still further. That year he opened the first video rental store, making viewing-on-demand a possibility. For the first time, the viewer controlled the market. Earlier in the 1970s, Hollywood executives had begun making feature-length movies available on videocassette, charging fifty dollars each. There were few takers. But Atkinson saw an opportunity, and with fifty movies that he purchased—including *The French Connection* (1971), *The Sound of Music* (1965), and *Butch Cassidy and the Sundance Kid* (1969)—he offered customers rentals for ten dollars. People came in droves.

Other innovations have followed—from the videocassette to the DVD and now streaming. In 1999, the packaging of DVDs with extra features began in earnest with the Wachowskis adding two documentaries to their DVD version of *The Matrix* (1999). By 2005, there were more than 24,000 video stores in the United States. Customers rented 2.6 billion DVDs and VHS cassettes in 2004, generating more than $8 billion in revenue. But in 2007, things changed again as Netflix introduced streaming services. A decade later, they had almost 50 million subscribers in the US and 93 million worldwide, even while video stores were shutting their doors. Amazon Prime and Hulu also began streaming movies for their customers, but these services seemed to be more complementary than competitive, with 54 percent of all Americans saying that in 2017 they had watched something on Netflix. America had become a digital culture.

The church's response to media's new possibilities has varied. A few have continued to resist (and have often, as a result, received media attention), believing that greater purity and a reassertion of doctrinal priorities is the best "defense" against what is (falsely?) perceived to be our culture's growing secularism. But a larger and increasing number of Christians have recognized that since the church's core message is a story, and since movies are our culture's primary storytelling medium, dialogue and interaction are a better response.

As Rodney Clapp observes, "In our very busy, overly hectic lives and society, people don't pause for any kind of contemplation or second thoughts about what's the meaning of life except in places like movie theaters. At my church, we have people who see films together and then talk about it."[21] And film viewing by Christians has not been limited to the Cineplex. Where just 4 percent of churches were using video clips in their programming at least once a month in 1999, just five years later the number had risen dramatically to over 20 percent. The percentage has continued to rise.[22] A church seeking social influence or hoping to relate even to its own members (particularly its youth), let alone communicate its story effectively to those outside its doors, increasingly realizes that it must creatively incorporate film in its various ministries.[23]

Support for the church's use of media and the arts has come from multiple quarters. Pope John Paul II, for example, in his December 1999 "Address to the Festival for the Third Millennium," asserted:

> People created in the image and likeness of God are naturally called to peace and harmony with God, with others, with ourselves, and with all creation. The cinema can become an interpreter of this natural propensity and strive to be a place of reflection, a call to values, an invitation to dialogue and communion. . . .
>
> The cinema enjoys a wealth of languages, a multiplicity of styles, and a truly great variety of narrative forms. . . . It can contribute to bringing people closer, to reconciling enemies, to favoring art and ever more respectful dialogue between diverse cultures.[24]

This pope, himself a poet and playwright who saw several of his plays turned into movies, also affirmed in an address to participants in the 2004 Pontifical Academies "the *via pulchritudinis* [the 'path of beauty'] as the best way for the Christian faith and the culture of our time to meet, besides being a valuable instrument for the formation of the young generations."[25]

The African American preacher Bishop T. D. Jakes, who appeared on the cover of *Time* as America's best preacher and whose R-rated movie *Woman, Thou Art Loosed* (2004) was reviewed favorably by the *New York Times*, was asked if cinema was the next frontier of evangelism. He responded, "It can be. The Gospel is not about standing and saying 'Come to me.' It's about going where they are, and the world is at the theater."[26]

As the church entered the twenty-first century, it was indeed trying to "go where they are." Richard Corliss, *Time* magazine's film critic, discussed the church's use of film in its ministries: "For decades America has embraced a baffling contradiction. The majority of its people are churchgoing Christians, many of them evangelical. Yet its mainstream pop culture, especially film, is secular at best, often raw and irreligious. . . . It's hard to see those two vibrant strains of society ever coexisting, learning from each other. Yet the two are not only meeting; they're also sitting down and breaking bread together."[27]

The church has increasingly begun to recognize that theology is often being done outside its doors. A spate of books and articles on faith and film have appeared since 1979, literature whose primary intention has been to bring movies into the church's life and witness. Terry Lindvall's bibliography of religion and film (2004, 2005) stretched to almost eighty pages and has continued to increase.[28] Some of the entries in Lindvall's bibliography had a more catechetical function, using movies to interpret the Apostles' Creed, for example.[29] Others used movies to illumine biblical texts.[30] Still others provided pastors help with their preaching.[31] Some of the most popular books and articles encouraging film's use in the church (though they were often quite superficial) were those intended to suggest appropriate clips that youth leaders might utilize.[32] There were also a growing number of books meant to facilitate group discussion with adults and teens,[33] and others seeking to be an aid to spiritual growth.[34]

While the interlacing of Christianity and film during the first twenty-five years following the rise of film rentals (1979–2004) emphasized books and periodicals, in recent years the dialogue between faith and film has largely moved to the internet. Christian websites that review movies or provide resources for study and reflection are legion. They now support and encourage the rapid adoption of film as a resource for Christian life and witness, for both individuals and churches. According to the Pew Internet Project, more than 82 million Americans (64 percent of all internet users) make use of the web for faith-related matters, and here, faith and film sites have found eager readers. Consider the following:

- Reel Spirituality (www.reelspirituality.com) is the website of Fuller Seminary's Reel Spirituality Institute in the Brehm Center. With a quickly growing library of theologically informed criticism of both TV and movies, podcasts, interviews, video essays, film festival reportage, and even a book series published by Wipf & Stock, the site is curated by Elijah Davidson and has become perhaps the leading academic website for theology and film.

- Spirituality and Practice (www.spiritualityandpractice.com) has also been an important site, launched by Frederic and Mary Ann Brussat in 2006. The Brussats strive to offer "a positive and spiritually progressive perspective on contemporary media, particularly books and film." An outgrowth of their Cultural Information Service, which began publishing material in 1972, the website presents insightful reviews and study material, recognizing that the spiritual dimensions of life are written in the texts of our experiences.

- Christ and Pop Culture (www.christandpopculture.com) is an online magazine with a special interest in film and television. Its authors engage all aspects of popular culture from a Reformed, Christian perspective.

- Hollywood Jesus (www.hollywoodjesus.com) might be considered the granddaddy of these sites. Started in 1997 by David Bruce, it had over 700 million hits in its first decade, reviewing a wide cross section of Hollywood fare. Currently, however, the site has narrowed its focus to films made primarily for a Christian audience, and many of its readers and reviewers have moved elsewhere.

These four sites represent something of the present range of "Christian" internet sites, but the variety is startling. Two omnibus sites are also worth mentioning:

- Patheos (www.patheos.com), founded in 2008, is notable as a substantial blogging platform for global dialogue about religion and spirituality. It has housed the blogs of such Christianity and film critics as Craig Detweiler (*Doc Hollywood*), Peter Chattaway (*Film Chat*), Jeffrey Overstreet (*Looking Closer*), Steven Greydanus (*Decent Films*), Ken Morefield (*1 More Film Blog*), Josh Larsen (*Larsen on Film*), and Rose Pacatte (*Sister Rose at the Movies*).
- The website of Gordon Matties (www.cmu.ca/library/resources.php?s =film), who is a professor of biblical studies and theology at Canadian Mennonite University, has been helpful in locating and organizing this growing maze of faith and film websites. The site provides access to what has at times been as many as fifty religion and film websites and an equal number of journals, film lists, and other resources. It provides close to one-stop shopping for anyone interested in faith and film.

The Present

Movies are recognized today as serving the church and the synagogue, the mosque and the temple. They are providing a resource for our personal and societal search for meaning and transcendence; they are helping those in the church develop a clearer understanding of how religion is both perceived and expressed today. They are also becoming the occasion for relating missionally with those outside the church, and they are helping those within to better reflect theologically.

Despite some excesses, both Hollywood and the church have matured in their depiction of spirituality on the screen. Religion has been portrayed not only for the niche market of Christian viewers—for example, *God's Not Dead* (2014) and *God's Not Dead 2* (2016)—but also for mainstream audiences. In 2016, a number of films waded into these waters. The Coen brothers' comedy *Hail Caesar* juxtaposed competing ideologies (including theism) within the structure of a passion play. Martin Scorsese's *Silence* was a profound drama about belief and doubt set in seventeenth-century Japan. Mel Gibson's *Hacksaw Ridge* told the true-life story of a Christian pacifist medic's lifesaving heroics in the midst of a World War II battle. Nate Parker's *The Birth of a Nation*, which won Best Picture at the Sundance Film Festival, told the true story of a slave rebellion in nineteenth-century America, where the Bible was repeatedly used to justify the slaves' oppression. And in *The Innocents*, French director Anne Fontaine tells the haunting story of a group of Polish nuns who were raped and impregnated by Russian soldiers during World War II.

In each of these movies, the characterization of Christians is complex and compelling, of interest to a much wider audience than only the "faith-based." In a context of increasing pluralism, where faith and doubt comingle for many, such movies provide viewers a significant space. As Alissa Wilkinson concludes in her perceptive review of 2016 movies, "Art provides a place for us to deal with our own fears and search for meaning. Entertainment lets us do this together. When we're trying to figure out one another while also sorting out our own beliefs about right, wrong, belief, doubt, and the transcendent, it looks, from 2016, like we've decided the screen is a decent place to start."[35]

In such a context, the dialogue between faith and film finds itself entering ever wider territory. Faith-based films are beginning, almost for the first time, to offer their viewers more complex and captivating stories that present real struggle and ambiguous answers. At the other end of the spectrum, tentpole superhero movies, thought by many to be simply entertainment devoid of spiritual depth, have also dared to show human vulnerability and spiritual complexity. In the process, both genres have become increasingly important resources for Christian reflection on faith and life.

By way of illustration, we can conclude this discussion of the church and the film industry by considering two quite different movies that came out on the same weekend in early 2017—*The Shack* and *Logan*. *The Shack*, directed by Stuart Hazeldine and costing approximately $20 million to make, is a faith-based movie seeking a crossover market; *Logan*, directed by James Mangold and costing $97 million to make, is the last (or perhaps not?) of a hugely profitable franchise created seemingly for mere entertainment. Because of their particular genres, both got mixed critical reviews. But both turned out to be audience favorites, returning handsome profits to their investors. Moreover, both films, in very different ways, demonstrated the continuing development of theologically relevant films, with many viewers finding in these movies important spiritual insight and resonance. Both help illustrate the changing state of the relationship between the church and Hollywood.

The Shack *(2017)*

A decade after Mel Gibson's surprise blockbuster *The Passion of the Christ* grossed $370 million in the US and Canada alone, studios and A-level talent have begun to successfully reach out to faith-driven consumers (a large and underserved market), while faith-based filmmakers are becoming better artists with substantial resumes. The result is a better quality faith-based film. Where movies with Christian-intended audiences have generally lacked the star power, narrative complexity, financial backing, and production quality necessary to compete with other theater releases, this has begun to change (even while the need for further improvement remains evident). Moreover, as American culture enters ever more strongly into a postsecular age, where spirituality is understood to be no longer the interest only of those explicitly connected to faith communities, finding that wider audience for faith-based movies is becoming necessary in order to be successful in the marketplace.

While organized religion might be losing adherents, spirituality is increasingly admired, so films with a spiritual core have become more culturally desirable. This trend might have begun with the 2011 movie *Soul Surfer*, the real-life story of a teenage surfer whose faith helped her overcome the loss of a limb in a shark attack. The movie, starring Dennis Quaid and Helen Hunt, grossed $44 million. By 2014 the direction of this trend was clear. In that year, *Heaven Is for Real* was a surprise hit, taking in $91 million in domestic sales. Leading studio producer Joe Roth hired Randall Wallace, a Christian and an A-list Hollywood screenwriter, to direct this movie, as well as Greg Kinnear to star. Two years later, Roth's colleague, producer DeVon Franklin, himself a Christian, hired Patricia Riggen, who had made the Chilean miner movie *The 33* for Warner Brothers, to direct *Miracles from Heaven* (2016). The movie starred Jennifer Garner and grossed $62 million. Riggen had tried consciously to expand the story's audience beyond the hard-core Christian base, and she was successful.[36] And in 2018, the surprise hit *I Can Only Imagine*, with a budget of $7 million, earned $83 million. Telling the story behind the hit song of the same name and focusing

The Shack (2017), © Summit Entertainment, LLC

on Bart Millard, the leader of the Christian music group MercyMe, the movie tapped into the song's popularity and the group's fan base.

Of course, not all such attempts at capturing both Christian and mainstream audiences have worked. The remake of *Ben-Hur* (2016) cost upwards of $100 million and returned $26 million, with both Christians and the wider public disappointed by the dismal production. Similarly, *The Young Messiah* (2016) failed to find an audience. Historical depictions of faith-oriented stories seemed to be less compelling to people wanting to know how faith works today.

The Shack, on the other hand, within its first three weeks earned more than double what it had cost to make. Final box-office results topped $97 million worldwide, with another $16 million in DVD and Blu-ray sales. Capitalizing on the success of William P. Young's Christian novel, which sold over 22 million copies and is the basis for the movie, *The Shack* sparked strong negative and positive reactions for its multiethnic and feminine portrayal of God. The book and movie follow the spiritual journey of Mack Phillips after the murder of his young daughter Missy. It turns out she has been abducted by a man wanted by the police, and the little girl's bloody dress is later found in a mountain shack. Here the movie's first act ends, having brought viewers into one of any parent's worst nightmares.

The second act, the heart of the movie, explores Mack's attempt to find answers for what has happened. He visits the shack once again, after he receives a mysterious invitation from "Papa" in his mailbox. Wrestling with survivor's guilt and filled with grief, Mack (Sam Worthington) meets an outdoorsman outside the shack who takes him to a nearby idyllic cottage (think of a sentimental Thomas Kinkade painting). There he meets a trio of divine figures—a matronly African American woman (played by Academy Award–winning actress Octavia Spencer) who is called Papa; her son, Jesus (played by the Israeli actor Aviv Alush), who is the Middle Eastern carpenter Mack has just met; and Sarayu, meant to be the Holy Spirit (played by Japanese actress Sumire Matsubara). When Mack stammers in asking each of them if they are God, all three answer, "I am" (an insider joke referencing the name of God in the Old Testament—Yahweh, which in Hebrew means "I am who I am"). Later, Sophia (Alice Braga), a personification, or embodiment, of God's wisdom (see Dame Wisdom in Prov. 1–11), meets Mack in a nearby cave, and Papa reappears not as a woman but as a gruff father (First Nations actor Graham Greene). This portrayal of Christianity's trinitarian God proved controversial to some (was it a tri-theism?), but to many others it was provocative and encouraging.

The movie is explicitly Christian themed, and many of the filmmakers were self-identified Christians. This is a "faith-based" film, not a studio film reaching out to a faith-based audience. But different than many earlier Christian-themed and Christian-sourced movies in which theological questions are never deeply explored, *The Shack* asks the difficult questions that all of humanity struggles with. How could God allow such a tragedy if God is "God"? As Mack seeks an "answer" from the three divine figures (the Holy Trinity in Christian theology), he asks them accusingly, "If you are God almighty, why did you let my girl die? How can you say you can help me (now), when you couldn't help her? You abandoned my daughter just like you abandoned your son! If you are who you say you are, all-knowing, why ask me?"

The resolution in the third act provides not so much answers to such questions as the dawning awareness of an answerer. Voiced by Tim McGraw and Faith Hill as the credits roll, the final song expresses Papa's/Sophia's wisdom—"Keep Your Eyes on Me":

> Ain't it just like love to leave a mark on the skin and underneath. . . .
> Keep your eyes on me, when you're lost in the dark.
> Keep your eyes on me when the light in your heart is too burned out to
>   see.
> Keep your eyes on me.

Giving narrative strength to the song is the fact that Tim McGraw is not only the singer but also plays the role of Mack's neighbor, Willie, in the movie. As narrator of the story, Willie fills in details for the viewer, including family secrets. The song thus functions as the story's final "truth" from someone all-knowing.

Another important framing device carries the story to its conclusion. While viewers are encouraged to believe that Mack visited the shack and learned to trust the love of God, we also discover at the end as Mack wakes up in the hospital that he has been hit by a truck while driving up to meet Papa. Thus, he never actually got to the shack. Much like the movie *Life of Pi* (also produced by Gil Netter), viewers are left with a choice as to which story to believe. Has everything they've seen only been a dream? If so, does it matter? Could not Mack have met God in such a vision? As the movie ends, Mack has experienced transformation. He has been able to forgive his daughter's murderer. He can again embrace his wife and be a father to his remaining daughter as she grieves. Whether real or dreamt, Mack's experience has proven radically transformative. Viewers are left to ponder which version of the story they will choose to believe.

Like *The Shack*, some movies function like a biblical parable (see chap. 7 for more on films as parables). Rooted in the everyday and compellingly told, its story invites a metaphoric interpretation that challenges audiences to perceive a spiritual truth about the human condition. It does this while functioning subversively, undermining certain contemporary beliefs (e.g., God is a male judge with a white beard) in order to invite s/Spiritual insight and personal transformation. Here is a movie that offers a bold, straightforward interpretation of the Christian faith. Rather than God being understood as a God of judgment, God is portrayed as a God of love (in contrast with the findings of a 2006 Baylor University study documenting that half of all Americans understand God primarily in terms of someone who punishes evildoers, whether now or in the afterlife).[37]

Yes, there remain too many clichés in this Christian-themed movie, and not all the metaphors work. Some will disregard the movie as religious kitsch.[38] Yes, the camera shots from above (from a godlike perspective), revealing a pattern instead of disorder, seem manipulative. The idyllic, Kinkade-like cottage is off-puttingly sentimental, while Mack and Jesus walking on the lake's water for fun is simply corny. And yes, the filmmakers seem to have been too tied to referencing (or reverencing?) the book and its apologetics, keeping the story consistently on the edge of mere platitudes rather than portraying greater theological complexity. At its worst, the movie's story is but illustrated argument. But despite such shortcomings, here is a movie that worked for many. Viewers (though not all) reported leaving the theater having experienced the ongoing love of God, and they were eager for postviewing discussion.

Logan *(2017)*

If *The Shack* seeks at times to transcend its genre, this is even more the case with the superhero movie *Logan*. The ninth (and seemingly final) Wolverine film since *X-Men* began the modern era of comic-book films in 2000, *Logan* once again stars Hugh Jackman. Logan is now an aging mutant who finds his powers on the wane and his seeming immortality questioned. The movie is uncharacteristically dark and violent for a Marvel movie, filled with angst, anger, and alcohol. Accepting life's moral ambiguity even while seeking to rise above it; graphically violent, even showing horrific acts willingly committed by the child Laura (Dafne Keen); and deeply personal in its soul-searching, even while dealing with such larger issues as corporate greed, immigrants, fatherlessness, and the limits of biotechnical engineering, *Logan* is much more than the prolonged chase scene that some have described it as. It is anything but popcorn entertainment.

Rather, *Logan* is an R-rated road trip, a surprisingly personal buddy story, in which the mutant Logan lives into his full humanity, even as he sacrifices himself out of love for his genetically engineered but biological daughter. Rather than being escapist fare, *Logan* is, as one reviewer put it, "an escape from escapism, a restoration of the human element in blockbusters."[39] Another reviewer has

Logan (2017), © Twentieth Century Fox Film Corporation / TSG Entertainment Finance, LLC

called this comic-book saga "a Christian fable disguised as a superhero story."[40] This might be somewhat of an overstatement, but the movie's overall narrative arc, its biblical allusions, and its clear Christ-imagery do give the comparison a certain credence.

It is commonplace to understand superhero movies as our contemporary westerns, helping this generation deal with the anxieties of our age.[41] But seldom is the connection between these two genres made as explicit as it is in *Logan*. (It should be noted that the director of *Logan*, James Mangold, also directed the 2007 remake of the western *3:10 to Yuma*.) The movie's chief referent is *Shane* (1953) and even includes a scene with Xavier and Laura watching that movie while hiding out in a hotel room. Later, Laura recites Shane's final monologue at Logan's grave: "A man has to be what he is. . . . You run home and tell them everything is all right." As Elijah Davidson writes, "Mangold uses the film to remind us who Wolverine was when we met him in *X-Men*, who he has been since we've been watching him for the past seventeen years, and ultimately who he will always be in this genre—he's the Superhero *par excellence*—violent, rogue-ish, sadly necessary and ultimately Good, but we're going to have to get along without him in the end."[42]

Viewers of *Logan* also might reference one of John Wayne's final roles in *The Cowboys* (1972), where Wayne plays a deteriorating rancher who reluctantly assumes a fatherly role among a group of schoolboys whom he has hired to help him drive his cattle to Montana. Viewers might also recall Wayne's role as Ethan Edwards in *The Searchers* (1956), a loner who rescues a young girl from those bent on subjugating her. Westerns share a common mythic shape, which also undergirds *Logan*. The conflict is between good people trying to live at peace and the corporate forces of evil who seek to destroy them. Into this context "rides" a cowboy/gunslinger who is reluctant to use violence to save the people but ultimately kills off the evil force before departing from the town.

In westerns, this "cowboy" is often a Christ figure, a savior figure who risks or even lays down his life that others might live in peace and harmony. It is no accident that after the children give their "savior" a funeral, Logan having died to free them, the movie ends with them placing a cross over his grave. Then in a final symbolic act (in case viewers missed it!) Laura tips the cross 45 degrees, creating an "X." Like Christ himself, this superhero has died that others might live.

We see additional biblical references in the film also. Logan/Wolverine has had, for example, a skeleton of adamantium (the allusion to Adam seems unmistakable) fused into him, a metal that is almost indestructible, making him both a feared killing machine and someone almost immortal. He would be "like God." But the adamantium is now poisoning him and limiting his body's miraculous healing properties. His body, it seems, can no longer bear "the weight of glory" (to use a phrase from C. S. Lewis about the sin of humankind's arrogant grasping to be God, a sin first perpetrated by Adam and Eve).

In this situation, Logan must choose whether he is going to die an angry man ("disappear into the potter's ground"), angry with God for his mistake in creating him, or whether he will "take of that last offered cup," as the final Johnny Cash ballad "The Man Comes Around" puts it. Will he live into his destiny as an X-Man? Or, as Logan tells his young traveling companion, Laura, do X-Men only live in comic books, "ice cream for bed-wetters"? By ending his film with this Johnny Cash song, the director, James Marigold (who also directed the Cash biopic, *Walk the Line* [2005]), makes the movie *Logan* its spiritual sequel. Like the movie's hero, Cash spent much of his life reveling in the larger than life, only to discover a gritty humility toward the end. One of his last compositions, this ballad wrestles with sin and salvation. Much like Logan himself, the ballad finds an analogue in the imagery of the Four Horsemen of the Apocalypse (imagery taken from the biblical book of Revelation).[43]

> Till Armageddon, no Shalam, no Shalom.
> Then the father hen will call his chickens home.
> The wise men will bow down before the throne.
> And at his feet they'll cast their golden crown.
> When the man comes around.[44]

The mythical superhero must be deconstructed; death, amorality, mystery abound in this world. No one is indestructible. But there still remains hope—the gift of redemption: the man comes around. Here, in one critic's words, is "a parable for the fleetingness of life and the hope that can be found in what we do not deserve."[45]

Discussion Questions

1. The movie critic Pauline Kael wrote that sin and cinema have always been intertwined in Hollywood. Is she correct? Or is it more complex than that?
2. Might selective censorship ever become an effective strategy for the church in its response to Hollywood? Should there be limits?
3. What recent movie might you identify that invites a "deep focus," one that opens out to the spiritual even if its theme is not overtly religious?

act i

film

3

fade in

a narrative lens

Is your life a story? Does it have a narrative arc? If so, who is the author? In *Stranger Than Fiction* (2006), Harold Crick measures his life in minutes. He is all about efficiency. A narrator describes how Harold brushes his teeth, secures his necktie, and marches to the bus stop every single workday. Will Ferrell plays the hapless IRS tax auditor who assesses his world as a constant cost-benefit question. Most poignantly, the narrator (Emma Thompson) tells us that after washing the dishes, Harold goes to bed alone at 11:13 every night. This routine is interrupted when Harold begins to audibly hear the narrator's running commentary on his life.

We've all heard cinematic narrators set a plot in motion. But what if a character could hear that voice-over and begin to see his life from the author's perspective? *Stranger Than Fiction* explores how writers "play God" with their characters' fates. It raises enduring questions of drama (and religion) such as whether we have free will or are subject to fate or divine providence. *Stranger Than Fiction* reveals the role of the author in crafting a story. It takes us inside both writer Karen Eiffel's mind and her character Harold's dilemma. We are invited to view life through a narrative lens.

Harold is so disturbed by the voice-over describing his life that he seeks out the expertise of English literature professor Jules Hilbert (Dustin Hoffman). The professor asks Harold, "What kind of story are you in?" There are only so many plots to choose from. Professor Hilbert notes how "some plots are moved forward by external events and crises. Others are moved forward by the

Stranger Than Fiction (2006), © Crick Pictures, LLC

characters themselves."[1] Is Harold subject to circumstance, or does he have the ability to alter the outcome of the narrative? The professor frames the tension with a quotation from novelist Italo Calvino: "The ultimate meaning to which all stories refer has two faces: the continuity of life, the inevitability of death." In tragedy, you die. In comedy, you get married. Harold's life could go either way. So many of us feel that tension on any given day. The fundamental question looming over the movie and the filmgoers: Is my life a comedy or a tragedy?

Stranger Than Fiction is also a meditation on romance. It asks age-old questions like, Why do opposites attract? The uptight tax auditor falls for a breezy baker named Ana (depicted with aplomb by Maggie Gyllenhaal). Dramatic sparks fly. Harold's inhibitions and fears are melted away by Ana's free-spirited artistry. As an audience, we begin to fall in love with and care for both characters. We root for their relationship and yet fear that things may not work out. Screenwriter Zach Helm puts his characters (and the audience) through an emotional wringer. To create drama, writers must be ruthless toward their protagonists, subjecting them to a series of life-threatening tests and decisions. The entertainment industry credo is "Kill Your Darlings." But Harold doesn't want to die. What actions can characters (and we!) take to alter the outcome? Can characters change their habits? Can they grow? How do we confront the peril of mortality?

Karen deals with her own struggles, wrestling with writer's block. Authors should become attached to their characters, birthing them out of love and respect. But Karen is a chain-smoking wreck, frightened by the ways her reputation for ingenious deadly endings looms over this unfinished story. From the simple words "Fade in" a screenplay can unspool in so many directions. Staring at a blank page can be paralyzing to a writer, but that space can also be filled with the most wondrous flights of fantasy.

Movies begin in writers' imaginations (like the creative brain of *Stranger Than Fiction*'s Zach Helm). Writing is usually a solitary act, rooted in months (even years) of research, brainstorming, outlining, writing, and especially re-writing. Some writers prefer to work with a partner, so they can bounce ideas and dialogue off each other. Hollywood will often hire numerous screenwriters throughout the development process to rewrite or polish a script. What began with a singular vision may dissolve into collective mush, unfocused and un-engaging. The most enduring films (and original screenplays) usually display all the hallmarks of the storytelling craft—a compelling character caught in a vexing situation that requires extraordinary creativity and resolve. In search of an ending for Harold's story, Eiffel tells her assistant Penny, "It came to me . . . like anything worth writing it came inexplicably and without method." Such is the mystery and wonder of storytelling.

This chapter will consider film (and life) through a narrative lens. We will endeavor to sharpen our storytelling and story-perceiving skills. Screenwriting gurus like Syd Field, Linda Seger, and Robert McKee increasingly shaped and codified story structure in Hollywood.[2] They tapped into how "the archetypal story unearths a universally human experience, then wraps itself inside a unique, culture-specific expression."[3] They reached back to the ageless question posed by Aristotle, "How should human beings lead their life?"[4] McKee notes how cynicism has undercut our confidence in the ability of philosophy, science, and religion to answer this question. He writes, "As our faith in traditional ideologies diminishes, we turn to the source we still believe in: the art of story."[5] Psychologists urge their clients to explore their personal narratives in search of meaning and wholeness. Gerontologists challenge senior citizens to engage in guided autobiographies as a way to put their lives in perspective. Increasingly, church leaders have begun to champion narrative theology as the best way to recover and understand the Christian story.[6] We are becoming more comfort-able talking about our personal story in relation to God's larger shaping story and narrative. A greater understanding of Hollywood narrative conventions can deepen our appreciation for Jesus's skills as a storyteller. We also share in Harold Crick's dilemma, endeavoring to discover what story we find ourselves in. What questions or critiques might we need to bring toward movies so we do not fall into the trap of measuring our life only in terms of story beats, plot twists, and happy endings?

Thanks to digital technology, there are almost no limits on screenwriters' creativity. Traditional hurdles regarding setting and time have been expanded by the pixels that can be manipulated on a laptop rather than a camera. It can be overwhelming to consider the myriad of possibilities inherent in a blank page. Yet screenwriters must resist the temptation to settle for provocation and special effects rather than genuine human drama. Hollywood agent Robert Newman suggests that despite all the big-screen blockbusters, "It's not about the blue-screen spectacle. Kids are going to see *Finding Nemo* for the same reason they went to see *Spider-Man* or *Titanic*. They relate to the unabashed romance and emotion and the complexity of the characters. That's what makes you want to go see a movie again and again."[7] While spectacle may draw us to the cinema, it is the plight of the characters that gets us invested in a story. We extend our hopes and fears to the people onscreen, struggling to solve a crime or resolve a romance. We hunger for heroes.

Building on the archetypes identified by Joseph Campbell, Hollywood films chronicle a hero's journey from bystander to active participant. Reluctant characters choose to get engaged, whether leaving their shire, coming out of retirement, or putting on the uniform again. Film critic David Thomson famously declared, "No matter the modern stress on special effects, there isn't a sight in movies as momentous as shots of a face as its mind is being changed."[8] In other words, the close-up still packs an emotional wallop. Roger Ebert declared, "Movies are the most powerful empathy machine in all the arts. When I go to a great movie I can live somebody else's life for a while. I can walk in somebody else's shoes." Through cinematic heroes, we discover the warrior, the advocate, and the romantic lurking within each of us. Truly moving pictures inspire us to examine our own lives, consider our own choices, reflect on our own story. Ebert celebrates how "the great movies enlarge us, they civilize us, they make us more decent people."[9]

Despite screenwriters' best efforts, empathy remains in remarkably short supply. Studio pictures can sink into stereotype, resting on established notions of good and evil, power and privilege, to reinforce preexisting tropes. We can come to consider ourselves the heroes in our own story, without ever considering the ways in which we may be propping up systems that deserve to be challenged and even dismantled. What if our happy ending comes at someone else's expense? We may need the leveling power of comedy to reveal such cultural blind spots. Movies can expose how frequently we embarrass ourselves and undercut our loftiest aspirations. We may sabotage our pursuit of love, fame, or riches. Or block others' pursuit. Like our onscreen comics, we may have to discover how humility and forgiveness serve as a prerequisite to honor and adulthood. From the days of Aristotle, comedy and drama have provided essential lenses for seeing ourselves as both fallen short of the glory of God and a little lower than angels.

The Elements of a Story

What are the elements of a compelling story? Wesley Kort, professor of religion and literature at Duke University, argues that the power and meaning of a story (as well as its relationship to religion) can best be understood by analyzing the story in terms of its constitutive parts: character, setting, plot, and tone (what we will call "point of view").[10] Some stories are more like parables and others like myths, but all share certain structural properties. Moreover, in any given telling of a story, one or another of these four aspects of the narrative will be emphasized or given precedence. By reflecting on a story's makeup, the audience can find a key to the heart of the story.

Character

Stories that emphasize *character* portray issues of human need or potential. They deal with the question of human nature by offering paradigms of possibility. What is it to be human?

Most screenplays start with a character in a crisis. The tension could be physical (aliens approaching) or existential (wrestling with a death in the family). American movies tend to follow two basic types—ordinary people caught up in extraordinary situations (consider heroic biopics like *Hidden Figures* or Oscar winners like *Forrest Gump*) or extraordinary people struggling to resist the forces that cause them to reveal their remarkable gifts (like *Star Wars*, *Harry Potter*, *The Matrix*, or every superhero franchise). It will often involve enormous stakes (like the future of the human race) but can also turn on the plight of an individual facing crushing personal circumstances (think of the determined adolescents in *Slumdog Millionaire* or *Lion*). We suffer with our onscreen heroes and share their pain, their fear, their triumph, their defeat. In a tragedy, external forces overwhelm the protagonist. We may lament and mourn the loss we see onscreen (in Oscar winners like *Titanic*, *Million Dollar Baby*, *The Departed*, and *No Country for Old Men*). These tragedies serve as cautionary tales to wake us from our slumber—to make us more vigilant and proactive in our daily lives.

We also love underdog stories about rising above harrowing circumstances (from *Rocky* and *Gladiator* to *The King's Speech* and *12 Years a Slave*). When we follow the travails of a protagonist into a cave or woods, we experience a similar sense of catharsis when they emerge victorious. *Wonder Woman's* (2017) journey of self-discovery may embolden us to leave home, to face our fears, to resist our enemies. It was fascinating to see Wonder Woman conquer her foes on the front lines of World War I via bracelets rather than bullets. Her heroism did not require guns to vanquish the weapons of war marshaled by the opposition. We may identify with our cinematic heroes' struggles and find points of contact that resonate with our own trials and temptations. From biblical heroes like David overcoming Goliath or Esther protecting her people to cinematic legends like Dorothy confronting the wicked witch or Frodo facing Sauron, we have always searched for role models to go before us and slay the dragons that haunt us. The wisdom they gain along the journey becomes a comfort to us as we seek to conquer our foes, whether internal or external.

We go to the movies to find ourselves in the stories. As Frederick Buechner has written, "My assumption is that the story of any one of us is in some measure the story of us all. . . . I suppose, it is like looking through someone else's photograph album. What holds you, if nothing else, is the possibility that somewhere among all those shots of people you never knew and places you never saw, you may come across something or someone you recognize."[11] We need screenwriters from many different cultures to tell stories that reflect their life experience and lens. They may question the hyperindividualism assumed in Hollywood narratives. Alternative values such as family, community, or equality may arise. In an acceptance speech at the 2017 Emmy Awards, Reese Witherspoon challenged studios to "bring women to the front of their own stories, and make them the hero of their own stories."[12] Barry Jenkins, the filmmaker of *Moonlight* (2016), saw his Oscar victory as a message of hope: "To anyone watching this who sees themselves in us, let this be a symbol, a reflection that leads you to love yourself."[13] From distinct cultural milieus begin to flow even more universal truths about the human predicament.

Setting (Atmosphere)

Another key question that screenwriters must answer involves *setting*, or *atmosphere*. Where and when does the action take place? A great setting will test the weaknesses and refine the strengths of a protagonist. Screenwriters move their characters from a relatively mundane everyday world (like Indiana Jones's university classroom) and drop them into a literal jungle. The setting should test the mettle of the main character, forcing them to face their greatest fears (like snakes). The atmosphere and milieu proves so important in a visual medium like the movies. Is the story set in the past, the present, or the future? If the story occurs in a time and place we are familiar with, then screenwriters will engage in rigorous research to (re)create a believable world. How did people dress, speak, and live in an earlier era? The screenplay serves as the blueprint for the thousands of choices regarding makeup, costumes, props, and locations that invariably follow. Many films are rooted in faithful re-creations.

Consider how important it was for Steven Spielberg to get the historical details right in *Schindler's List* (1993). The story is dominated by the real-life specter of anti-Semitism, the movie's fundamental "atmosphere." Its presence is not up for debate—only how characters will respond, given its ghastly reality. We see fear in the eyes of Jewish people as they are herded into railcars. We see Jews stripped naked and, heads shaved, led to the "showers" of the concentration camp. We see the commandant force a young Jewish woman into sexual slavery. The atmosphere and setting are appropriately drab, dank, and depressing.

As Oskar Schindler (Liam Neeson) comes to care for his Jewish workers over the course of the film, we witness his growth as a human being. What is going on is bigger than just Schindler. What is at stake is the very sanctity of human life itself. When his workers give him a gold ring made from the fillings of their teeth, on which is engraved, "Whoever saves one life, saves the world entire," we sense that Schindler's resistance to Nazi anti-Semitism has a larger meaning than even he knows. The movie ends with streams of people, some actors in the movie and some the Jews Schindler rescued, together with their descendants, walking by his grave. Anti-Semitism will not have the final word. Humankind's survival depends on our resistance to such tyranny. Here is the power of this story.

In *Hotel Rwanda* (2004), the quiet, desperate courage of Paul Rusesabagina (Don Cheadle), the hotel manager who rescued more than a thousand from certain death during the genocide of a million people in Rwanda, is demonstrated over against the inexplicable, incorrigible evil of tribal hatred. Viewers are left speechless, wondering whether we would have had such courage given the inevitability of the situation. In all these movies, we are not *simply* dealing with interesting and/or compelling characters. Rather, the stories find their energy in confronting something larger than characterization alone—a backdrop against which moral choices must be made.

Fantasies and sci-fi are also subject to the same high standards of research, but screenwriters have a freedom to imagine a new world. They must still consider the physics and rules for how their cinematic universe operates. *Jurassic Park* (1993) and *Jurassic World* (2015) are not just dinosaur movies but stories about the re-creation of lost worlds. From *The Wizard of Oz* (1939) and *E. T.* (1982) to *The Lord of the Rings* and *The Hobbit* trilogies, many stories are shaped around the notion of homecoming. The filmmakers go to great lengths to establish a believable and heartwarming home before the adventure kicks in. For *Mad Max: Fury Road* (2015) to work, we need to understand how rare water has become in the postapocalyptic setting. What has happened in the past to create the current conditions? The filmmakers knew they needed to find the driest climate possible, which took them to Namibia, to film the story.

Characters' bravery or treachery is linked to the setting, a world without enough water or fuel to survive. Atmosphere is more than just the prevailing mood or emotional element of a story. It is the entire high-stakes setting within which the characters are forced to take action.

Plot

Once the character is established within their world, audiences want to know what's going to happen. What is the *plot*? What is the movie about? Most American movies can be reduced to a fairly succinct logline: Two friends vie for the affection of a girl. Foes race to recover a bag of money (or diamonds or gold). Parents attempt to rescue a kidnapped child. Clear, measurable goals drive the plot. We know who we are cheering for and how their success will be measured. The playwright Lillian Hellman has described the difference between plot and story in this way: "Story is what the characters want to do and plot is what the writer wants the characters to do."[14] Plot is the way the movie constructs and conveys the unfolding of action over time. Movies that portray how our existence in time might be thought significant, how our lives reveal patterns that can take on meaningful shape, have plot as their center.

American movies tend to follow a three-act structure rooted in Aristotle's *Poetics*. Screenwriting guru Linda Seger notes that whether we have a Greek tragedy, a five-act Shakespearean play, or a four-act dramatic television series, "we still see the basic three-act structure: beginning, middle, and end—or set-up, development, and resolution."[15] Events unspool in a linear and logical fashion. One choice or clue leads to the next. Louis Giannetti states, "In the American cinema especially, the story reigns supreme. All the other language systems are subordinated to the plot, the structural spine of virtually all American fiction films, and most foreign movies, as well."[16] We want our pictures to move, to take us somewhere. We prefer action to dialogue, plot to pondering. The downside of our addiction to what happens next is that we resist narratives that require extended reflection. Films that leave space for us to consider our relationship to each other or to God are often bypassed for an easily digestible action adventure. We prefer films that come at us rather than stories that draw us out (what Paul Schrader calls the "transcendental style"). Movies that are light on plot, that cause us to pause, are too easily dismissed as boring.

Tone (Point of View)

Audiences have become so familiar with Hollywood's classic narrative arc that screenwriters are working much harder to subvert the three-act structure.

Some of the most satisfying films play with time or upend audience expectations via unreliable narrators. They alter the traditional understanding of *point of view*. Tone is established by the implied narrator's attitude toward the story's subject and audience. A voice-over or monologue can immediately tell us how a character (and usually the audience) should feel about the situation. Tone can also be conveyed through the movie's cinematic language—its editing, photography, composition, music, pace, and lighting (we will discuss these formal aspects of movie's tone in the next chapter). Point of view is how a story is framed, the lens through which it is told.

Audiences are so accustomed to a linear narrative and a reliable narrator that postmodern filmmakers figured out how to exploit our expectations for dramatic surprises. *Pulp Fiction* (1994), *Fight Club* (1999), and *Memento* (2000) broke away from narrative conventions in original ways. They forced audiences to look more closely and think more carefully about what they've seen. As the movie ends, we realize that our understanding has barely begun. The cinematic tricks employed by M. Night Shyamalan in *The Sixth Sense* (1999) and *Signs* (2002) caused audiences to play back the story in their minds, looking for clues they missed the first time around. We begin to question our perception: How could we have failed to see what seems so obvious in hindsight? The German film *Run Lola Run* (1998) unspooled like a video game, resetting the story for viewers multiple times. It offers three retellings of the same story of a young woman who has twenty minutes to get her hands on one hundred thousand deutsche marks in order to save her boyfriend's life. The pace is frenetic as Lola literally runs through the streets, racing against the clock. Lola goes through a complete cycle before starting over with a little more knowledge and understanding each time. Her race within a temporal purgatory is a cinematic delight. These puzzling films are so prevalent that they became their own mind-blowing subgenre.

What makes a story work, enabling it to rise above cinematic conventions and audience expectations? A clever plot full of unexpected twists may still prove unsatisfying. Great movies must answer the question, why? Why should we give you our attention and even affection? Why should I bother? Why should I care? If characters are not compelling, audiences will not care how many effects and explosions occur onscreen. We must be invested in a character's plight before we dare to follow them down a dark road. Massive megastories like *The Lord of the Rings* or the intertwined *Star Wars* universe are dependent on audiences' investment in following characters' struggles across time. Once we know and love Harry, Hermione, and Ron, we will follow their efforts to solve almost any of J. K. Rowling's plots. The *what* of a stirring story begins with the *who* we are asked to follow. The *why* of a story gets at those large overarching themes of good versus evil and the choices we face every single day. Who are we and what are we called to do? These are core questions of good drama—and also of daily discipleship.

The Building Blocks of Film

In a well-told tale, we are so swept up in the drama that we may not notice the seams of how the story is constructed. We are so busy enjoying the story that we do not take the time to analyze how it is made or why it is effective. Given the importance of storytelling across our daily lives, we feel compelled to sharpen our skills as story analysts. Although some may not want to know how movie magic is created, we believe that a greater understanding of the building blocks of film leads to an even deeper appreciation of and potential for masterful storytelling.

The standard unit of measurement in cinematic stories is one reel. From the earliest days of moviemaking, the physical limits of film resulted in movies being shot and projected in ten-minute increments—one reel at a time. In the silent era, only so much footage could fit on a reel of film loaded into a camera or projected onto a movie screen. A cameraman or projectionist had to monitor the playback, watching closely for when the reel would run out. Early films were reduced to one reel—ten minutes of screen time—until a second projector was added. Then a projectionist could synchronize the switch from one projector to another in a seamless manner. The multi-reel movie was born. Having been inspired by big-budget spectacles in Italy like *Cabiria* (1914), D. W. Griffith pushed the boundaries of what was possible with his lengthy epic *The Birth of a Nation* (1915). A film's story was no longer limited to one or two reels but could be expanded to "feature length," which was two or even three hours (with the reels still changed every ten minutes).

Feature films began to be crafted in ten-minute sequences. Each *sequence* had its own goals or tensions, from introducing a character's backstory in act one (once upon a time), through to the climactic chase scene and happy reunion in act three (they lived happily ever after). Each sequence comprised discrete but related *scenes*. Each scene comprised particular dramatic *beats*, moments when the thoughts or actions of one or more characters turned or shifted. Ideally, then as now, each scene and each sequence contains a twist to surprise audiences, arousing our curiosity enough to sustain our interest. A smart beat will energize a good scene. A surprising scene will fuel an entire sequence. A brilliant sequence will carry us through to the next act. Sequences, scenes, and beats are the dramatic building blocks of film.

American movies are built on a three-act structure. Feature films are constructed out of eight or nine sequences that each last ten to fifteen minutes. While the overriding goal of the story may remain clear, the tensions and obstacles confronting the lead character will shift with each sequence. In action films, these big "set pieces" are quite obvious and may involve, say, breaking out of a prison cell or breaking into a bank. The setting and goal will be distinct within the sequence. The end of the sequence (and the achievement or frustration of the goal) will usually be accompanied by a change of place and time. Scenes will shift from day to night or night to day. Setting will move from Bangkok to Bucharest. New allies or foes may be introduced and a fresh set of plans set in motion. Think about any film within *The Fast and the Furious* franchise. They are always switching locales and automobiles. As our heroes hop into cars around the globe, we may be so dazzled by the setting that we fail to think about why the plot has seemingly shifted from Plan A to Plan B. The screenwriter's goal is to simply keep the story moving forward.

In act one, the screenwriter has approximately ten minutes of screen time (ten pages in the screenplay) to introduce the character's everyday life. We will likely see where they live, how they start their day, who they're related to, and where they work. To make them more endearing to audiences, they might even pet a dog. This is the setup. At the end of the first reel, an external force or catalyst will disturb their status quo. It may be a theft, a kidnapping, an invasion, an escape, a diagnosis, a spider bite. By the twenty-minute mark (twenty pages in), a protagonist will face a turning point to make a choice, to leave the comfort of home and break their routine. The catalyst must be large enough in size and urgent enough in timing to propel a story forward for two more acts. The stakes will be spelled out clearly, allowing the audience to ponder whatever the film's central question or tension may be: Will our hero find true love? Will our heroine escape the island before the tsunami arrives? Will the earth be saved?

In act two, the protagonist chooses to embark on a journey to find a treasure, recover a lost love, return a ring. The middle of the movie may take a full hour (sixty pages of a screenplay) for all complications to set in before a second turning point or twist sends the story in a new direction. The middle of a story tests our hero or heroine. Best-laid plans fall short. Strategies to trap the villain or win a potential mate's heart do not work. Hope fades. Depression and panic enter. The protagonist will discover their weaknesses and learn about their limitations. With Plan B, C, and D exhausted, Plan E will have to be adopted. Are the characters learning from their mistakes or doomed to repeat them? By the end of act two, we should have a strong sense of whether our protagonists are heading toward a hard-won victory or a disaster (of their own making). Out of failure, our desperate protagonist will hopefully emerge with a fresh perspective borne of humility. A fatally flawed character will make decisions rooted in even greater hubris and folly.

In act three, the protagonist will face their greatest challenge and hopefully vanquish their most ardent foe. This is the dramatic climax of the story, the ultimate test of creativity, mettle, or resolve. The final twenty minutes should leave us a little breathless, swept up in a combination of fear and delight. The finale traditionally concludes with a chase, a fight, a race against the clock to defuse the bomb, save the world, or make it to the church on time. When we care about the characters, we become invested in the outcome, rooting for Rocky to defeat his challenger. We may find ourselves shouting at the screen, warning the hero to duck, to not make the same mistakes that vanquished them in an earlier confrontation. Special skills planted earlier in the movie (a secret weapon) will be summoned and pay off in a satisfying manner. If we are disconnected from the hero's plight, climactic fight scenes feel interminable. We cannot wait for the film to end (and put us out of our misery). If done right, though, a story should create a sense of catharsis—tension released in a deeply satisfying way. The final sequence will usually bring the character back home to friends and family. They will be battered and bruised, but deepened. Wisdom will arise from the arduous journey. The resolution may be open-ended, but we sense how much we as an audience have learned and experienced by witnessing the character's struggles.

What kind of story are we watching? A comedy will end with a wedding or graduation; a tragedy often concludes with a funeral. A simple story will telegraph that ending in the opening scenes. The poster or the trailer may have revealed too much. We can already predict who will be battling in the third act (and who will prevail). A complex plot will surprise us with twists that we didn't expect (but that we can still appreciate as both logical and inevitable). We may expect romance to blossom, but perhaps it will not occur with the characters we expected or in the manner we envisioned. The films in Richard Linklater's *Before* trilogy do not resolve in a tidy manner, but we sense that love lingers beneath the surface in sublime ways. Characters' goals, one hopes, will shift over the course of a film (or series of films), signaling growth and recognition that mirror the audiences' expanding understanding as well.

Analyzing Stories—Acts, Sequences, Scenes

During Craig's time at the University of Southern California's film school, all aspiring directors were required to take a film analysis class taught by Czech screenwriter and legendary professor Frank Daniel. The structure of the course was remarkably simple. Watch a film, dissect the story, and outline every act, sequence, and scene. How did the students sharpen their skills? By watching the same film two weeks in a row. Frank Daniel put no pressure on them to analyze the story in week one. The students, with cinematic delight, simply let the plot twists of classic films happen to them. But a week later, already familiar with how the story would unfold, they were much more aware of how the story worked. Over time, they could spot the structure of films that ranged from the thrillers of Hitchcock to the comedies of Mel Brooks. Let's consider the structure of two highly acclaimed but very different features.

The poetic Oscar-winning *Moonlight* revels in film's three-act structure. It is based on Tarell Alvin McCraney's semiautobiographical play *In Moonlight Black Boys Look Blue*. Miami-born filmmaker Barry Jenkins expanded the forty-five-minute play, simplifying the elliptical story where scenes and remembrances faded in and out across time.[17] He also added a new third act. The resulting film retains poignant scenes of learning to swim in the Atlantic Ocean, enjoying a reunion meal, kissing on a moonlit beach. But the formal plot remains quite linear. To anchor the "experimental" story, Jenkins makes the three distinct eras of this boy's life abundantly clear. Title cards separate each section of the film. The main character is known by three different names: as an innocent boy, "Little"; as a troubled adolescent, "Chiron"; and as a hardened adult, "Black." Three actors are employed to make the eras even more distinct. What a bold choice, to force the audience to leap across three eras in an effort to understand the challenges of this boy's life.

The stark changes in the character's persona—from the playful Little, to the tentative Chiron, to the world-weary Black—are shocking. We are invited to watch closely, in search of clues for how a gentle young man can end up committing assaults in a classroom or pushing drugs on the streets. *Moonlight* humanizes young men we all too easily dismiss as criminals. We witness the hellish descent of Chiron's mother, Paula (Naomie Harris), from capable nurse to crack addict over the three acts. The introduction of a father figure like Juan (Mahershala Ali) provides some much-needed structure to the struggling boy's life. We also notice Juan's unannounced and unexpected absence. Jenkins, explaining why he left Juan's exit so open-ended, says it was "because of the structure of the source material. It's meant to be immersive to the audience. It's supposed to function as part of his pain—'you have to walk a mile in my shoes.' All across the US there are these young men like Chiron, and there are these father figures like Juan who take them under their wing. And one day, Chiron came home and Juan was gone, with no explanation. I wanted the audience to feel what that was like."[18] How many equally bright black men end

Moonlight (2016), © A24 Distribution, LLC

up either dead or in prison? We feel for Chiron because we see how characters and circumstances shift around him. This beautifully filmed story is painful to watch, but it forces us to consider how we would respond under equally trying conditions.

We also follow Chiron's evolving relationship with his best friend, Kevin. Here is one source of solace amid a world of chaos and confusion. And yet, it comes with its own social challenges. In the third act, we wonder, will the hard exterior of Black reveal the tender side of Chiron and even Little that has been stuffed down so deep in order to survive? *Moonlight* is a love story that unfolds remarkably slowly. It rewards patient viewing. Barry Jenkins and Tarell Alvin McCraney won the Oscar for Best Adapted Screenplay because they figured out how to focus our attention across time—via a clear, three-act structure.

The outrageous style and furious pace of *Mad Max: Fury Road* (2015) disguise a profoundly simple story. *Fury Road* follows the beats of a classic escape story, chronicling what it takes to run away from a tyrant. Director George Miller did not work from a traditional screenplay. Charlize Theron, who plays Imperator Furiosa, explains the process: "There was a script; it just wasn't a conventional script in the sense that we kind of know scripts with scene numbers. Initially it was just a storyboard, and we worked off that storyboard for almost three years."[19] Miller explains, "I got in touch with Brendan McCarthy, a wonderful artist who had sent me some terrific drawings of Mad Max. I asked if he wanted to come down and work on it. . . . We sat in a room and basically laid out 3500 panels."[20] The "script" for *Fury Road* was essentially a giant comic book.

Set in a postapocalyptic future, the story conforms to the structure of a western, where a small community, led by an outsider, reclaims its home. Miller told NPR, "Basically, they're allegorical stories in the same way I guess that the classic Western was that. And Max is a character who gets swept up into this story. He's sort of wandering the wasteland looking for some sense of meaning in a very stark world, and he gets caught up in this story."[21] The plot also juggles notions of knights, castles, and damsels in distress. But *Fury Road* follows Furiosa on her hero's journey far more than it follows Max.

As the story begins, environmental disaster and scarcity hover in the atmosphere. Mad Max (Tom Hardy) is captured and thrown into a dungeon, serving as a blood bag for a War Boy. Blood, oil, milk, and water are all in short supply in this harsh, elemental setting. Imperator Furiosa and five women break away from the Citadel in a big rig truck full of precious fuel, in search of an idyllic Green Place. *Fury Road* is a chase story with the bloodthirsty Immortan Joe pursuing his childbearing harem with full force. This is the setup in act one.

As the story unfolds, our heroes Furiosa and Max must martial all kinds of creativity to escape Joe's minions. They gradually join forces and win over Nux, the War Boy, to their cause. A confrontation with the Bullet Farmer takes place within a dark blue night that results in him being blinded. Only when they reach their Edenic goal in the desert do they (and we) realize that they must turn around and face their tormentors. This is the literal turning point that concludes act two. An army of determined grandmothers, the Vuvalini, join the revolution. In act three, the hunted become the hunters. Instead of escaping to an elusive paradise, they decide to storm Joe's castle and reclaim it for all who are oppressed. The movement of the story is simple: from point A to point B and back again. How they return to point A is deeply satisfying. A ballet of motorcycle stunts, high-wire pole-vaulting, and automotive force overwhelm the dialogue. In *Mad Max*, actions are much louder than words. *Fury Road* is all about the hunger for home—for Max, for Furiosa, and for the women seeking a safe haven within which to raise their children.

Mad Max: Fury Road (2015), © Warner Bros. Entertainment Inc.

The longing for love, for a stable home for our children, for a sustainable earth—these are core values that animate our lives across cultures and religions. These make up the human story from Genesis onward. As our institutions have lost their cultural cachet, stories have emerged as our primary medium for making meaning. Our hunger for story corresponds to our growing transcendence gap. Moviegoers (and increasingly churchgoers) recognize that "story reigns supreme." Metaphorically, it reflects a "three-stage journey of courage, heartbreak and redemption."[22] Paul Woolf, screenwriting professor at the University of Southern California's film school, explains this pattern in the classroom:

> So I say to my students, take my word that this pattern exists. If you look, you'll find it. Why do you think it exists? Because some screenplay writer invented it? Is it a formula? Finally, someone in my class thinks about it, and says, "It's there . . . because it is life." Movies are life. That's why we go. We're hoping the characters will do teshuvah [i.e., come back to something you once were, return to God, journey homeward] because we want to know it is possible.[23]

Frederick Buechner reminds us that the gospel can be read as tragedy, comedy, or fairy tale.[24] Life can be extremely cruel, as we witness in *Moonlight*. Despite the specter of death, we may still find moments of comic relief, as in *Stranger Than Fiction*. Sometimes, we may find the deepest truths about the human condition—from our capacity for self-destruction to our remarkable drive to survive—in a fairy tale like *Fury Road*. We must never sugarcoat the complexities of life. There is a tragic dimension to Jesus's story. The cross is a deadly symbol until we encounter the comedic reversal of the resurrection. Sometimes the beauty of creation and redemption can only be captured in a fairy tale. May we develop eyes to see the story we find ourselves in.

As we train our hearts and minds to digest films in ten-minute increments, we may also be training our souls to measure our lives in similar ways. We may think of our lives as eight sequences of ten years each. Our first ten years of childhood may have a certain simplicity and innocence that is altered in adolescence. Our twenties feel like a time of experimentation, trying on adulthood, flirting with potential mates, and trying on careers. By our thirties, we may be starting to settle down, to have financial stability and commitments. Middle age is comparable to the middle of the movie, where things can get a little slack, the pace may slow down, and we may need a big twist to propel our attention forward. By fifty or sixty, hopefully, we've learned enough about ourselves and our lives to make wise decisions. There may still be time to try a different approach to marriage or parenting. The arrival of grandchildren may offer a restart. At retirement, we may have to face some of our biggest foes—like answering questions about the meaning of life. Our final years may not involve guns, car chases, or bank robberies, but they may require our greatest clarity and resolve. The ending may be beautiful, tragic, or bittersweet. Like Harold Crick, we may not know whether we are in a comedy or a tragedy until the final act.

Discussion Questions

1. Think about a favorite film, one you have watched many times. To what degree and in what ways do the characters, the setting, the atmosphere, and the point of view sharpen the story?
2. Try to identify the three distinct acts that create the structure of the film. Break the story down into eight or nine sequences. What does the resulting outline look like? Can you see how the goals and tension change in each sequence?
3. What kind of story do you seem to find yourself in now? Tragedy? Comedy? Fairy tale?

4

sights and sounds

an audiovisual lens

A title card announces that, in space, "There is nothing to carry sound. No air pressure. No oxygen."[1] Into the roaring silence comes the faint echo of voices over radio waves. An astronaut is engaged in a space walk, while two mission specialists service their space shuttle *Explorer* orbiting around Earth. The casual banter of shuttle pilot Matt Kowalski (George Clooney) with mission control in Houston (the voice of Ed Harris) lulls us into a false sense of ease. Mission specialist Dr. Ryan Stone (Sandra Bullock) deals with the pressures of zero gravity while replacing a panel for a scanning system. An errant bolt floats toward us in stunning 3D. Earth appears as a vibrant presence reflected in the astronauts' visors. While mission specialist Shariff laughs with delight at the wonder of space, Kowalski asks Stone, "So, what do you like about being up here?" She answers, "The silence." The camera pans across the blue planet, Earth, serving as the primary light source for the scene (and for the astronauts' work). All is peaceful for the first ten minutes of *Gravity*, until we hear reports of a missile strike and see debris approaching from a Russian satellite torn apart. Houston offers two harrowing words: "Mission abort."

Debris zooms past the astronauts and across the screen. The music follows the same frightening path from left to right. Disaster literally strikes as mission specialist Shariff and Dr. Stone are cut off from the shuttle. Stone swings from a mechanical arm careening toward us like a gyroscope gone wild. The bass rumble from a subwoofer rattles our seats. The astronauts struggle to survive amid the resulting chaos. The camera pans and twirls as Stone spirals away

Gravity (2013), © Warner Bros. Entertainment Inc.

toward deep space. She turns at a dizzying pace, and the sound rotates with her. Only a distant voice keeps her connected. An objective close-up on Dr. Stone's face in panic, gasping for breath, morphs into a subjective experience. We move inside her space suit, flipping around Earth, searching for the shuttle, through her disoriented point of view. We see the status updates on her visor; we hear her shortness of breath, the fading sounds of radio noise. As she cries out, "Houston, do you copy? I am drifting," the lights on her face change to intense reds and greens. Darkness and silence descend as Dr. Stone is cut off from her traveling companions. She floats into a void. With her oxygen dropping, she—and the viewer along with her—faces death. Until Kowalski reappears and they are tethered together in a bracing survival pact.

Lights, cameras, and actions are all synchronized in the harrowing cinematic ballet that opens *Gravity* (2013). Director Alfonso Cuarón and his creative team create a seamless nineteen-minute shot. Because there are no edits or cuts in this masterful *plan-séquence* (a long take that constitutes an entire scene), audiences are swept up in Dr. Stone's dilemma. The contrasting sounds, from eerie quiet to raucous ruckus, also contribute to our unease. When we drift with Sandra Bullock into deep space, cut off from her oxygen supply, the long wait for rescue feels almost interminable. The sights and sounds in *Gravity* take us inside the astronauts' life-and-death struggle. It takes so much work and planning to coordinate this cinematic dance between the actors, the cameras, and the effects. As a nail-biting roller-coaster ride, *Gravity* earned Academy Awards for its achievements in cinematography, directing, film editing, sound mixing, sound editing, visual effects, and original score.

This chapter will analyze how sights and sounds combine to create such intense cinematic experiences. Film is a collaborative art, or rather a collection of arts. It draws on painting, photography, architecture, and set design to create spectacular sights. Yet the theatrical arts of acting, music, and dance are also employed to create equally compelling sounds. We will trace the three stages of how movies are made—from preproduction to production through postproduction. Rigorous preproduction and planning come to fruition during long, pressure-packed days on location. Once the shooting concludes, the postproduction crew edits both picture and sound, adding effects, graphics, and music to create a highly polished picture. Savvy filmgoers note how color, costumes, and silence distinguish key scenes and themes and enhance a movie's meaning. This chapter will consider what that long list of credits at the conclusion of Oscar winners like *Gravity* mean. We will highlight key members of the creative team for each stage—from art directors and cinematographers to composers and sound designers. We will employ an audiovisual lens to grasp how images and sounds enhance a story and deepen our theological appreciation of cinema.

Preproduction

The script serves as the blueprint for a film. It takes a massive crew and herculean effort, however, to turn that blueprint into a finished film. Once the script has been approved, a director is hired to bring that story into vivid reality. Directors are responsible for the overall look and feel of the film. In preproduction, they may communicate that vision via sketches, storyboards, color swatches, or mood boards. These will be developed in consultation with their principal creative collaborators—the production designer and the cinematographer.

Visual Palette

This power trio of director, production designer, and cinematographer will spend months developing a particular visual palette for the film that corresponds to the type of story they're telling. A chilling drama may come across in shades of black, blue, and gray, while a sunny comedy may feature bright pastels or vibrant shades of red, orange, and yellow. Consider the green glow of a computer screen that dominates the production design in *The Matrix* (1999) or the drab brown grass that surrounds the spooky psychiatrist's home in *Get Out* (2017). After a tornado, the sepia tones of farm life burst into Technicolor for Dorothy in *The Wizard of Oz* (1939). As she and her friends travel the bright yellow brick road, the poppy fields are vibrantly red and the Emerald City green (matching the skin of Margaret Hamilton's wicked witch!). Dorothy responds to this new splendor with words that have taken on a whole afterlife: "Toto, I have a feeling we're not in Kansas anymore."

Color can have both a psychological and a symbolic effect on the story being told. It can be conveyed through how the story is filmed and by what is filmed. Inspired by the colors of the French flag, Krzysztof Kieslowski created the masterful Three Colors trilogy: *Blue* (1993), *White* (1994), and *Red* (1994). Each film is distinguished by tightly controlled production design and lighting to explore the distinct themes of liberty, equality, and fraternity. Director and cinematographer of *Traffic* (2000) Steven Soderbergh used different coloration in the film itself to tell his three interwoven stories about drug trafficking. The bureaucratic world of the government's war on drugs has the hue of a cold, sterile blue. The corruption of sunny suburban San Diego is photographed as overexposed and washed out. And the earthy Mexican world of violence and death is given a golden brown glow. These distinctive colors allow viewers to follow the complex, intercut story lines without feeling lost.

The martial-arts epic *Hero* (2004) retells the same story three times: how an anonymous assassin in ancient China defeats three rivals. A cinematographer-turned-director, Zhang Yimou is renowned as a visual stylist, including his vibrant staging of the opening ceremony at the 2008 Beijing Olympic Games. *Hero* uses bold colors in costume and setting to distinguish each recollection. One of the retellings is thus given a red hue; another, blue; and the last, white. Viewers also see a number of flashbacks that are cast in strong greens, and a framing tale is dominated by shades of black. The cinematographer, Christopher Doyle, said about the movie: "Part of the beauty of the film is that it is one story colored by different perceptions. I think that's the point. Every story is colored by personal perception."[2] Color can be a means to create a narrative spine.

Production Design: Setting the Stage

While directors are rightly credited for the overall vision of a film, they depend on designs and decisions made by key members of their creative team. When Spike Lee was interviewed at the 2018 Cannes Film Festival, where his *BlacKkKlansman* premiered, he likened himself to the manager of a basketball team whose job is to encourage the creativity of the players toward a common goal. In preproduction, the look of the film is often determined by the art director and set designer; they oversee the production design. The over-the-top style of Baz Luhrmann's films is distinguished by the skills of his Oscar-winning spouse, Catherine Martin. In *Moulin Rouge!* (2001), Martin made Nicole Kidman and Ewan McGregor singing atop an elephant while being serenaded by the moon seem not just plausible but delightful. Martin was also honored for her imaginative art direction and retro costume design in *The Great Gatsby* (2013). In her capable hands, the 1920s in West Egg roared again. While Wes Anderson's films all have a distinctive look, the rich colors of *The Grand Budapest Hotel* (2014) were created by the Oscar-winning team of art director Adam Stockhausen and set decorator Anna Pinnock. The pink exteriors, the red elevator, and the purple bellboy suits were all meticulously planned to enhance the comedy. For *La La Land*, director Damien Chazelle was inspired by the primary colors in *The Umbrellas of Cherbourg* (1964). Los Angeles provided a magical backdrop as production designer David Wasco and set decorator Sandy Reynolds-Wasco placed Emma Stone in yellow, red, blue, and green dresses alongside Ryan Gosling in his stylish skinny ties. Through rigorous research and planning, production designers of any good film ensure that costumes, makeup, sets, and props all contribute to the desired feeling of joy (or sorrow) within each scene. Thousands of creative decisions are made before the actors arrive.

Preproduction is an opportunity to play God, to create an entire world. It is comparable to the work of Genesis 1, when God sets the stage for Adam and Eve to enter. Yet the production designer (traditionally credited as the art director) and their team must create a believable world within the limitations of money, space, and time. For example, producers and studio execs want to know how much it will cost to create or secure the primary settings. Decisions must be made to film either on location or on a set (or some of both). For the first *Harry Potter* movie, the historic Leadenhall Market in London stood in as the backdrop for Diagon Alley. Alnwick Castle in Newcastle, England, initially served as the exterior of Hogwarts. The old steam train *Jacobite* on the Glenfinnan Viaduct on the west coast of Scotland was transformed into the *Hogwarts Express*.[3] What about the film's interiors? Carpenters crafted a three-dimensional world to specifications overseen by production designer Stuart Craig and set decorator Stephanie McMillan. So much detail went into the creation of eight Harry Potter movies that tourists can now tour the sets for Diagon Alley and Hogwarts at the Leavesden studio outside of London.[4] Fans who cannot travel overseas can relish the attention to detail within the Wizarding World of Harry Potter at Universal Studios (also designed by Stuart Craig).

Films must satisfy our voyeuristic eye. If sets, costumes, hair, and makeup look cheap or cheesy, we are likely to lose interest in the story. Credibility depends on plausibility, even in fantasy and science fiction.[5] While J. R. R. Tolkien was free to describe a Middle Earth full of hobbits and orcs in fanciful detail, imagine how much pressure accompanied the creation of the cinematic *Lord of the Rings* trilogy. Thousands of sketches and drawings preceded the creation of props, costumes, and wigs. The preproduction design team had to decide the shape of Gandalf's hat, the length of his staff, the cut and color of his beard. What about Bilbo Baggins's home in the Shire? Peter Jackson and his collaborators scoured New Zealand in search of the ideal location before finally discovering an unassuming family farm. The grass, the hillside, the ponds could work for Hobbiton. But those tiny Hobbit holes still had to be drawn and built to exacting detail. As with Harry Potter's world, Hobbiton movie set tours outside Auckland allow fans to walk in Bilbo Baggins's steps and even take photos outside the green door of Bag End.[6]

What about the dramatic backdrops and environments for those sets? The art of matte painting was developed to save time and money. In *Black Narcissus* (1947), one image could be dropped in front of a camera lens to provide the illusion of the Himalayas. Actors could occupy a small portion of the frame, while an artist's vision tricked audiences into believing nuns were living outside Darjeeling, India. Nowadays, most backdrops are added in postproduction via digital enhancement. More and more, the director, cinematographer, and production designer must work with the effects team to pre-visualize how the finished film will look. This process of pre-visualization ("pre-viz") borrows from the art of animation, where teams from Pixar and Disney rely on animatics to see how their proposed story might actually look and flow. The walls of Pixar's studio in Northern California reveal the importance of storyboard, pre-viz, and animatics for the finished film.[7] The color contrasts between scenes are worked out before the project moves forward. The camera angles and movement of the characters are coordinated before the detailed drawing begins. So many potential production problems are solved (or avoided) in the preproduction phase.

For *Gravity*, each shot and scene was planned beforehand on computers.[8] Cuarón brought his ace cinematographer Emmanuel "Chivo" Lubezki into the script development process. They worked on the look of *Gravity* for four and a half years prior to production. After working with his visual effects supervisor Tim Webber and his Framestore team on *Harry Potter and the Goblet of Fire* (2005), Cuarón brought them into the creative process early for *Gravity*. They went through ten months of pre-viz before actors were brought into the process. Artistic choices involving complex physics and camera movements were tested via computer simulations.

When the script and storyboards are proven to be compelling in the pre-viz process, the filmmakers shift to the challenges of production—turning best-laid plans into stirring performances captured on camera.

Production

Rigorous preproduction sets the stage for performers like Sandra Bullock and George Clooney to be truly in the moment. Attention to costume and props beforehand allows the actors to create believable characters. Successful pre-production sets up viewers for a vicarious experience, for entering into actors' predicaments.[9] With our critical eye satisfied by the reality of the scenario, we can extend our emotions toward the characters' plight.

Acting: Making Believe to Make Us Believe

On set, as the actors try to summon genuine fear or love, the camera focuses in to capture each glance or gesture. When the performance is believable, audiences respond with compassion—suffering with them. A close-up on an evocatively lit human face can create the greatest movie magic.

Actors engage in make-believe so that audiences may believe what they are seeing. Hours of sitting in makeup, being changed into a dwarf, an elf, or a wizard every single day, enables actors to inhabit their role. It is so much easier to become Mad Eye Moody, Bellatrix Lestrange, or Lord Voldemort once in costume for the *Harry Potter* movies. Think of the fanciful wig and eye shadow that make Johnny Depp's first appearance in *Pirates of the Caribbean* (2003) so delightful. Jack Sparrow steps onto a set when all the elements for piracy are already in place. The Oscar-winning hair and makeup that transformed Meryl Streep in *The Iron Lady* (2011) go a long way toward convincing audiences that she is British prime minister Margaret Thatcher. As the film begins, we wonder, "Is that what she looked and sounded like?" Hopefully, we forget that it is Meryl Streep playing a part. As dramatic complications rise, we ask, "What should she do?" The ultimate goal of a good drama is to inspire us to consider, "What would I do?"

Some actors make it purposefully hard on themselves, daring audiences not to care. Consider how Tom Hardy often hides behind masks or constrains his voice. As the villainous Bane in *The Dark Knight Rises* (2012), Hardy communicates almost solely through his shoulders and his eyes. In *Mad Max: Fury Road* (2015), Hardy's eponymous character is bound and gagged for the first third of the film. Even when he is cut loose, Max lets his actions speak rather than words. In *Dunkirk* (2017), Hardy's heroism is obscured by the oxygen mask that covers his fighter pilot's face. As he stands before his burning plane, back turned to the viewer, we are invited to share in his bond with the vehicle that enabled him to save countless soldiers' lives. Perhaps Hardy's finest performance takes place on a long, overnight drive in *Locke* (2013). Hemmed in behind the wheel, Locke responds to a series of phone calls that plunge him deeper into a personal crisis. Alone in his car, Hardy has only disembodied voices to interact with. Audiences lean toward the screen, watching carefully for clues that reveal the depths of Locke's dilemma. As the colors of the highway glide across his face, we are drawn into his self-induced spiral. Hardy has perfected the art of withholding, preserving an aura of mystery around his characters (and himself as an actor). Retaining a layer of secrecy, not giving audiences all they want to know, keeps us coming back for more. We wonder, "Should I care about this person?" The minimal information keeps us wrestling, reaching deeper to summon our own empathy.

Cinematography: Painting with Light

A great cinematographer can convey what a character is feeling through the use of lighting, focus, framing, and movement. As the actors and director rehearse a scene, the cinematographer, focus puller, gaffer, key grip, and crew will also make marks, tweak lights, and coordinate their movements. The camera might be mounted on a dolly or a crane, or it might be handheld. Camera moves have an expressive quality that can enhance a performance and invite viewers even further into a vicarious experience. When the camera responds to what characters and audiences are feeling (maybe through a zoom, a close-up, a slight push into a human face), we enter further into the human drama and all the love and sacrifice, the dejection and elation that are inherent in life. An effective camera operator captures believable performances and magical movie moments that invoke empathy or awe in filmgoers.[10] Rodrigo Prieto, director of photography on *Silence* (2016), says, "I believe shooting a movie is an act of love. My goal is for every scene in each film to move the audience emotionally in the right direction."[11] The right dance between actors and cameras on set can generate tremendous compassion in audiences.

Cinematographer John Alton described his role on classic films ranging from luscious musicals like *An American in Paris* (1951) to stark film noir like *The Big Combo* (1955) as "painting with light." Alton shared his trade secrets as director of photography for those "who also delight in capturing bits of light at rest on things of beauty."[12] Cinematography, Alton says, is about the interplay of light and shadow on sets, props, and people. Comedies employ high-key lighting, where almost everything and everyone is visible. But for mysteries and horror, the drama arises from what we cannot see, where our imagination starts to take over. "Sometimes, it's not what you light, it's what you DON'T light."[13] Film noir focuses on the shadow side of humanity—our depravity. Alton connected the art of cinematography to the paintings of Rembrandt, who demonstrated how to play with shadows and light in order to communicate character. Amid so many digital effects in movies, we may easily forget that film arose as a photographic art. The challenge for painters and cinematographers is to capture the three-dimensional wonders of God's creation on a flat surface like a canvas or a screen.

Orson Welles famously shared his title card and credit as director of *Citizen Kane* (1941) with his cinematographer, Gregg Toland. They altered film history with the introduction of "deep focus," a photographic technique that overcame the limitations of camera lenses. It was thought that a camera could only see so much within a single shot. Objects further away appear blurred or fuzzy because of the distance that light has to travel to reach our eyes. But what if the light was boosted on distant objects? Through careful composition and extreme lighting, Toland and Welles demonstrated how much depth of field and vision was possible even while working with seemingly primitive cameras, lenses, and film stock. By placing characters in focus within the foreground, midground, and background, Toland allowed viewers to study the power dynamics that drove Charles Foster Kane to a tragic demise.

Consider three famous shots from *Citizen Kane*. Inside a log house, his mother makes a key decision to send young Charles away to boarding school while, seen outside through a distant window, the boy plays outside in the snow. The gap between mother and son will only widen after this fateful scene. Or in another dramatic turning point, Kane finishes a scathing review of his wife's operatic debut on behalf of his best friend, Jedidiah Leland. While Kane types in the foreground, the drunken Leland stumbles into the frame from

Citizen Kane (1941), © Turner Entertainment

a distant doorway of the newsroom. Deep focus suggests how much separates the two former friends who are about to permanently part ways. And finally, the growing estrangement between Kane and his second wife, Susan, is emphasized by the depth of field between them in his mountaintop castle, Xanadu. The gap between Kane and his closest companions is underscored by our ability to see how distant he has become from those who cared about him. The story and performances in *Citizen Kane* became much more complicated and intriguing because the audience could literally see so much more due to Toland's deep focus.

From Alton and Toland to now, the craft has been so dominated by men that Rachel Morrison's nomination for *Mudbound* in 2018 marked the first time a woman had ever even been nominated for an Academy Award for Best Cinematography.[14] Historically, the director of photography (DP) was referred to simply as "cameraman." In a creative act of resistance, Kristen Johnston entitled her brilliant cinematic autobiography *Cameraperson* (2016). Barriers of gender are slowly being broken on set. The same is true for race. Mexico's Emmanuel "Chivo" Lubezki recently enjoyed the most remarkable and lauded creative streak in the history of cinematography with three consecutive Oscars for his work on *Gravity* (2013), *Birdman* (2014), and *The Revenant* (2015). We see his groundbreaking innovations in the seamless merging of visual effects with human performances in *Gravity*; in the long, continuous takes in *Birdman*; and in the remarkable use of natural light in *The Revenant*. Chivo has mastered cinematic technique.

Lubezki's experimentation with long takes reached initial heights in *Children of Men* (2006). Anglican writer P. D. James imagined a postapocalyptic future where the miracle of the nativity takes on renewed relevance. With grimy sets and a foreboding atmosphere, director Alfonso Cuarón anticipated the refugee crisis that has gripped the world since the film's Christmas 2006 release. He challenged Chivo to figure out how to film three key sequences as a single, nail-biting shot. The opening breakfast scene is punctured by a terrorist attack in London. A drive through seemingly sylvan woods is interrupted by a bloody motorcycle chase. A march through a bullet-riddled building becomes a sacred occasion. In a poetic tracking shot, a different kind of holy family brings a fleeting moment of peace to a weary war-torn world. The technical expertise necessary to choreograph these scenes is staggering in complexity.[15] And yet, Chivo and his camera team make the extraordinary look almost effortless. John Tavener's haunting score, "Fragments of a Prayer," provides a plaintive audio juxtaposition to the visuals of a bloody, urban London battlefield.

In a sci-fi film like *Gravity*, Cuarón and Lubezki needed to coordinate even more moving parts. The first production problem to be solved was the illusion of zero gravity onscreen.[16] How to make the actors float in a believable manner on film sets that are still bound by the laws of gravity? Sandra Bullock and George Clooney did not want to be hoisted in the air, dangling from wires that would be digitally removed afterward. So instead, the *Gravity* team kept the actors stable within a rig while robots controlled the camera swirling around them. What about the lights of outer space? How to convey the flicker of space debris or spinning above the earth? The actors were dropped into a light box, with LED lights rotating around them. Lubezki and his gaffer (the head electrician) pre-lit each scene in a computer for four months prior to filming. They incorporated research regarding the rotation of the earth.[17] In the ninety minutes of screen time, the characters experience two sunsets and two sunrises on their trips around the globe. The colors shift with each scene. Sometimes the earth emits a crystal ocean blue; over Egypt, the astronauts take on an orange glow. *Gravity* is a cosmic dance of lights, cameras, and performances.

When the technical challenges of coordinating camera and effects rise to maddening heights, Lubezki retreats to the wilderness. *The Revenant* was a grueling physical challenge for actors Leonardo DiCaprio and Tom Hardy—as well as for the crew facing the elements of ice, wind, and snow. Miles from city lights and creature comforts, Lubezki and director Alejandro Iñárritu and their team were constrained by natural light. Like the characters in the historic western, the crew had to work with the conditions presented by rural Montana and British Columbia. When winter ran out in North America, the production even moved to Argentina to find sufficient snow for the climatic scenes. Lubezki had already worked with natural light on Terrence Malick's productions of *The New World* (2005) and *The Tree of Life* (2011). With Malick, he created two of the most beautiful and transcendent films in cinematic history by shooting at sundown—during magic hour—when the natural world is aglow. They were literally chasing light, every day of production. Lubezki took the same rigorous aesthetic into the frozen rivers and snowy hillsides of *The Revenant*. Audiences were immersed in the life-threatening conditions western pioneers like Hugh Glass faced because the entire crew also flirted with hypothermia. In the wilderness, with the sun setting, the director, cinematographer, and actors all faced real-world pressure to perform. Careful planning in preproduction surrendered to conditions at hand. Creative decisions needed to be improvised in the moment. Every so often, in the splash of water or blood or breath on a lens or in a flare of sunlight, the camera recorded something magical. The results may be truly miraculous, a tribute to creativity and endurance—God smiling upon a scene.

Postproduction

Who will comb through the hours of footage captured in production to find the most memorable moments? Welcome to the meticulous realm of postproduction. Filmmakers toy with audiences via the juxtaposition of images and sound.

Editing: Creating the Rhythm

The art of editing arises from affinity and contrast.[18] Viewer anxiety or satisfaction rises and falls with the manipulation of time, space, and pace. Sounds and images that share an affinity of shape, style, and substance are soothing. Dramatic tension rises when color, light, angle, music, or subject changes between shots or scenes. Editing (both sounds and pictures) depends on a sense of rhythm. It is comparable to orchestrating a symphony. As Alfred Hitchcock famously declared, "I enjoy playing the audience like an organ."[19]

An early Russian filmmaker, Lev Kuleshov, conducted a famous experiment that showed on the screen an actor with an expressive but neutral look. He used the same footage of the actor but juxtaposed a shot of him with contrasting images in order to trigger different emotions in the audience. Spliced between identical images of Mosjoukine, the well-known actor, were scenes of a crying baby, a bowl of soup, and even a coffin. Not knowing that the shots of Mosjoukine were identical footage, the audience praised the actor for his performance, noting how well he displayed a father's love, a man who was hungry, and a person in mourning! Through editing, the same expressive face had taken on appropriate connotations to match the context. Audience members read into the actor's face what they would have felt if they had been in his place.[20] This phenomenon, known as the Kuleshov effect, illustrates how the arrangement of images can alter our perception, understanding, and emotions.

Sergei Eisenstein, another pioneering Russian filmmaker, called such juxtapositions of film images "montage." He wrote that "two film pieces of any kind, placed together, inevitably combine into a new concept, a new quality, arising out of that juxtaposition."[21] Eisenstein's theories were famously realized in *Battleship Potemkin* (1925), especially in the bloody Odessa Steps sequence. Civilians celebrating the mutiny of sailors in the Ukraine are caught in a cross fire between the czar's militia and encroaching Cossacks. As shots are fired, Eisenstein captures the chaos by juxtaposing the approaching soldiers with victims of all ages. Long shots of the panicked crowd fleeing down the steps are intercut with close-ups of shots fired and boots marching over dead bodies. As a mother is shot, her baby in a carriage is plunged down the steps. An elderly woman grimaces as she is shot in the eye. Static shots of the lion carvings on the steps serve as a counterpoint. They witness but do not comment on the slaughter. An overall mood of oppression and despair is captured not by focusing on a particular character, but by contrasting the jackbooted soldiers with innocents lost. For Eisenstein, the joining of one image to another results in a greater meaning: $1 + 1 = 3$. The French expanded upon Eisenstein's notions by referring to the entire process of assembling images as *montage*. Americans use *montage* to describe a short sequence that compresses time and advances the plot. We call the overall craft *editing*. It is the visceral side of filmmaking, when images hit us in the gut rather than the head or heart.[22]

Both picture and sound editors refer to their craft as "cutting" a film. It has roots in the physical act of cutting and splicing film shots and sound effects together. While the European montage tradition is comfortable calling attention to these cuts, the Hollywood style tries to make editing invisible. We rarely talk about editing in America because editors are encouraged to make their work seamless and unnoticed. Among the most honored editors in cinematic history are Michael Kahn, whose work on *Raiders of the Lost Ark* (1981), *Schindler's List* (1993), and *Saving Private Ryan* (1998) moved millions of viewers, and Thelma Schoonmaker, whose editing put the punch in *Raging Bull* (1980), *The Aviator* (2004), and *The Departed* (2006). So many hours are spent together, poring over footage in a darkened room, that acclaimed filmmakers like Steven Spielberg and Martin Scorsese turn to these underappreciated collaborators again and again. We speak of the fight sequences in *Saving Private Ryan* or *Raging Bull* as having been constructed, but editors must search through so many shots to find the key take, performance, or angle. Editing is a selective and reductive art. Whether we speak of building a sequence or removing sounds and images, the goal is the same: the construction of narrative meaning in a movie.

There are few better examples of the power of editing than the shower scene in Alfred Hitchcock's *Psycho* (1960) and the baptism that ends Francis Ford Coppola's *The Godfather* (1972). Both are repeatedly used as examples in film textbooks, yet they became textbook examples via divergent means.[23] In *Psycho*, Hitchcock begins the scene with an appeal to prurient interests. Viewers are placed in the uncomfortable position of voyeur. The initial shots of a naked Marion intercut with close-ups of the showerhead and sounds of the water running arouse complex, sexualized feelings. How much are we about to see of actor Janet Leigh onscreen? The shot of Marion showering is static until a shadowy figure emerges through the door. The camera pans in slowly, until the curtain is ripped aside and a knife is lifted. Marion turns and screams. The camera zooms in on her mouth agape, frightened to death. A barrage of images, cut by longtime Hitchcock editor George Tomasini, follows. There is seemingly no real continuity to the actual attack. The knife strikes from several directions; Marion struggles; water and blood begin to mix around her feet. All is chaos and panic. The repeated staccato screech of violins—emulating the stabbing motion—adds to the sense of horror. Hitchcock used seventy-eight different camera setups and ultimately spliced fifty-two different shots into one harrowing minute of screen history.[24] This is visceral filmmaking.[25] The pace of the editing unfurls with its own kind of violence, each cut within the scene approximating the slashing knife of the murderer. The dissolve from blood and water running down the drain to Marion's eye swirling in this sudden death is chilling. Although in *Psycho* we never see the knife pierce Janet Leigh's flesh, we feel as if we have been victimized, the scene creating a palpable fear in us. This montage unleashed a wave of imitators who have been mixing sex and onscreen violence against women in gruesome and often reprehensible ways ever since.

Now, consider Francis Ford Coppola's epic finale in *The Godfather* (1972), a film that uses the Mafia as a metaphor for America itself. In the movie, the church is portrayed as oblivious to the seared consciences of the Corleone family. As the film reaches a dramatic climax, we see a high-church baptism going on with all its pomp and formality. An organ plays as the ritual commences. The sprinkling of water is contrasted with the preparations of gangsters loading their weapons. Michael Corleone is asked by the priest on behalf of his godson, "Do you renounce Satan?" The organ rises dramatically. Michael responds strongly, "I do renounce him," just as the movie crosscuts to show the first of a number of brutal gangland executions, effective in establishing Corleone as the new Godfather. (One victim is caught inside a revolving door that is jammed, another in a barbershop as he is being shaved, still another while being massaged in a steam room.) Between these murders, the priest repeatedly asks Michael the baptismal questions: "And all his works?" "I do renounce them." "And all his pomps?" "I do renounce them." The baptism is notable for its ritual formality; the slayings, for their gruesome reality. The baby's cries are contrasted with piercing gunshots. In its juxtapositions of sights and sounds, the scene is breathtaking. Through cut after cut, continually jumping back and forth between the gangland executions and the baptismal vows, both the killings and the sacrament rivet the viewer. The hypocrisy of the scene—the immorality of Michael's orchestrated violence contrasted with the impotent ritual of the church—leaves audience members speechless as they exit the theater.

Both sequences juxtapose cleansing water with bloody violence. The calm of a shower or the purity of a baptism creates expectations that are shattered by grisly murders. The contrast between the images makes them far more jarring and horrific. They demonstrate the power of affinity and contrast to shock. But these filmmakers adopted vastly different approaches to crafting their sequences. Hitchcock relied on storyboards to plan the shower scene before

The Godfather (1972), © Paramount Pictures

shooting began. The film was nearly finished in his mind before production even began. On location, Coppola shot from multiple takes and angles before starting to find the film he was looking for within the postproduction process. Coppola's famously out-of-control production of *Apocalypse Now* (1979) was "found" through the editing process by the legendary sound and picture editor Walter Murch. As one of the most erudite editors in film history, Murch describes the difference in approach: "There are two kinds of filmmaking: Hitchcock's (the film is complete in the director's mind) and Coppola's (which thrives on process). For Hitchcock, any variation from the complete internal idea is seen as a defect. The perfection already exists. Coppola's approach is to harvest the random elements that the process throws up, things that were not in his mind when he began."[26] A rough cut can arrive through rigorous advance planning or months of working with the footage to find the movie. Affinity and contrast can be orchestrated beforehand or discovered within the editing process.

The second factor in editing involves the manipulation of time and space. Picture editing, sound editing, and musical soundtracks are all connected by rhythm. *Run Lola Run* (1999) is a literal race against the clock, where Lola has only twenty minutes to secure the money to save her boyfriend's life. It is cut to the relentless beat of rave music; pulsating intensity alternates with chill-out scenes in which the characters (and viewers) catch their breath. Andrey Tarkovsky describes editing as "sculpting in time," which he considers "the essence of the director's work." "Just as a sculptor takes a lump of marble, and, inwardly conscious of the features of his finished piece, removes everything that is not part of it—so the film-maker, from a 'lump of time' made up of an enormous, solid cluster of living facts, cuts off and discards whatever he does not need."[27]

Tarkovsky's films, such as *Andrei Rublev* (1966) and *Solaris* (1972), unspool at a deliberate pace that invites contemplation. Three hours in a Tarkovsky movie may feel like three days for impatient viewers. He wants to expand hearts and minds, so his films consciously slow us down. Thrillers like *Psycho* often compress time, leaving viewers breathless. Hitchcock creates tension through multiple cuts and shifting points of view. He explains his approach: "The screen ought to speak its own language, freshly coined, and it can't do that unless it treats an acted scene as a piece of raw material which must be broken up, taken to bits, before it can be woven into an expressive visual pattern."[28] Moments that are captured on set, during production, can be extended or protracted in the postproduction process. Time can be lengthened or compressed depending on the director's desire to shock or soothe the audience. Long, languid shots with limited edits (like the candle scene that concludes Tarkovsky's 1983 film *Nostalgia*) will calm viewers' minds, creating a meditative state. The quick bursts of images and sounds in *Psycho* and *Run Lola Run* make audiences' hearts race. Editing is the crafting of pace and rhythm.

Sound: Ears to Hear

While it is easy to see excellent directing, cinematography, and film editing, it is often tough to hear and appreciate the art of sound editing, sound mixing, and film scoring. Good sound is rarely noticed (nor should it be). Bad sound is a telling sign that a production is amateur, low budget, or student made. Only after a picture edit is locked do sound engineers and composers "spot" the film for moments that need effects, ambient backgrounds, or music cues. Producers and directors may assume that dramatic problems can be "fixed in the mix." Yet the final stage of postproduction—sound editing and mixing—is often subject to time constraints. On the other hand, excellent sound begins early in the process, in thinking through the story, getting clear recordings on set, and allowing sound designers and musicians ample time to add their magic to the finished film. While the tools of the boom operator and sound mixer on the set, the Foley artists in the pit, and the rerecording mixers behind the console are constantly changing, the artistic and scientific principles of sound remain the same.[29]

Consider how different the cinematic experience of a classic like *Raiders of the Lost Ark* (1981) would be with subpar sound. At the University of Southern California's film program, Craig's graduate education began with a sound workshop taught by Professor Tom Holman. In the first session of the class,

Holman showed the opening sequence from *Raiders*, where Indiana Jones steals the golden idol from an ancient temple (and triggers a furious fusillade of rocks, arrows, and boulders). Holman replayed the famous sequence without the sound. No piercing sound of darts flying, no rumble of boulders rolling. It was less than thrilling. Slowly, via multiple playbacks, he added in first the original dialogue, then countless sound effects, and finally John Williams's rousing score. In stripping these four minutes of film down to their core, Holman enabled the students to hear the essential role that dialogue, effects, and music have in the final sound mix. Over the course of the semester, the class also came to appreciate how THX sound arose for Lucasfilm: it was the Tomlinson Holman Experiment.

While millions of children have tried to imitate the whoosh of a light saber or the growl of Chewbacca in their backyards, they didn't realize those cinematic sounds were created by renowned sound editor Ben Burtt. As sound designer for every *Star Wars* movie (as well as the *Indiana Jones* films, the *Star Trek* reboots, and *Wall-E*), Burtt and his team were tasked with creating the overall sound plan as well as the particular effects necessary to make these fantasies believable. To create the sound of light sabers, Burtt was inspired by the hum of the motor of an old film projector at USC (whose film program he graduated from). He combined that with the buzz from an old cathode-ray television tube. But how to convey a sense of fighting and movement? Burtt drew upon his undergraduate degree in physics. He played the hum through a speaker and then waved a microphone across it, up and down, side to side, in sync with the onscreen movement of Darth Vader and Luke Skywalker. He tapped into the Doppler effect first described by a physicist in 1842.[30]

Chewbacca's voice was created from the growls of bears, lions, badgers, and walruses that were eventually synchronized with the actor's performance. Darth Vader's heavy breathing was created by recording breath through a scuba regulator and mask—no underwater bubbles necessary. For the big boulder in *Raiders*, Burtt recorded a Honda Civic station wagon rolling over baseball-sized rocks without its motor running.[31] To create the wheezy voice of the beloved E. T. the Extra-Terrestrial (1982), Burtt recorded his wife sleeping while she had a cold. The possibilities of creating movie magic via sound effects are endless. Sounds may be recorded in the wild or on a Foley stage (where an artist mimics the movements within a scene, like footsteps), or taken from a library of prerecorded effects or backgrounds (like rain, crickets, or hospital sounds). But the overall goal is to make convincing and realistic sounds, even for fanciful characters or sci-fi films.

The recording of sound (whether dialogue captured on set or sound effects added in postproduction) is merely the first step toward blending the dialogue, effects, and music into a satisfying mix. Gary Rydstrom, a protégé of Ben Burtt at Skywalker Sound, has been honored with Oscars for both sound effects editing and sound mixing on *Terminator 2: Judgment Day* (1991), *Jurassic Park* (1993), and *Saving Private Ryan* (1998). Speaking to the Motion Picture Sound Editors guild about his groundbreaking work on *Jurassic Park*, Rydstrom described sound design as comparable to knitting or quilting. It involves so much interweaving of elements, making sure that the effects and music do not distract from the dialogue. It requires a quilter's art (and a sophisticated ear) for blending potentially clashing things into a cohesive and artistic whole. Rydstrom also compared his work to orchestrating music. He told his fellow sound editors, "When you're writing music for an orchestra you pay attention to frequencies and harmonics."[32] When composer John Williams heard what the raptors would sound like in *Jurassic Park*, he steered away from the use of cellos in his orchestration because of the similar frequencies they occupied. The work of John Ottman, picture editor and composer for *The Usual Suspects* (1995), *Superman Returns* (2006), and *X-Men: Days of Future Past* (2014), demonstrates the relationship between music and images. The rhythm between images, dialogue, and music must be carefully orchestrated. We often don't realize how sensitive and perceptive our ears can be.

The most esteemed maestro of sound *and* film editing is Walter Murch. He made classic films directed by George Lucas and Francis Ford Coppola sparkle. Murch figured out how to use 1950s rock and roll in a natural way in *American Graffiti* (1973). He wove it into the film through songs playing on car radios, at a diner, and within a radio station. *The Conversation* (1974) follows the travails of a surveillance expert hired to spy on a woman who may be cheating on her wealthy husband. The film comments on the paranoia that surrounded the Watergate era of tapes secretly recorded in President Nixon's White House. The movie plot allowed Murch to reveal how conversations can be clandestinely recorded and manipulated in playback for all kinds of dramatic purposes. The secrets of sound recording were revealed within the film itself. The Academy recognized Murch's contributions to both the picture and the sound editing on *Apocalypse Now* (1979) and *The English Patient* (1996).[33] Murch made massive and poetic leaps in time and space through the use of sound. In the opening scene of *Apocalypse Now*, the whirl of a helicopter blade contrasts with Jim Morrison and the Doors' Indian raga track, "The End." The helicopter blade dissolves into a fan overhead and a soldier lying on his back, upside down, staring at the ceiling. The effect is hypnotic. Later, the juxtaposition of Wagner's orchestral "Ride of the Valkyries" with helicopter attacks over Vietnam makes the war seem both grandiose and absurd. It is a visceral rush until we see napalm incinerate villages. Beauty turns to horror. As with picture editing, sound often works best in stark contrasts.

To understand the power of sophisticated sound, watch the thriller *A Quiet Place* (2018), or study the opening getaway scene of *Drive* (2011) in which no dialogue is necessary to communicate the resolve of the nameless driver played by Ryan Gosling. The action is narrated by two competing play-by-plays. A police radio tracks the character's movements while a radio announcer describes a Los Angeles Clippers game. The roar of his Chevy Impala's engine and the rattle of police helicopter blades overhead shatter the relative calm. Efforts to hide are interrupted by a piercing police siren. As the countdown begins on the basketball game, the driver barrels toward the Staples Center parking lot in downtown LA. While police sirens close in, the driver parks the car and walks away. The hubbub of victorious fans allows Gosling to escape unnoticed and anonymous. Sound tells the story in remarkably compelling ways.

Music: Enhancing Characters, Underlining Emotions

How many amazing movie moments are elevated by brilliant song selections? The right musical cue can rouse emotions in audiences that dialogue would never deliver.[34] As with film and sound editing, greater impact is often achieved via counterpoint—doing the opposite of what viewers may expect. Directors and editors often establish the rhythm of a scene or the traits of a character via a song. Quentin Tarantino used Chuck Berry's "Never Can Tell" to bring out the playful side of the ill-fated Vinny and Mia during their famous dance in *Pulp Fiction* (1994). Retro songs like "Come and Get Your Love" made the sci-fi universe of *Guardians of the Galaxy* (2014) instantly cool, establishing the Starlord's character via his playlist. The meticulously choreographed coffee run that opens *Baby Driver* (2017) with the "Harlem Shuffle" went a long way toward selling the groundbreaking concept of a musical/film noir mash-up. Music supervisors are tasked with finding such pop chestnuts and securing the rights to use them within a film. However, the cost of merging music with movies can be prohibitive. Richard Linklater spent more money licensing Aerosmith's "Sweet Emotion" for *Dazed and Confused* (1993) than he spent on his entire first film, *Slacker* (1991)!

Original scores can add needed texture to the overall film experience, though. Composer Aaron Copland offered a useful summary of five functions of film music, outlined by Pauline Reay in her helpful book *Music in Film: Soundtracks and Synergy*: "(i) It conveys a convincing atmosphere of time and place; (ii) it underlines the unspoken feelings or psychological states of the characters; (iii) it serves as a kind of neutral background filler to the action; (iv) it gives a sense of continuity to the editing; (v) it accentuates the theatrical build-up of a scene and rounds it off with a feeling of finality."[35]

Great film scores complement rather than compete with the performances onscreen.[36] Bernard Herrmann's music heightens the eerie atmosphere of Hitchcock's *Vertigo* (1958), *North by Northwest* (1959), and *Psycho* (1960). Ennio Morricone's compositions for *Fistful of Dollars* (1964) and *The Good, the Bad, and the Ugly* (1966) create such mystique around Clint Eastwood's Man with No Name. A musical theme or leitmotif may represent a place, a person, an idea, or even a shark. John Williams's score for *Jaws* (1975) establishes the shark as an ominous threat with a two-note ostinato: "Duunn dun . . . dun dun."[37] In *Close Encounters of the Third Kind* (1977), scientists play five simple notes to communicate with the spaceship hovering above Devil's Tower in Wyoming.

In the *Star Wars* movies, Williams employed leitmotifs to distinguish recurring characters, as with Darth Vader's imposing "Imperial March." Musical figures like this also connect each new installation with the ever-expanding Star Wars franchise, appearing as it does in *Episode VII: The Force Awakens* (2015), *Rogue One: A Star Wars Story* (2016), *Episode VIII: The Last Jedi* (2017), and *Solo: A Star Wars Story* (2018). Williams penned equally poignant musical moments for Luke Skywalker, and even a sprightly motif for the Force. Effective film scores enhance actors' performances and deepen the story.

In the musical genre, each number of the original score marks a key relationship, represents a character, or celebrates or laments pivotal episodes. While music functions in similar ways in all films, it happens explicitly—with the audience's full appreciation—in musicals. The rebirth of the movie musical begun by Disney in animated films from *Beauty and the Beast* (1991) to *The Lion King* (1994) has crossed over into live-action remakes like *Beauty and the Beast* (2017) and *The Lion King* (2019). A generation raised to sing along with musicals is now creating its own in movies like *La La Land* (2016).

Music should underline rather than telegraph the emotion onscreen. Classical musical training was often necessary when studios hired symphonies to record a score. Today, though we still have John Williams's compositions, directors increasingly turn to popular musicians working with synthesizers to create atmospheric soundtracks. It is tough to separate Tim Burton's quirky visions from the jaunty music composed by former Oingo Boingo front man Danny Elfman. Devo's lead vocalist, Mark Mothersbaugh, created the playful score in *The Lego Movie* (2014). Jonny Greenwood of Radiohead brought haunting tones to *There Will Be Blood* (2007). Nick Cave and Warren Ellis generated an elegiac, contemplative mood in *The Assassination of Jesse James* (2007). Trent Reznor of Nine Inch Nails won an Oscar (with Atticus Ross) for Best Original Score for songs riddled with angst and regret in the cautionary tale *The Social*

Network (2010). Directors have also incorporated more diverse sounds by hiring, for instance, Argentina's Gustavo Santaolalla to score *Brokeback Mountain* (2004) and A. R. Rahman to create the music for *Slumdog Millionaire* (2008). Yet, even while we marvel at the art of film scores, we also lament the fact that, as in almost every craft we've highlighted, the paucity of women working in the field is rather shocking.[38] In the blockbuster remake of *A Star Is Born* (2018), Lady Gaga found a brilliant vehicle to showcase her talent as actor, singer, and composer. But her success story is unfortunately still an exception.

The opening sequence of *Gravity* is a great study in the way sound effects and music can complement each other. There are no picture edits in the first nineteen minutes—so how does the film create tension? The challenge for the filmmakers was how to raise audience anxiety. We hear the characters' distant voices before we see them. A country and western song adds a comic air to the scene. Breathing is used to both calm viewers and add to the suspense. When Kowalski and Stone grab onto the space shuttle, we hear the sounds of their hands touching the metal. We hear the sounds inside the astronauts' space suits. When the music of composer Steve Price is introduced, it resembles a sound effect. The strings travel across the screen in a pattern that approximates the space debris flying by. The music travels around the theater with the characters. When Stone spins, the music rotates with her. The art of sound placement has become more sophisticated with the rise of Dolby Atmos and multiple speakers in front of, behind, and now above the audience.

Gravity can be studied as a cinematic symphony with the rhythm of breathing and heartbeats interrupted by staccato blasts of music and sound effects. When Ryan Stone starts to lose her will to live, it is sounds that revive her. Having crawled into a Russian capsule, Stone reaches out on the radio, begging for someone, anyone, to hear her cry. She does not know how to pray. Finally, amid her despair, a voice from Earth, self-identified as "Aningaaq," responds. While Aningaaq does not speak the same language as the astronaut, he is surrounded by sounds on Earth that are universal and familiar. His dog barks. Stone howls back with recognition and delight. A baby cries in the background. The grieving, motherly side of Stone is reawakened. She sheds a tear that floats through the capsule. Stone confronts her mortality. The most basic, everyday sounds from Earth allow her to appreciate the gift of life and accept the inevitability of death.

Amid the challenge of mechanical failure, music composer Steve Price turned to human sounds to amplify the pathos in *Gravity*.[39] He hired Alasdair Malloy to play wine glasses with water in them to approximate the music of the spheres—earth, moon, and sun. You can hear his human skin on the glass. It is an inherently emotional sound. Price's score pulsates with a heartbeat that breathes with the characters. For his bass rumble, Price did not turn to synthesizers but to a human voice slowed down. When Ryan Stone cries out in lament for her lost daughter, Price accompanied the scene with the plaintive voice of Ireland's Lisa Hannigan. Both the character onscreen and the singer in the soundtrack are alone. As Stone rises to the occasion and summons the courage to continue, the music builds with her. Price composed a melody for reentry that includes a church organ. He wanted religious power to accompany Stone's urge to live. As her capsule enters Earth's atmosphere, a choir of voices rise up, communicating that Stone is no longer isolated. She is reentering the human community. The composer took his emotional cues from the action onscreen and found musical ways to complement the movie's themes of grief and loss, recovery and rebirth.

The postproduction process is guided by the same question that drives the preproduction process. The fundamental question throughout is, what story are we telling? Some members of the crew focus on satisfying our voyeuristic instincts; they focus on what we see. On set, the director focuses on performance, trying to capture genuine emotion. This appeals to viewers' vicarious instincts. In postproduction, what we hear also comes into play. Quick cuts and jarring sounds can offer gut-level visceral thrills. Or time may slow down and silence set in for moments of contemplation or even transcendence. Our eyes focus, our ears sharpen, and our hearts expand. Movie magic occurs when sights and sounds merge in a glorious symphony.

Discussion Questions

1. What film(s) do you recall as having a distinctive look? How did that align with and even amplify the themes of the film? To what degree did the visuals communicate the movie's message?

2. Are there particular shots or sequences throughout your film-viewing history that stand out in your mind? What made them especially impactful? The lighting? The framing? The contrast? The rhythm?

3. What is the most effective use of film sound you can recall? Did it arise from silence, from contrast, or from a particular song or sound effect?

5

where form
meets feeling

a critical lens

Mrs. Chan glides down a narrow Hong Kong alley where steam rises. Restaurants serve piping-hot bowls of noodles. Her elegant cheongsam dress belies the work-a-day setting. As she carries the noodles back to her painfully quiet apartment, Mr. Chow passes, heading to an equally lonely dinner. His hair is close cropped, his suit impeccable. A seemingly casual glance is loaded with feeling. They are next-door neighbors in a cramped apartment building, both being cheated on by spouses who are engaged in an ongoing affair with each other. As Shigeru Umebayashi's evocative "Yumeji's Theme" plays on the soundtrack, the jilted man and woman glide past each other in slow motion. Their nightly rituals form a waltz laden with longing. Smoke, rain, food, glances, hallways, phone calls, and missed opportunities loom over director Wong Kar-wai's re-creation of Hong Kong circa 1962. *In the Mood for Love* (2000) may be the most romantic film about adultery, betrayal, and disconnection in cinematic history. The scenes and songs of heartache sear themselves into our memory.

Once a decade, film critics and directors from around the world are asked by the British Film Institute to submit a list of their top ten films of all time to *Sight and Sound* magazine. *Citizen Kane* topped the aggregated list for decades until it was displaced by Hitchcock's *Vertigo* in 2012. Only two films created in the twenty-first century were among the top fifty films. David Lynch's mind-bending nightmare *Mulholland Drive* (2001) resided at number 28. Critics

89

placed Wong Kar-wai's *In the Mood for Love* at number 24, the highest-rated film of the new century.

In the Mood for Love may have attained "classic" status because it exemplifies the qualities discussed in previous chapters. We have seen so many movies chronicle illicit love affairs, yet Wong Kar-wai follows those left home alone. It is an original take on a genre we've seen many times before. The performances by Tony Leung as journalist Mr. Chow and by Maggie Cheung as secretary Mrs. Chan are loaded with unspoken emotion. Empathy abounds as they get to know each other and imagine how their spouses met and fell in love. Like most of Wong Kar-wai's films, *In the Mood for Love* plays with time, with memory, with how a shift in moments can forever alter our personal histories. The stellar production design, gorgeous period costumes, remarkable camera movements, and a soundtrack suffused with heartache all work together to deepen the story. The rich red color palette matches the characters' passionate, unspoken feelings. Each shot down their long hallway is beautifully composed as a frame within the frame. Each scene of Mr. Chow smoking while he waits and wonders is perfectly paced. Dialogue is nearly unnecessary amid such a steamy atmosphere. The period songs from Nat King Cole say more about desire and disappointment than the potential lovers can ever admit. *In the Mood for Love* is pure cinema, a remarkable marriage of form and feeling.

While critics raved about the look and feel of Wong Kar-wai's ill-fated spouses, *In the Mood for Love* escaped widespread public embrace. Why is there often a gap between critical notice and box-office receipts? Are critics inclined toward snobbery, championing the obscure rather than the popular? There may be an air of superiority that comes through, denigrating public taste. Critics can ruin a perfectly good "bad" movie with a cranky review. Yet *New York Times* film critic A. O. Scott suggests that exactly the opposite is true. He contends that "criticism, far from sapping the vitality of art, is instead what supplies its lifeblood."[1] Scott lifts up criticism as "the defense of art itself." A new generation of thoughtful Christians—such as Justin Chang (*Los Angeles Times*), Alissa Wilkinson (*Vox*), and Josh Larsen (*Filmspotting* podcast)—have risen to the task, becoming esteemed film critics.

Nowadays, the internet is loaded with critics, but few are getting paid to write.[2] On the Internet Movie Database (IMDb), anyone with an account can chime in and offer a capsule review. Viewers rate movies on a one-to-ten scale, with the highest-ranked films given special status as among the top 250 films of all time. What do IMDb users around the globe think about *In the Mood for Love*? It is currently ranked among the finest films in the history of cinema![3] Perhaps the critics' praise has had an effect. As we all become amateur critics, questions arise: What criteria should be used in determining a film's worth? Are

In the Mood for Love (2000), © Block 2 Pictures Inc.

special skills needed to become a film critic, or can anyone develop a discerning eye? What makes a truly moving picture?

This chapter will survey the history of film theory in an effort to bridge the perceived divide between critics and audiences. We will trace the origins of ongoing tensions between those who analyze the formal aspects of film and critics who champion cinema's ability to depict reality. We will consider four particular aspects of film criticism that have become dominant: (1) *Genre criticism* examines the common form and mythic shape of film. (2) *Auteur criticism* attends to the movie's "author." (3) *Cultural criticism* focuses on a film's social context. And (4) *thematic criticism* compares film texts. We will consider films through these critical lenses in order to deepen our appreciation for the art of cinema and place the growing discipline of theology and film in context. We hope that a solid grounding in established film theories will sharpen our perception of spirituality in cinema, thus allowing theology to serve as a new critical lens.

Film Form: Eisenstein on the Power of Montage

Film criticism was forged in the tension between form and feeling, ideas and emotions. In 1929, Sergei Eisenstein declared that "cinema is, first and foremost, montage" and championed the intellectual possibilities inherent in this new visual art form.[4] He highlighted the pioneering techniques of D. W. Griffith, the first director to organize and capitalize on the unique grammar of film.[5] Griffith and his cinematographer, Billy Blitzer, explored the possibilities of a moving camera via pans, dollies, and traveling shots. Their pictures actually moved! Griffith also employed close-ups on irises to focus viewers' attention on particular elements of the plot. A simple shot of a gun being drawn raised audience awareness and anxiety to unprecedented heights. Griffith combined dollies and close-ups to arouse sympathy for his actresses, such as Lillian Gish. His actors developed a more naturalistic style, in keeping with the intimacy of the camera, and his films took on a lyrical quality, appealing to unabashed sentimentality. Griffith's advanced technique forced audiences to get emotionally involved. Superior form enhanced audience feeling.

Griffith also mastered cinema's greatest innovation: crosscut editing. He understood the possibilities of parallel action across multiple locations. While exhibitors worried that viewers would be confused by Griffith's juxtaposition of a heroine-in-peril with help rushing toward the scene, audiences found his new techniques invigorating. His controversial and landmark *The Birth of a Nation* (1915) featured thrilling, epic battle scenes. Griffith defined cinematic conventions, showing dueling armies enter from opposite sides of the screen. He surmised that soldiers crossing the frame from right to left would appear to face more overwhelming odds since Western audiences' eyes were trained to read from left to right. Our ongoing notions of continuity and film logic stem from Griffith's innovations. His crosscutting raised tension in his audience, forcing viewers to wonder, Who will win? Will she be saved? Will they make it in time? He also mastered flashbacks and flash-forwards, demonstrating a complete understanding of cinematic space and time. Griffith's moving images heightened reality.

Pioneering Russian filmmakers like Vsevolod Pudovkin and Sergei Eisenstein celebrated Griffith's innovations, heralding cinema as an original, purely visual art form. Eisenstein wrote that Griffith's work "contained the rudiments of the art that, in the hands of a constellation of Soviet masters, was destined to cover Soviet filmmaking with undying glory in the pages of history of world cinema, thanks to the novelty of ideas, the unprecedented plots and the perfection of form in equal measure."[6] (Humility was not Eisenstein's gift.) Griffith's ability to shift locations, to cross time and space, suggested that movies could be much more than a filmed play. While films *could* perform an archival or scientific function, they proved capable of far more than Aristotle's notion of mimesis. Griffith moved audiences to rage, to sorrow, and to action (including the lamentable revival of the Ku Klux Klan).

How could silent movies evoke such dramatic responses? The Russians suggested that juxtaposing two images via the editing process created a powerful and unique third experience (tertium quid). Eisenstein found parallels in the Japanese language; their written words are a literal combination of representative Chinese symbols.[7] Combine the hieroglyph for "dog" with the symbol for "mouth" and you have "to bark." A knife and a heart mean "sorrow." Film editors create the same types of complex words by juxtaposing shots. But individual images and shots are not the foundation for a cinematic language. For Eisenstein, the building block of this new visual form of communication was montage. The ability to manipulate space and time (and audiences) via editing made movies unique. Through contrast, parallelism, or simultaneity, film editors tell viewers what to feel and when to feel it. Eisenstein and Pudovkin pushed the form to a new aesthetic and philosophical conclusion. Film was rooted in signs and symbols, offering artists the chance to create a new kind of abstract, intellectual art.

In films like *Strike* (1924), *Battleship Potemkin* (1925), and *October* (1928), Sergei Eisenstein put his theories into practice. He juxtaposed unlikely images, as in *Strike*, when the shooting of workmen is intercut with shots of a bull being slaughtered. In *Potemkin*, a sailor scrubs a plate inscribed with the words, "Give us this day our daily bread." This prayer rouses the hungry sailor to anger. Yet, rather than showing him smash the plate in a single action, Eisenstein breaks a few seconds of screen time into eleven shots.[8] It makes the scene longer, the action more violent, and the protest more explicit. The Odessa Steps sequence in *Potemkin* endures as exhibit A in all subsequent discussions of the power of cinema as dialectic, a purely visual medium. Eisenstein emerged as a film theorist who put his ideas regarding film form into action. He not only told; he showed.

Under Eisenstein, silent films reached their artistic apex, serving as a visual Esperanto, a common language that crossed borders, cultures, and customs. Films communicated to audiences irrespective of their age, education, or interests. Movies may have adhered to a dramatic story, but along the way they provoked emotions and called audiences to action. Working within the newly formed Soviet Union, Eisenstein and Pudovkin were encouraged to exploit cinema's ability to serve as an effective propaganda machine. Images of the emerging Soviet people could be placed alongside shots of nobility, power, and grandeur to elevate the perception of the common man: victory via visual association.

Eisenstein also communicated through disassociation. He chronicled his antireligious intentions in *October*, which shows a series of images of the divine, ranging from a baroque Christ to an Eskimo idol. By juxtaposing disparate representations of god, Eisenstein hoped to inspire "individual conclusions about the true nature of all deities."[9] His dialectic attempted to create a "gradual discrediting of it in purposeful steps."[10] Eisenstein admitted that his visual argument "is most suitable for the expression of ideologically pointed theses." He aspired to wake up viewers via cinematic montage, challenging them to quit settling for false idols (or shadows). By highlighting the formal elements of filmmaking, the Russian theorists borrowed (at least) a page from Plato's cave analogy. Film was far more than mere entertainment; it was a portal to a higher plane, a rallying force rooted in core issues of creativity and artistic freedom.

Film Realism: Bazin on the Grace of Mise-en-Scène

The introduction of synchronized sound escalated tension between those who viewed film as a visual polemic and those who were part of a new wave of critics inclined to see film's greatest gift as documenting real life. To filmmakers and critics steeped in montage, sound undercut their still burgeoning art form.[11] Eisenstein noted the inherent tension between the acoustic and the optical. While acknowledging talking pictures' ability to avoid annoying intertitles, the Russian theorists worried about the destruction of their culture of montage. They advocated the use of contrapuntal (counterpoint) sounds as an additional opportunity for juxtaposition and artistic commentary. Eisenstein, Pudovkin, and Grigori Alexandrov suggested that "with this method of construction the sound film will not be imprisoned within national markets, as has happened with the theatrical play and will happen with the 'filmed play.'"[12] Nevertheless, filmmakers and audiences in the 1930s could not resist the temptation to tell their stories through monologue, dialogue, and voice-over. The global Esperanto of silent pictures faded almost overnight. The fluid moving camera, grabbing images for fast-paced montages, once again became stage-bound, anchored to the floor in an effort to capture actors' lines. Now, cameras had to be housed in soundproof booths or wrapped in barneys. Whatever freedom film had found apart from its theatrical roots was dissipated.

Yet, for filmmakers striving for mimesis, the addition of sound served as a natural evolution, an essential innovation. If great art was meant to re-create nature, then it must do more than re-create an accurate look. It must capture voices, tones, inflections, and natural sounds. When characters walk onscreen, we should hear their footsteps, not an organ. While the Russians begrudged such limitations, a French critic rose to the defense of naturalistic filmmaking. As a prophet for cinematic realism, André Bazin declared, "Sound has given proof that it came not to destroy but to fulfill the Old Testament of the cinema." He contrasted directors "who put their faith in the image and those who put their faith in reality" and declared war on "the tricks of montage."[13] While Russians bemoaned the rise of sound as the death of cinema, Bazin celebrated the 1930s and '40s as film's golden age, a natural maturity.

In his influential 1945 essay, "The Ontology of the Photographic Image," Bazin connected the invention of photography and cinema with "the great spiritual and technical crisis that overtook modern painting around the middle of the last [i.e., the nineteenth] century."[14] According to Bazin, "Perspective was the original sin of Western painting." He suggested that film could resolve painting's dueling ambitions—aesthetics and accuracy. The great artists combined both callings. But the rise of photography allowed painting to relinquish its role as duplicator or preserver of the natural world. Painters could now concentrate on aesthetics, "the expression of spiritual reality wherein the symbol transcended its model." Film would satisfy our innate obsession with realism. Cinematographers must aspire to objectivity, a goal made even clearer by the French word for "lens": *objectif*.[15] Bazin insisted that "the aesthetic qualities of photography are to be sought in its power to lay bare the realities. . . . Nature at last does more than imitate art: she imitates the artist."[16] Consequently, he praised unfussy camera work that attempted to record nature, rather than manipulating viewers with quick cuts that failed to establish a sense of place. Bazin preferred long, static, master shots or *mise-en-scène* over *montage*. He celebrated anything that allowed viewers to recognize natural behavior or perspective.

Bazin praised the understated slices of life offered by the Italian neorealists and directors like Jean Renoir, a fellow Frenchman. Renoir's films, such as *La Règle du Jeu* (*The Rules of the Game* [1939]), *The Southerner* (1945), and *The Diary of a Chambermaid* (1946), were domestic dramas that unspooled at a leisurely pace. While the Russians called attention to certain signs and symbols via close-ups, Renoir allowed audiences to find their own rhythm within the space. He gave viewers room to roam, to seek out telling details. Bazin noted how Renoir "forced himself to look back beyond the resources provided by montage and so uncovered a secret of a film form that would permit everything to be said without chopping the world up into little fragments, that would reveal the hidden meanings in people and things without disturbing the unity natural to them."[17] Renoir's drawing-room stories often drew from literary sources and chronicled characters' everyday lives. His films feel stage-bound, with a static camera and elaborate indoor sets. For Bazin, Renoir's genius resided in detailed rehearsals, careful camera placement, and meticulous blocking. To add tension to these drawing-room stories, Renoir employed deep focus, allowing audiences to observe minute shifts in an actor's posture or gestures. The human dynamics within the mise-en-scène drive the drama. Renoir encouraged actors to simply "be" before beginning to express themselves. Acting flowed from action rather than projection. With everything in focus, viewers could finally approximate their life experience, becoming literal flies on the wall. We zoom in or out from a fixed position, duplicating our eye's remarkable ability to shift focus (the technical term for this camera trick is *rack focus*). Renoir placed his faith, as did Bazin, in the audience rather than the artist.

Bazin also celebrated the innovative camera work of Gregg Toland. In films like *Citizen Kane* and *The Little Foxes* (both from 1941), Toland managed to keep foreground and background figures in clear, deep focus. The potential for visual contrast within a shot thrilled Bazin. With deep focus, the filmmaker's primary building block returned to the single shot, rather than the crisply edited montage. As Charles Foster Kane gradually loses his power and influence, Toland shifts the focus in the scenes from the foreground to the background. Orson Welles's performance as Kane is strengthened via composition and shot selection rather than editing. The magic happens before viewers' eyes, not in the editing room. In one striking shot, his wife's medicine resides in the foreground, her bed in the middle ground, and Kane and nurses enter in the background. The focus within the shot is blurred, reflecting the troubled state of Kane's depressed wife, Susan. As we read the shot, we understand that she has overdosed in an attempted suicide. The camera allows us to grasp the narrative at our pace. For Bazin, deep focus reintroduced ambiguity into filmmaking. In *Citizen Kane*, "The uncertainty in which we find ourselves as to the spiritual key or the interpretation we should put on the film is built into the very design of the image."[18] Viewers are put into a moral quandary alongside the characters and given space to decide for themselves where their sympathies should reside. Is Susan a victim of Kane's overreach, collateral damage to his character flaws? Thanks to Bazin, Aristotle's notion of story structure and catharsis experienced resurgence.

Bazin also admired the sophisticated master shots and deep-focus photography found in *The Little Foxes* (1941). Based on Lillian Hellman's stage play, *The Little Foxes* refers to "the little foxes, that spoil the vines" in the biblical Song of Songs (2:15 KJV). Solomon's wisdom becomes a vivid and painful reality in this enduring classic. Director William Wyler preserved the theatrical roots of the material; almost all the action takes place in a single house. Without Toland's deep focus, the film may have felt static and claustrophobic. Bette Davis gives a riveting performance as the selfish and greedy matriarch of the Hubbard-Giddens family. Her iron grip eventually corrupts her family and kills her husband. Director William Wyler's meticulous planning for cinematography, sets, and blocking allows viewers to measure the subtle, complex interrelationships for themselves. Bazin notes how "director and cameraman have converted the screen into a dramatic checkerboard, planned down to the last detail."[19] As greed infects this stately Southern family, the distances within the household grow (both physically and emotionally). For Bazin, the best directors never call attention to their craft. Their touch appears objective and invisible.

Bazin became a formidable foil for the Russian formalists. While they promoted a preexisting political agenda, Bazin admired artists who appreciated nature more than themselves. If his Aristotelian understanding of art wasn't offensive enough, Bazin's Catholic faith must have frustrated his communist critics. While Bertolt Brecht's self-conscious art drove the intelligentsia, Bazin stuck to his preferences for naturalism over artifice. He saw cinema as an unobstructed window on the world. He believed motion pictures were more than a technological breakthrough or a scientific problem to be solved. Movies sprang from humanity's deep, abiding need to recognize and re-present reality. Like the myth of Icarus, "It had dwelt in the soul of everyman since he first thought about birds."[20] Bazin's critics may have argued that films like *Citizen Kane* and *The Little Foxes* came with a preexisting agenda rooted in a clear moral center. Yet Bazin's faith placed morality into the fabric of the created order. Released against the backdrop of World War II, the films' distinctions between good and evil undoubtedly resonated with audiences trying to make sense of their world. Audiences may have loved hating the protagonists, but greed wasn't rewarded and pride did not pay. Bazin's influence arose alongside the moral quandary presented by Hitler's Germany and Mussolini's Italy. In a time of clear enemies, Bazin's call to a spiritual cinema resonated with audiences.

Genre Criticism and American Exceptionalism

With the advent of sound, Hollywood film studios began to systematize their production process. Bazin noted how five or six major kinds of American films were emerging with particular tropes, rules, and expectations during the 1930s. Bazin praised American comedies, musicals, gangster films, psychological dramas, horror and fantasy, and westerns for their "overwhelming superiority" in form and content, especially when compared to national cinemas (with France a close second).[21] While Bazin and Eisenstein argued about the nature of cinema, Hollywood studios dove into the business of making movies (and money). Genre categories established during the Golden Era of Hollywood, the 1930s and '40s, are still prevalent today. Whenever we scroll through Netflix in search of a film to watch, we are engaging in a form of genre criticism. It is a system of orientation for both the filmmaker and the film viewer, a means of communicating expectations and conventions. These expectations usually correspond to our prior experience with movies. Genre films adhere to a form (if not a formula).

While some may consider genre as a reduction of cinematic art, forcing stories into a preestablished box of conventions, an appreciation of genres may deepen our understanding of how films enable us to navigate cultural tensions. Film scholar Leo Braudy notes, "Critics have ignored genre films because of their prejudice for the unique."[22] Genre films may be criticized "because they appeal to a pre-existing audience."[23] Sure, romantic comedies or horror films may be marketed toward film viewers' expectations. Yet, Braudy argues, genre films can "arouse and complicate feelings about the self and society that more serious films, because of their bias towards the unique, may rarely touch."[24] Martin Scorsese, reflecting on the history of cinema for an American Film Institute documentary, comments: "The most interesting of the classic movie genres to me are the indigenous ones: the Western, which was born on the Frontier, the Gangster Film, which originated in the East Coast cities, and the Musical, which was spawned by Broadway. They remind me of jazz: they allowed for endless, increasingly complex, sometimes perverse variations. When these variations were played by the masters, they reflected the changing times; they gave you fascinating insights into American culture and the American psyche."[25]

We may learn more about our conflicted feelings toward America's founding principles through a study of westerns. Shifts in gender politics may be reflected in Hollywood's romantic comedies and musicals. Genre criticism gives us a template through which to notice subtle changes in art and audiences across time.

Genres are a form of contemporary myth, giving expression to the meaning of everyday life. Each genre carries an intrinsic worldview. Gangster films present a closed universe where evil often triumphs over good. Through repetition, a certain imagery, story line, and characterization of gangsters become archetypal. The genre tropes established by depictions of Al Capone's Chicago in *Scarface* (1932) are reset for the Miami drug trade in the 1983 *Scarface*. As we become familiar with the codes and rituals of criminals, we sense a pattern or model that gives shape to or provides options for interpreting our violent reality. In their most artful form, gangster films like *The Godfather* can become iconic meditations on the American Dream.

Romantic comedies reflect the mating rites that continue to fuel our hopes and cause such high anxiety. In analyzing films from the 1930s and '40s, Stanley Cavell calls the American comedy of remarriage "parables of a phase of the development of consciousness at which the struggle is for the reciprocity or equality of consciousness between a woman and a man."[26] Those onscreen battles of the sexes reflect cultural tensions generated by the women's suffrage movement. More recent romantic comedies like *No Strings Attached* (2011) and *Friends with Benefits* (2011) deal with complications arising from contemporary hook-up culture where relationships may start with sex before seeking love

and commitment. Genre conventions arise from universal conflicts that allow viewers to participate vicariously in the basic beliefs, fears, and anxieties not only of their own age but of all ages. Genre films tap into how human nature plays out, causing us to wonder, does crime pay? Will I find true love? Artistic variations on a genre offer insight into shifts within our collective psyche.

The evolution of the western on the screen provides a clear illustration of a genre's ability to shed light on the culture in which it was created. The typical plot for a western prior to World War II centered on the hero as rugged individualist who rode into town from the outside and solved the problem out of a sense of what was right, or perhaps for the love of a girl. Think of John Wayne as the Ringo Kid in *Stagecoach* (1939). The westerns of director John Ford chronicled how the West was won and community achieved (even if the lone hero had to ride off into the sunset). Starting in the 1950s, the dark side of this morality play was explored. After witnessing so many atrocities during World War II, some wondered if Americans were still noble. Was this Hollywood myth true to the American experience? In John Ford's *The Searchers* (1956), Ethan Edwards (John Wayne), the hero, is motivated in his sadistic violence not by a sense of rightness but by vengeance, and in Arthur Penn's *The Left-Handed Gun* (1958), Billy the Kid (Paul Newman) is a juvenile delinquent. To quote Scorsese again, Billy is "a suicidal antihero who sought his own death. Neither a vicious killer nor a sympathetic outlaw, Billy was a rebel without a cause. His rage and confusion had more to do with the malaise of adolescents growing up in the 1950s than with the realities of the old West."[27]

In the 1960s, American culture changed again, becoming more corporate and professional in nature. Thus, it should come as no surprise that the typical western plot changed with it. The individual hero became multiple heroes (as in the original *Magnificent Seven* [1960]), and they often worked for money. They were specialists (typically hired professionals, sometimes outlaws) who formed a group to solve the problem (consider *True Grit* [1969], *The Wild Bunch* [1969], and *Butch Cassidy and the Sundance Kid* [1969]).[28] American society had changed, and with it, the western. This change in the structure of many westerns (though not all, since genre is fluid) signaled a change in the attitudes and expectations of the movie audience. And this has continued. Few westerns are being made today. Disillusionment within American culture has allowed little room for the classic, mythic struggle between good and evil, at least in this form.

American society has changed since the days of John Wayne. We all know too well the mixed motives for establishing civilization on the frontier and the consequences that resulted. Yet the genre is not completely dead. Clint Eastwood has continued to use it to great effect by riffing on his own iconic image as the

Man with No Name in seminal spaghetti westerns. *Unforgiven* (1992) explores our society's present ambivalence toward violence and guns. As Eastwood's character, an old gunslinger, says to a young kid who is practicing his draw, "You've got to be careful when you talk about killing a man, because you're not only taking his life, you're taking all that he was and all he's gonna be." Even though the story is set in the 1880s, it echoes contemporary concerns. If you commit violence, what does it really accomplish? Does it do something to you, diminish you, as well as the victim? In the Coen brothers' remake of *True Grit* (2010), Jeff Bridges steps into John Wayne's shoes as the boozy but lovable Sheriff Rooster Cogburn. What emerged was a darker vision of the American West and the price that everyone paid to settle it, especially young Matty Ross. As we consider current questions of borders and immigration and Native rights, the western has risen again as a remarkably relevant meditation on American soul and soil.

Auteur Theory: Forming a Pantheon of Directors

In emphasizing the power of the well-framed shot, Bazin inadvertently elevated the director's eye to unparalleled critical importance. The more detailed the planning, the more ambitious the master shot and mise-en-scène, the more praise Bazin heaped on the finished product. In an attempt to celebrate the unobtrusive artist, Bazin forged a school of thought that gave film directors unparalleled credit for the finished product. Perhaps this explains how Bazin's periodical, *Cahiers du Cinéma*, became the primary locus of the *politique des auteurs*—the auteur theory. Bazin and his followers wanted to propose an artistic pantheon that could serve as an alternative to stuffy French conventions. In the process, they promoted the director to godlike cult status.

At *Cahiers* in Paris, Bazin rallied a cadre of young *cinéphiles* (film lovers), including François Truffaut, Claude Chabrol, and Jean-Luc Godard. They lauded underappreciated cogs in the Hollywood machinery, like directors Howard Hawks, John Ford, and Alfred Hitchcock. The French appreciation of American auteurs crossed the Atlantic via critic Andrew Sarris and his influential 1962 essay, "Notes of the Auteur Theory," and subsequent book, *The American Cinema: Directors and Directions, 1929–1968*. Sarris acknowledged the politics and power behind the theory and how "Truffaut used American movies as a club against certain snobbish tendencies in the French Cinema."[29] He called the auteur theory "a highbrow gambit of elevating lowbrow art at the expense of middle-brow art." It saluted those directors who left a personal stamp on genre films generated within the studio system. San Francisco film critic Pauline Kael famously countered that in focusing on "the frustrations of a man working against the given material," the auteur theory glorified trash.[30] It is tough to re-create this era of heated debates in serious film journals. Despite the limitations of Sarris's study, since the 1960s, films have been discussed and analyzed almost exclusively in terms of the director as author. An initial cinematic canon was established. Sarris's pantheon of directors successfully navigated Hollywood and "transcended their technical problems with a personal vision of the world."[31]

From their work at *Cahiers*, Bazin's stable of film critics led the renowned *Nouvelle Vague*, the French New Wave. His studious theorists became gifted practitioners, transformed from *cinéphiles* to *cinéastes*. Bazin's appreciation for the unvarnished slice of life inspired Truffaut and Chabrol to take up arms—or at least their handheld cameras—into Paris's streets. They reclaimed the mantle of the Lumière brothers, using untrained actors and filming with a documentary eye for detail. Their back-to-basics, low-budget productions brought a feeling of authenticity lacking in studio-bound projects. The spontaneous feel of New Wave films served as an implicit critique of Jean Renoir's elaborate cinematic plans. Films like *Les quatre cents coups* (*The 400 Blows* [1959]) have a poignant real-world quality; humor and tragedy coexist in every frame. Truffaut borrowed liberally from his own childhood in creating *400 Blows*—auteur as autobiographer. We follow the emotional journey of Antoine as he wanders from indifferent parents to an abusive home for delinquents. He skips school, mocks his teacher, and engages in petty crime. But his intelligence and decency are never in question. He lacks love and the influence of a caring adult. In Antoine's concluding escape and run toward the ocean, Truffaut captured the essence of the *Nouvelle Vague*. The director and his surrogate character both long for freedom, for fresh air, the next wave. Bazin inspired his disciples to rediscover the joy of cinema, the vibrant sense of being alive that characterizes the most infectious movies.

New Wave directors like Jean-Luc Godard rediscovered the power of editing. His films are elliptical, allusive, freed from the bounds of space or time. Godard's use of jump cuts, freeze frames, and voice-over in *À bout de souffle* (*Breathless* [1960]) underscored the director's artistic interference. While Bazin sought to limit editorial influence, Godard cut with a heavy hand. Film became a personal essay, a chance to explore the director's personal psyche and boyhood experience. The characters in *Breathless* share Godard's affection for American gangster films. The movie serves both as homage to film noir and as subversive satire. Godard often cast his current wife or mistress as the lead actress. Scenes began to mean more to the artist than to the audience. Godard supplied voice-over for his movies, commenting on the plot or action with a monologue addressed directly to filmgoers. Over time, Godard's movies became a megaphone linked to political debate.

Against the backdrop of the Vietnam War, Bazin's predilections seemed sentimental and quaint, part of ancient history. His disciples, like Godard, abandoned their master, resolving to destroy cinema as audiences had known and loved it. In films like *Pierrot le Fou* (1965) and *Weekend* (1967), Godard reintroduced film as political essay (à la Eisenstein). His works were more manifesto than entertainment—or at least politics as entertainment. As his faith in film waned, Godard's vision grew darker. The free-flowing fun of *Breathless* gave way to the paranoia of *Alphaville* (1965). Young punks play-acting like movie gangsters in *Bande à part* (*Band of Outsiders* [1964]) devolve into a bourgeois couple focused on collecting their inheritance in *Weekend*, which depicts the contemptible Roland and Corine cheating on each other and willing to resort to murder to get what they want. In opposition to Bazin's fondness for depth of field, Godard constructed an elaborate ten-minute tracking shot for *Weekend*. The camera tracks alongside a massive traffic jam as Parisians head for a weekend in the country. Godard offers audiences a single perspective from which to view an endless procession of cars. Despite the variety of makes and models of automobiles, the extended scene suffers from a suffocating sameness. It is flat and boring, just like the bourgeois values (cars, families, vacations) Godard is attacking.[32] Roland ends up consumed by a band of revolutionary cannibals. By the conclusion of *Weekend*, Godard undercuts cinema itself. A title card at the conclusion of the film announces nothing less than the "End of Cinema."[33]

Even the earnest Truffaut slipped into self-analysis and reflexivity. In *La Nuit Américaine* (*Day for Night* [1973]), Truffaut portrayed the behind-the-scenes melodrama of a film crew. He plays himself, a director, trying desperately to complete a movie while backstage traumas threaten to unravel his efforts. The title refers to the cinematic trick of shooting night scenes in daylight. He pays tribute to his cinematic idols—Hitchcock, Ford, and Hawks—in a cinematic essay. Truffaut bypasses the perspective offered by surrogate characters like Antoine Doinel. The director has become not only the auteur but also the subject. Brecht must have been proud. The artifice inherent in the cinematic process has become the plot. The postmodern meta-cinema was born.

Quentin Tarantino represents the apotheosis of auteur theory and postmodern filmmaking. His liberal "borrowing" of all that has gone before demonstrates the possibilities and limits of self-referential (and self-reverential!) cinema. He is the ultimate film fan, aware of film history and striving to secure his own place within it. In naming his production company "A Band Apart," Tarantino consciously identified himself as Godard's disciple. Tarantino's acclaimed first film, *Reservoir Dogs* (1992), borrows tropes from American film noir that Godard had stolen from hard-boiled directors like Sam Fuller and Nicholas Ray. *Cinephilia* came full circle. The French paid tribute to American B movies, and an American becomes an international sensation by stealing from Frenchmen obsessed with American gangster films. Tarantino fractures the narrative, playing with time, in a manner that Eisenstein would have respected. Yet he often locks off of the camera (i.e., makes it static) for extended riffs from his quirky characters. He respects his characters and highlights the written and spoken word. Tarantino composes poetic, profound, and profane prose that would make Bazin blush. With long takes and minimal editing, Tarantino revived the caper film.

Pulp Fiction (1994) embodies all sorts of postmodern contradictions. It is horribly violent and deeply spiritual. Professional hit men talk casually about hamburgers while en route to a contract killing. They commit atrocious crimes and become witnesses to miracles and epiphanies. Such seemingly irreconcilable impulses are presented as utterly normal in Tarantino's universe. A gangster film can become an occasion for common grace, a theological touchstone for an emerging church. *Pulp Fiction* fuses images from our collective pop cultural history. At Jack Rabbit Slims, a 1950s-style café, waiters dress like Marilyn Monroe and James Dean. The most famed dancer from the 1970s, John Travolta, brushes off some moves with an icon of 1990s cinema, Uma Thurman. They win the dance contest and audience sympathy. Most moviegoers did not realize that Tarantino lifted the style and tone of this scene from Godard's *Bande à part*. Tarantino resurrected art cinema by wrapping it in B-movie genre conventions. He became a star in the process, the most celebrated auteur of his era. His dedicated followers founded the Church of Tarantino, labeling him "A God among Directors."[34]

Not all movies lend themselves to auteur analysis; the creative process is at times so collaborative and chaotic, and so corporate, that no clear artistic voice can be heard. But many films do. When the creative effort of a moviemaker is dominant, a recognition of the auteur allows new insight into the power and meaning of the movie itself. There are, of course, dangers in adopting auteur criticism. We can lose the uniqueness of an individual movie by submerging it in the whole corpus of a director's work; we can reduce film analysis to autobiography; and we can overlook individual brilliant movies that have no parallels in a director's other works. But used with a modicum of common sense, auteur criticism can help us uncover the full significance of an individual film within a director's overall oeuvre. The list of directors with a body of work that invites analysis and intertextuality (a conversation between the movies or "texts") is rich, even overwhelming.

Cultural Criticism: Embedded Ideologies

From the politically charged atmosphere of the 1960s arose Christian Metz's study of the semiotics of the cinema, *Film Language* (1974).[35] He fused psychoanalysis, linguistics, and Marxist politics into a potent intellectual stew. While Eisenstein identified the building blocks of film, Metz and subsequent postmodern film critics deconstructed cinema. Metz adopted scientific methods rooted in Ferdinand de Saussure's semiotics. Special attention focused on contradictory signs and symbols residing within a single shot. The scientific observations of Aristotle met the intellectual idealism of Plato. Much optimism about the power of film theory followed. Finally, an objective system for studying film had been found! Metz aspired to nothing less than forging a science of cinematic signs.

But shots, like words, are rather complex, full of multiple shadings, histories, and interpretations. A new wave of film theorists called attention to the cultural politics of film. They emphasized the power dynamics at play within the Hollywood style, recognizing that the studio system of invisible editing may hide what's really happening (both on and off the screen). An understanding of subtext became as important as the story itself. As an example, for *In the Mood for Love*, director Wong Kar-wai borrowed from his own autobiography as a boy in Shanghai relocated to Hong Kong after the Communist takeover of mainland China. Viewers reading subtitles who do not speak Shanghainese or Cantonese may miss the subtle cultural tensions. The same goes for the cheongsam dresses worn by Maggie Cheung that evoke a timeless Chinese beauty and remembrance. Wong set the film in the past as a safe means to comment on the present political setting in Hong Kong. It is a story about desire and restraint made at a time full of anxiety as the British handed the rule of Hong Kong to the People's Republic of China. As the married characters grapple with infidelity onscreen, the audience in Hong Kong worries about broken political promises of independence and self-rule. Each shot of unconsummated love operates on multiple levels.

Cultural criticism looks at film in terms of its social and psychological contexts. It studies the entire apparatus of film, from production to distribution to reception. With regard to a movie's reception, for example, it desires to know what effect a movie has on its viewers, its impact on their attitudes, emotions, or behaviors. It also considers how the viewers' social situations or competencies influence their experience of a movie.

How, where, and when viewers see often determines what viewers see. Despite directors' best intentions, what matters most may be what is communicated and received rather than what is intended. Metz shifted the focus in film studies from the auteur to the audience. The move toward reader response gave underrepresented voices an invitation to join the critical debate. Histories of the screen depictions of all types of minorities followed. In *The Only Good Indian* (1972), Ralph and Natasha Friar traced how Hollywood westerns misrepresented Native Americans. Molly Haskell chronicled the evolving onscreen roles for women in movies in her groundbreaking book *From Reverence to Rape* (1973). The stereotyping of African Americans was unspooled in Donald Bogle's *Toms, Coons, Mulattoes, Mammies and Bucks* (1974) and in Daniel Leab's *From Sambo to Superspade* (1976). Vito Russo's *The Celluloid Closet* (1987) brought the history of homosexuality on film into the open. We have come to understand how our sexuality, race, and gender will determine how we perceive and receive a film.

These landmark studies coincided with major cultural and political shifts. The movements toward civil rights, women's rights, and gay rights were aided by newfound critical awareness of underrepresentation and misrepresentation in the movies. These issues were also raised in theological circles, with black theology, feminist theology, and liberation theology combining political, religious, and sociological categories with relative ease. Were film critics and theologians responding to cultural shifts or initiating them? The general foment of the era forced politicians to wrestle with the academy and forced artists to confront politics. Theory and practice merged in a heady and confusing era loaded with combustible possibilities (not unlike our own combative postmodern context).

The study of filmed images became more political than ever, with particular emphasis on issues of power and ideology. Classic films like *The Birth of a Nation* were reexamined from an African American perspective. Sequences that had been analyzed in terms of craft were now seen as slanted, racist, and contemptible. Film history books were rewritten to expose the ideologies embedded in the technique. In *From Reverence to Rape*, Haskell surveyed the treatment of women in the movies and how Hollywood reinforced the big lie of women's inferiority.[36] Thanks to astute critics like Haskell, we began to identify how films colonized our imagination and influenced our thoughts regarding gender, class, and whomever we might consider "the other."

Laura Mulvey incorporated elements of psychoanalysis to demonstrate how predominately male directors objectified actresses through their choice of camera angles and framing. Her influential essay "Visual Pleasure and Narrative Cinema" served as the catalyst for the gender studies that followed.[37] She pointed out the power dynamics inherent in the male gaze. Alfred Hitchcock may have been one of the most gifted directors in film history, but his subjective camera forces audiences to act as voyeurs, spying on women in *Rear Window* (1954) and *Vertigo* (1958). In both films, Jimmy Stewart plays a lead character with a physical weakness. Whether suffering from vertigo or trapped in a wheelchair while recovering from an accident, he is handicapped in his ability to save the blonde object of his desire. Hitchcock did not disguise the central tension of his films—a man eager to save women from harm, but unable to perform. But Mulvey questioned the way Hitchcock fixates on certain objects or clues, like the spiral formed in Kim Novak's blonde hair. Women in Hitchcock's films appear faceless, distant, and unreachable. They are reduced to either a series of objects like a pendant or become an object/goal in and of themselves.

While Hitchcock's obsession with blondes undoubtedly appealed to many male viewers, Mulvey rightly pointed out how damaging and dangerous such fetishistic fascination can become through repeated, desensitizing exposure. Mulvey alerted viewers to the seductive power of cinema. The writing of author bell hooks pushed such concerns even further, toward active resistance and an oppositional gaze.[38] She explained why African American women had to place themselves "on guard" against offensive depictions sure to unspool on most movie screens. In raising issues of black female spectatorship and calling for self-representation, hooks empowered pioneering directors from Julie Dash to Ava DuVernay. People of faith and conscience could undoubtedly connect with Mulvey and hooks's criticism, lobbying for a cinema that treats all people with equal dignity. Film theorists united around the common ground of human rights. Gender studies from the 1970s paved the way for today's Bechdel-Wallace test, which asks whether a work of fiction (e.g., a movie) includes at least two women who converse together about something other than men.[39] Film critics raised important questions regarding representation and identity. Film studies aspired to shift us from passive spectatorship toward active and savvy film-going.

Unfortunately, film studies also became almost the exclusive province of left-wing academics attacking bourgeois values and beliefs. In an effort to atomize and analyze film, Metz and his associates sometimes turned film criticism from a joy into a burden. Overly technical language kept readers out of the conversation that swirled around our most inclusive and populist art form. The Marxist prejudices that informed most cutting-edge film critics of the 1970s looked questionable by the time the Soviet Union collapsed. Their theories fell along with the Berlin Wall. In the twenty-first century, rising economic inequality has made questions of power and ideology relevant again. We've needed scholars to question how Hollywood depicts Arabs and Muslims and economic refugees.[40] It is prudent to analyze how Hollywood has altered its products to please its funding sources—for example, making heroes of the Chinese in global franchises like *Transformers*.[41] Unfortunately, film studies has continued to occupy rarified air, removed from most filmmakers and filmgoers. The clubiness of academia may have given theorists what they desired: their own corner of a universe where few enter.

Not all critics took this route, however. Contrarian critics like Pauline Kael and her devoted followers (dubbed "Paulettes") sought to reclaim film as populist entertainment. "We generally become interested in movies because we enjoy them," Kael reminded us, "and what we enjoy them for has little to do with what we think of as art."[42] In her influential essay "Trash, Art, and the Movies," Kael insisted that "movie audiences will take a lot of garbage, but it's pretty hard to make us queue up for pedagogy. At the movies we want a different kind of truth, something that surprises us and registers with us as funny or accurate or maybe amazing, maybe even amazingly beautiful." From her prime position as film critic at the *New Yorker*, Kael inspired a fresh wave of film reviewers who reveled in the simple pleasures that movies offer. In the 1980s and '90s, Chicago-based newspapermen Roger Ebert and Gene Siskel took their film reviews to the mass medium of television, inspiring a new generation of film fanatics to debate the merits of movies and boil their feelings down to a thumbs-up or thumbs-down. At the dawn of the twenty-first century, websites like Rotten Tomatoes and Metacritic began to aggregate critical reviews. Filmgoers could quickly check whether a new film was certified "fresh" or not. With the advent of social media, word of mouth became the most important aspect of movie marketing. Audiences discovered the thrills available in *The Blair Witch Project* (1999), *Paranormal Activity* (2007), and *Get Out* (2017) without the studios' marketing. Critical reviews could not undermine public enthusiasm for these low-budget breakthroughs. In the internet era, the pedigree of an individual film critic has come to matter far less; friends' recommendations are equally likely to translate into box-office gold. How do we retain a critical eye during a profit-driven era of corporate blockbusters?

Focusing Our Critical Lenses: A Case Study of *Wonder Woman*

Amid the overlapping lenses of genre conventions, of filmmakers' intentions, and of cultural receptions, it is easy to lose sight of the film itself. Most filmgoers are inclined to talk about a movie's theme, what the story meant (rather than how it may fit into a director's oeuvre or reinforce certain cultural hegemonies). How do we apply the various critical lenses to films built for a global mass market? Thematic criticism, the fourth major critical lens, refers to the content of the movie. It focuses on the movie itself rather than on the moviemaker, the audience, or the embedded worldview. A professor or film student may look for a movie's theme and then compare it with the way a similar theme plays out in another text. Most often that companion text is another movie, but because intertextual dialogue also has value, a film might be compared to a philosophical essay, a biblical text, or perhaps the novel, play, or comic book from which it was adapted. We will conclude this chapter by applying genre, auteur, cultural, and thematic lenses to the spectacularly successful *Wonder Woman* (2017).

Wonder Woman exemplifies the superhero genre, especially the origin story. It offers scenes of Diana's extraordinary skills, even in childhood; her training by a fierce and beloved mentor, Antiope; and her place within the overriding mythology of the Amazon warriors. Her idyllic life on the hidden island of Themyscira is shattered when an American spy's plane crashes and German soldiers land on the beach. *Wonder Woman* follows the adult Diana (Gal Gadot) as she clarifies her calling as defender of humankind from the specter of Ares, the God of War. Like so many other cinematic superheroes, Diana must take up the sword (dubbed the "god killer"), tap into her superpowers, and vanquish the villain to restore order and fulfill her mandate.

Wonder Woman diverges from genre conventions in its gender politics. The male lead, Steve Trevor (Chris Pine), must be rescued from drowning by Diana. When she marvels at his appearance, "You are a man," Steve responds defensively, "Don't I look like one?" While nursing his wounds in a bath, a naked Steve is ogled by a curious Diana. She wonders if he is a typical example of manhood. While nervously covering his penis, Steve boasts that he is "above average." Their discussion of his watch masks the sexual subtext. Diana wonders, "Why do you listen to a little thing that tells you what to do?" Filmgoers delighted in this role reversal, with a naked man squirming defensively under a woman's gaze. Later, when Steve asks Diana whether she knows about the pleasures of the flesh, she disappoints him by deeming men unnecessary for pleasure. She heeds the words of her mother, Amazon queen Hippolyta: "Be careful in the world of men, Diana. They do not deserve you."

While a close reading of Allen Heinberg's screenplay reveals clear cultural commentary, director Patty Jenkins received rave reviews for her firm handling of the material. The battle scenes of Amazonians brandishing swords, leaping off shields, and unleashing arrows are thrilling. When Diana steps into "no *man's* land" to confront German soldiers on the western front, our admiration swells with the musical score. Diana repels bullets with her bracelets, deflecting German firepower with her rousing strength and shield. She stages a nonviolent intervention in fields ravaged by war.

Jenkins credits her peripatetic childhood as the daughter of an Air Force fighter pilot and Silver Star Vietnam veteran with empowering her. She also praises her environmental scientist mother, a second-wave feminist, because "the way she raised me was both super aware that there had been sexism but

Wonder Woman (2017), © Warner Bros. Entertainment Inc. / Ratpac-Dune Entertainment, LLC

also: 'Congratulations—thank you, now I get to do whatever I want, Mom.'"[43] How did Jenkins feel about becoming the first woman to helm a big-budget superhero film? She admits, "It never occurred to me that I couldn't be a director, that I couldn't be a successful director. And not a woman director, just a director. And so it's stunning to me now [to think]: 'I'm the first person to do this—how did that *happen*?'"[44]

The audience embrace of *Wonder Woman* broke records for the biggest opening for a film directed by a woman and the highest box-office gross for a female-helmed feature.[45] Critical consensus was equally rapturous. Richard Brody of the *New Yorker* compared it to "wisdom literature that shares hard-won insights and long-pondered paradoxes of the past with a sincere intimacy."[46] Ann Hornaday of the *Washington Post* lauded the cast, especially Gal Gadot: "Cool, solemn, her eyes often welling with tears at the human waste and destruction she witnesses, Gadot's Diana is the very opposite of a cartoon character: She's soulful and utterly credible, even when she comes out bracelets blazing."[47] Thanks to such positive reviews, *Wonder Woman* ranks second on Rotten Tomatoes' aggregated list of the sixty best superhero movies of all time (surpassed only by the beloved *Black Panther* [2018]).[48] It also rescued the embattled DC Comics' cinematic universe from both critical and public scorn.

Not everyone, though, applauded the girl power expressed at the box office. Sold-out screenings held at the Alamo Drafthouse for "People Who Identify as Women Only" were met with praise and outrage.[49] For every think piece that celebrated *Wonder Woman* as a feminist icon, another questioned whether the sexualized violence merely reinforced American militarization and exceptionalism. James Cameron dared to denigrate *Wonder Woman* as "an objectified icon" and "a step backwards" from his own cinematic heroines like Sarah Connor in

Terminator 2 (1991).[50] Before the inevitable sequel launched, Gal Gadot leaned into her newfound box-office power by refusing to act until executive producer Brett Ratner, a widely accused sexual harasser in Hollywood, was scrubbed from the production.[51] As a proactive response to the #MeToo movement, *Wonder Woman 2* was announced as the first feature to implement the Producer's Guild of America's new Anti–Sexual Harassment Guidelines.[52]

Aspiring reel theologians viewing *Wonder Woman* through a textual, genre, auteur, or cultural lens discover how many relevant issues surface even among Hollywood's biggest blockbusters. These critical lenses help us unpack a movie's power and meaning and prepare the way for honest and constructive analysis of spiritual themes including vocation and calling, love and sacrifice.

Having identified a film's story structure, highlighted the cinematic crafts, and surveyed the many critical lenses available, we now turn to another set of critical lenses to sharpen our focus: the theological.

Discussion Questions

1. Are there particular websites or critics you turn to and trust? Do you prefer to read reviews before or after seeing a film?

2. Are you more drawn to the formal aspects of film criticism (à la Eisenstein) or the more narrative side of storytelling (via Bazin)? What can you learn from the other?

3. What recent cultural lenses (psychological, racial, gender, etc.) do you find helpful in understanding movies?

act ii

theology

6

a diverse church responds

an ecclesial lens

The cinema and religious traditions of various stripes have sometimes seemed to be in competition with each other. Paul Woolf, a screenwriter and *maggid* (an ordained Jewish storyteller who teaches people about God), tells of growing up Jewish in Brooklyn. He had a strong commitment to the Jewish faith even as a young boy, but the rabbis at synagogue did not connect with him. The spiritual experiences that he had were more often the result of simple things. He remembers, for example, walking down the street when he was four, holding his mother's hand and realizing that he was in the presence of God. His consciousness seemed enlarged to the point that he could hear every bird singing and every leaf rustling.

When Woolf was fourteen, he went into Manhattan to see *Spartacus* (1960). Woolf sat transfixed as he watched Kirk Douglas, the gladiator Spartacus, say to his wife, played by Jean Simmons, "Anyone can kill, can be taught to fight; I'm not interested in that. I want to know where the wind comes from . . . why we are here." Woolf describes that all of a sudden there was this "incredible flight of questioning about life. In a film, no less." As the movie ended, the audience just sat there, stunned. Woolf concludes, "On the train ride back to Brooklyn, I kept thinking, how can this be? Why had I never experienced this in a house of worship? That's when I made my decision. I said to myself, I'm going to Hollywood to make movies."[1]

Woolf's story rings true for many. Perhaps the best known example is from the movie *Cinema Paradiso* (1988; English version, 1989, which won an Oscar for Best Foreign Language Film in 1990). In the movie, Salvatore (known as "Toto") reminisces about his childhood friend Alfredo, the projectionist at the local theater, The Paradiso. While church services put Toto to sleep, movies captivated him, and Alfredo became his mentor. The young, impressionable Toto would peek into the theater as the local priest would censor all motion picture kisses from the upcoming movies by ringing his bell to cue the projectionist where to cut. At the end of the film, Salvatore, now a famous filmmaker, returns home for Alfredo's funeral, receiving as a bequest a gift from the projectionist: a montage of all the movie kisses the church forced Alfredo to excise. As Salvatore watches these wonder-filled moments, viewers share with him a rich joy, tinged with sadness. How could the religious establishment be blind to such ordinary, yet luminescent pleasures?

Today, movie viewing by Christians is typically more like Woolf's experience with *Spartacus* than Salvatore's experience growing up in Sicily. But the church's response to film remains wide-ranging. A variety of lenses continue to be used by the church and its members to watch cinema. Christians, both individually and institutionally, at times (1) preach avoidance, (2) express caution, (3) enter into dialogue, (4) appropriate insight, or (5) are surprised by God's presence. These five responses can be depicted graphically on a linear timeline:

Figure 6.1 The Theologian/Critic's Posture

And though these approaches developed more or less chronologically over the last century, all also continue to have advocates today who find support for their positions both in Scripture and in the theology of their faith communities.

We can graph these theological approaches to Hollywood using a matrix to show (1) whether a given theologian/critic begins his or her reflection with the movie itself or with a theological position and (2) whether a given response centers on the movie more ethically or more aesthetically (see fig. 6.2).

Christian theologians who articulate an *avoidance* strategy do so not from an aesthetic posture but from an ethical one (often their books even have words like "morality" and "values" in their titles). Moreover, those preaching avoidance almost always move from their given theological perspective to the film

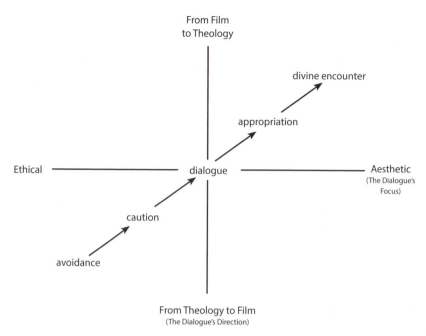

From Film
to Theology

divine encounter

appropriation

Ethical ——————————— dialogue ——————————— Aesthetic
(The Dialogue's
Focus)

caution

avoidance

From Theology to Film
(The Dialogue's Direction)

Figure 6.2 The Theologian/Critic's Approach

under consideration, rarely vice versa. On the other hand, those open to a *divine encounter* through film most often begin their reflections with the film itself, not with their theology. The film's themes serve as the springboard to attempt theological judgments. Any criticism they offer begins with aesthetic judgments about the film itself and not with ethical positions they bring to the film.

Three other positions emerge along the diagonal we have drawn between these contrasting approaches. Those expressing *caution* take the film with some seriousness, but still focus their responses on the film's ethical stance, beginning their deliberations from a given axiological/theological posture. Those wishing for theological *dialogue* want theology to inform their film viewing and want film viewing to inform their theology in a lively two-way conversation that is both ethical and aesthetic in nature. And those open to *appropriating* a movie's insight begin their deliberations with the movie itself, while bringing their own life experiences more strongly into the conversation than those who would explore divine encounters.

One should remember in the discussion that follows that these five "types" of Christian responses to film are just that—types. They are artificial constructs used to help identify discernible options despite recognizable fluidity and messiness. In real life, Christian theologians/critics often prove more eclectic in their approach than this graph might suggest. But most moviegoers do tend in their religious response to the movies to focus on one dominant perspective toward the movies. To these varied responses we now turn.

The Church's Varied Responses

Avoidance

The stance of some Christians today has continued the boycott mentality that characterized many conservative Protestants and Catholics of an earlier era. John R. Rice, the famous fundamentalist preacher, saw his small book *What Is Wrong with the Movies?* (1938) go through fifteen editions. It begins, "A mother in deep distress of mind came to see me, her pastor, to ask my prayers and counsel concerning a daughter who had been led away from the church, away from the Bible, away from Christian living and joy, by the movies."[2] Rice continues: just as there might be good food in the garbage, so there might be an occasional good in some movies. But you don't send your kids to eat garbage. Rice's advice? Avoid going to the movies.

Bryan Stone, author of the book *Faith and Film: Theological Themes at the Cinema* (2000), begins his case for the importance of cinema becoming a dialogue partner for Christians by recalling, "I grew up in a conservative Christian denomination that taught that it was wrong to go to the movies. The cinema was spelled s-i-n-ema, and Hollywood, we were taught, was an industry that was as opposed to Christian values as anything could be."[3]

Such rhetoric seems mainly to come from a bygone day, certainly one before the advent of television, which brought the "movie theater" into everyone's living room. More typical today than such blanket condemnation is the argument for a selective boycott of those films judged to be particularly objectionable. It is, after all, difficult to condemn *The Sound of Music* (1965) or *Inside Out* (2015). So, church organizations have continued to use boycott, but only as an occasional strategy for dealing with Hollywood, particularly when a movie treats a religious theme or institution in what is considered an objectionable, even blasphemous, manner. Movies like *The Last Temptation of Christ* (1988), *Life Is Beautiful* (1997), *El Crimen del Padre Amaro* (2002), and *The Magdalene Sisters* (2002) have all incurred the rejection of the church.

A particularly interesting example of such boycotting is the movie *Dogma* (1999), against which the Catholic League for Religious and Civil Rights mounted a vigorous campaign. When Kevin Smith's irreverent yet God-affirming movie opened at the New York Film Festival in October 1999, it did so over the loud objections of Cardinal John O'Connor and Mayor Rudolph Giuliani, a faithful

Catholic layman. What makes this opposition unique is that the movie exuberantly affirms the existence of God and tells the story of a woman's recovery of faith. It is also the case that Smith was a practicing Catholic. All this was thought irrelevant to the protesters, however, for organized Christianity seemed to be mocked and theology questioned.

In the movie, a thirteenth apostle (played by Chris Rock) claims to have been cut out of the Bible because he is black! There are pot-smoking prophets; the crucifix is replaced by the statue of a "Buddy Christ" winking and giving the thumbs-up; and scatological and sexual humor abound. The plot revolves around two fallen angels, banished from heaven and now living in Wisconsin, who seek to reenter heaven against God's wishes through a loophole in church dogma. The story, like the humor, is irreverent; but it also affirms the importance of faith, the benevolence of God, and the divinity of Christ. Here is a movie that is not agnostic or un-Christian in viewpoint, even if it is sacrilegious and sexy in design.

Why this paradox? Smith said he wanted "to do something full of faith that was entertaining enough to keep [viewers] in their seats."[4] A spokesperson for the Catholic League for Religious and Civil Rights, however, was unconvinced, finding "the entire plot [to be] one situation after another of making fun of the Catholic faith,"[5] with comedian George Carlin cast as the cardinal and alternative rock singer Alanis Morissette as God. The League instituted a letter-writing campaign urging a boycott, while the United States Catholic Conference of Bishops gave the film its worst rating of "O" ("morally offensive"). But such "moral admonition" seemed to have little influence on the wider public. As the headline in the *Los Angeles Times* announced following the movie's opening, "*Dogma* Opens in New York to Protesters' Jeers, Audience Cheers."[6]

Caution

Given the ineffectiveness of most religious boycotts in the West, avoidance has become a less tenable response to the perceived sensationalism and materialism of the cinema than it was in the 1930s. Thus, a more common attitude among conservative Christians today has become that of caution. Since the advent of television, few Christians have continued to argue for abstinence as a viable strategy. But many have continued to worry over the entertainment industry's "negative" influence. They have, for this reason, wanted to curtail Hollywood's societal reach (recall the rhetoric, for example, of some evangelical Christians during the 2016 presidential campaign).

For example, writing about the Academy Award nominations in 2005 for Best Picture (*Crash; Munich; Good Night, and Good Luck; Brokeback Mountain;*

and *Capote*), conservative Protestant leader Chuck Colson complained that "the films Hollywood chose to honor had little to do with quality and everything to do with philosophy and worldview." Quoting Barbara Nicolosi, a conservative Catholic, both religiously and politically, who teaches at Azusa Pacific University, he said, "Hollywood's choices affirm, once again, 'just how very, very sick America's storytellers have become.'"[7] Nicolosi's comments were, in part, her reaction to the Academy's snub of Mel Gibson's *Passion of the Christ* (2004), a movie that affected her deeply. But her language was unguarded and hyperbolic. She even suggested in the article Colson quoted that it might be a sin against the Holy Spirit for the industry to be "throwing accolades at films that are essentially depraved in their themes."[8]

Both Colson and Nicolosi would be quick to add that Hollywood can sometimes get it right, but they more typically bemoan the fact that the percentages are so low. As Colson writes, "Yes, there are too many bad movies out there—films that celebrate depravity. But there are good ones too. Films we can use to teach our kids and our neighbors good lessons."[9] Discrimination certainly is called for when choosing a movie; Colson and Nicolosi are correct on that count. But sensitivity is also called for in our film *viewing*. Social agendas do play into the viewing of any movie, yet because film focuses on life in both its particularity and its universality, this does not necessarily negate the quality of a movie.

Colson was a socially conservative Protestant; Nicolosi is a socially conservative Catholic. It is not only those on the religious "right," however, who suggest caution relative to a film's social or religious stance. Those on the religious "left" can be equally suspicious, and as a result risk being equally poor film viewers. Margaret Miles, the former dean of the Graduate Theological Union in Berkeley, received a large grant to identify and analyze the values imaged in films. In her book *Seeing and Believing* (1997), Miles argues that Hollywood continues to shape our attitudes toward race, gender, class, and sexual orientation through its patterns, stereotypes, and symbolic markers.[10] Even as a child, Miles understood from movie marquees that fat people were laughable, people of color were subservient, and beautiful, heterosexual people were the norm. The attitudes portrayed in movies "are not accidental or incidental to religious perspectives but," she argues, "as a concrete way religious perspectives are articulated, are central to religious values."[11]

Miles, like Colson and Nicolosi, approaches film from an ethically driven theological stance. Hers is a hermeneutic of suspicion, like that of her conservative counterparts. And though she seeks to be a student of film, she ends up not always being able to see a movie on its own terms. As John Lyden comments at the end of his discussion of Miles's book, "It is ironic that leftist critics of culture may find themselves in harmony with right-wing conservatives in their wholesale denunciation of popular culture."[12]

Miles, Colson, and Nicolosi all have a sense of style and discrimination with regard to their movie judgments, even if the authors of this book find them too often confined to an ideological straitjacket that dictates how they view a particular movie. Each comes to film from a defined theological perspective and thus finds a one-sided imbalance between Hollywood and the church, between movies and theology. For the most part, they believe that movies are too often in the business of theological subversion (though how "subversion" would be defined differs greatly). Thus, they advise caution for the religious viewer.

———— ·◆· ————

Our comments about avoidance and caution no doubt already signal the direction we believe a Christian response to movies might more helpfully go. Some movies are morally repugnant and should be avoided. (Pornography or snuff movies are obvious examples.) Reading the reviews of other movies might also suggest at times a response of caution and selectivity. But to typically begin one's interaction with a movie by first staking out one's theological and/or ethical position before experiencing the story on its own terms risks both theological imperialism and faulty artistic judgments. C. S. Lewis, in his insightful monograph *An Experiment in Criticism*, observed, "We are so busy doing things with the work [the movie] that we give it too little chance to work on us. Thus increasingly we meet only ourselves."[13] Better that the Christian moviegoer should first view a movie on its own terms before offering a theological judgment on it. Coming to a movie in a spirit of judgment, presuming to know ahead of time the proper religious/ethical response to a story, undercuts a story's ability to convey its unique power and meaning effectively. The movie remains stillborn, something capable only of an autopsy.

Instead, the movie experience, like all play activities, functions best when it is experienced first as a "parenthesis" within life's ongoingness. That is, when people enter the theater (or go to the opera or the ballpark, or play basketball, or dance), they must temporarily set aside the issues of the larger world around them and be caught up in the movie experience itself. Whether listening to Beyoncé or watching a Christopher Nolan film, the audience is asked to focus exclusively on being present, if the artistic experience is to work its charm. In a sense, the real world must for a time stand still. Unless moviegoers give to the screen their "as-if" assent, entering wholeheartedly into the movie's imaginative world, its power and meaning will remain unknown.

At the Cineplex, moreover, such a posture of openness usually happens naturally, as the darkness of the theater and the community of viewers, not to mention the surround sound and oversized screen, combine with the images and story to help capture the audience's attention. To give movie viewing this epistemological priority in the dialogue between film and theology—to judge it advisable to first look at a movie on its own terms and let the images themselves suggest the direction for theological dialogue—is not to make theology of secondary importance, though some have mistakenly concluded that is what we have done.[14] No, religious faith remains primary. The nature of both movie-going and religious faith suggest that film viewing be completed from a theological perspective. But such theologizing should follow, not precede, the aesthetic experience.[15]

We thus turn from those approaches that begin theologically, judging movies from a predetermined norm, toward those critical perspectives that view a movie on its own terms. The first of these options we have labeled *dialogue*.

Dialogue

Even those who express caution with regard to film viewing recognize that some movies have identifiably religious themes or elements and thus invite or even demand dialogue from a theological perspective. Like *The Passion of the Christ* (2004) or *Noah* (2014), they might be about biblical characters or, like *Sister Act* (1992), might center their story on the nature of the church. Others find in Christ's sacrificial love a model for the narrative shape of authentic human life (*Logan* [2017], *Calvary* [2014]). Some movies portray a preacher's redemption, as in *The Apostle* (1997); others might center on a clergy's apostasy, yet faith, as in *Silence* (2016). Critics are not imposing an outside perspective on these movies when they enter into theological conversation with such films. Rather, the movies themselves explicitly deal with religious matters and thus invite (perhaps even require) a theological response.

A dialogically centered approach to theology and film is not limited to such obvious examples, however, as previous chapters in this book have already demonstrated. Any good story can invite our theological gaze. Beginning with Joel Martin and Conrad Oswalt's *Screening the Sacred: Religion, Myth, and Ideology in Popular American Film* (1995) and Clive Marsh and Gaye Ortiz's edited volume, *Explorations in Theology and Film: Movies and Meaning* (1997), the last twenty-five years have produced a spate of dialogically directed books that demonstrate just that.[16] Although these books present diverse individual perspectives, they share a commitment (belief/understanding/perspective) that film and theology invite a two-way conversation.

Roy Anker's trilogy of books—*Catching Light: Looking for God in the Movies* (2004), *Of Pilgrims and Fire: When God Shows Up at the Movies* (2010), and

Beautiful Light: Religious Meaning in Film (2017)—uses the metaphor of light to suggest that film can be a vehicle that presents divine Light itself.[17] Craig Detweiler's *Into the Dark* (2008) notes how the sacred appears in the top films of this century's first decade, while Kutter Callaway's *Scoring Transcendence* (2013) focuses on how a film's music conveys theological meaning.

Richard Blake, in his book *Afterimage: The Indelible Catholic Imagination of Six American Filmmakers* (2000), notes the continuing influence, or afterimage, of the Catholic faith on a number of film directors who might no longer identify themselves as part of that church.[18] Robert Johnston's *Useless Beauty: Ecclesiastes through the Lens of Contemporary Film* (2004) provides an example of intertextual dialogue, using films like *Run Lola Run* (1999) and *Magnolia* (1999) to bring to life an enigmatic wisdom book in the Old Testament, and using Ecclesiastes to illumine the paradoxical portrayals of life's misery, yet wonder, found in these movies.[19]

Dialogue between theology and movies can thus take many forms. The examples above provide only a small sample. One can note the explicit theological themes of given films or dialogue with spiritual motifs embedded in them. One can bring film and biblical (or theological) texts into conversation, or one can compare and contrast the Christ of the Gospels with the metaphorical use of a Christ figure to advance the meaning of a given movie. Whatever the shape, the common denominator in such approaches is the attempt to bring film and theology into two-way conversation, responding to what the movie presents, while letting both sides be equal partners in the dialogue.

Appropriation

While dialogue as an approach to film viewing focuses its attention on the film's text (its content and theme), appropriation, on the other hand, concentrates more on the film's effect on the viewer, on the potential religious significance of movie watching for the receptor. In his keynote address at the 2001 Conference on Religion and Cinema at Princeton University, the experimental filmmaker Nathaniel Dorsky spoke of how he has attempted for almost forty years to create a "devotional cinema." A movie, Dorsky believes, has "the potential to be transformative, to be an evocation of spirit, and to become a form of devotion." His concern, both in his avant-garde films and when viewing other films, has been with those "moments of revelation or aliveness," when the film evokes "something meaningfully human." Dorsky suggests that a movie's shots and cuts (its montage, the juxtaposing of absolute and relative time, the uncompromising and self-confirming "present" of a film, as well as the illuminated room) all contribute to producing "health or illness in an audience."[20]

That is, it is not simply a movie's words but also its images that work to create transformation in the viewer. We agree.

For those open to appropriating insight from a movie's story, the focus is not so much on better understanding God as on discovering that which is human, our spiritual center.[21] Movies can tease out for their viewers greater possibilities for being human and can present alternative selves not otherwise available to the movie watcher. Viewed in this light, the goal in relating theology and film is not, first of all, to render moral judgments or even to deepen theological understanding, as was the case with the earlier options we have considered. Rather, it is to gain spiritual insight by quickening the human spirit.

In *God in the Movies* (2017), Catherine Barsotti and Robert Johnston provide multiple examples of such appropriations. In his chapter on the movie *Field of Dreams* (1989), for example, Johnston speaks of an interview he heard with Phil Alden Robinson, the film's writer and director. Robinson said he had no explicit theological intention for the movie but recognized it had spiritually affected thousands of people by encouraging reconciliation between parents and their children. Respectful of the possibility that this film might have had a spiritual influence despite his lack of religious intention, Robinson spoke humbly and thanked those who had shared what the film meant to them.[22]

In his foreword to Gareth Higgins's personal reflections on how movie-going had affected him, *How Movies Saved My Soul: Finding Spiritual Fingerprints in Culturally Significant Films* (2003), Tony Campolo comments, "What Gareth offers is not so much a series of interpretations as it is a methodology for engaging movies. He calls upon us to engage films with hungry eyes, and he echoes Jesus in saying that those with eyes to see will see truths in films that speak to the existential conditions of our times and to the spiritual conditions of our [own] souls."[23]

While many such testimonies in *God in the Movies* and *How Movies Saved My Soul* are personal and anecdotal, Clive Marsh's *Cinema and Sentiment: Film's Challenge to Theology* (2004) stands back from the process and assesses the theological relevance of cinema-going and film watching, something studies in theology and film have only recently begun to investigate. Marsh recognizes a religion-like function in film watching. "Something happens, or can happen, to people who watch films because of how films work, because of where they are watched, and who they are watched with."[24] Films provide narratives through which people find themselves and make choices about how to live. When people watch films, they do so for reasons that are "more than entertainment, and not just to get themselves educated." They do so, thinks Marsh, as "an exercise in spirituality."[25]

Divine Encounter

As the millennium turned, Western culture evidenced an increased interest in spirituality. We moved into what some have labeled a neoromantic era. And as the first years of the millennium have gone by, the momentum has simply continued to grow. It is not surprising, therefore, as the Roman Catholic scholar John May perceptively commented, that from an earlier concern with the morality of film (the categories of avoidance and caution, discussed above), those engaged in the field of religion and film turned first to the explicitly religious elements of film and to one's theological conversation with this (i.e., dialogue), and now more recently to a focus on the humanistic (i.e., appropriation) and the aesthetic (what invites divine encounter).[26] Writing in 1996, May believed this possibility of experiencing the Transcendent would prove most important in the coming decades. Time has proven May correct.

Thus, to give but one example, Jeffrey Overstreet, in his book *Through a Screen Darkly* (2007), becomes "a spiritual bloodhound, rabidly tracking the voice of God through his own experience" at the movies.[27] For example, after seeing *The Story of the Weeping Camel* (2003), he writes, "Sticky cushions, talkative teens, annoying big screen commercials—it's all worth enduring for those occasional moments of revelation. It's like waiting through a season of disappointing baseball just to be there at that magic moment when the angle of the pitch and the timing of the swing meet with a crack that will echo in your memory for days. And yet, unlike a home run, this occasion on the big screen doesn't merely change the score. It changes you."[28]

Movies have, at times, a sacramental capacity to provide the viewer an experience of transcendence. One of the best books arguing this position is Jonathan Brant's *Paul Tillich and the Possibility of Revelation through Film*.[29] Here, as we have observed, was Rob's experience with the movie *Becket* and Craig's with *Raging Bull*. Here also was the experience of one of our former students while watching the movie *Magnolia* (1999).

Magnolia ends with Aimee Mann's song "Save Me" ("You look like the perfect fit / for a girl in need of a tourniquet / But can you save me / come on and save me") being sung as Jim goes to Claudia, the fragile young woman who has suffered sexual abuse at the hands of her father. While the song continues, "If you could save me / from the ranks of the freaks / who suspect they could never love anyone," we look over Jim's shoulder at Claudia. Over the song, which is foregrounded, we faintly hear Jim's voice saying, "You are a good and beautiful person." The camera remains focused on Claudia as she struggles to accept Jim's gift of love. Miraculously, she smiles briefly for the first time just as the movie ends. Our student commented that this final moment was a divine revelation for him. "It let me know there was still grace available because I had long given up hope that there was." In the margin of his paper on the movie, he wrote, "I see a lot of myself in Claudia's character and a lot of Jesus in Jim. The fact that Anderson kept Jim out of the frame for much of this scene while his voice bestowed grace from off camera was simply brilliant. This enabled the scene to transcend the film and become a conversation between me and Jesus. This film served as a catalyst for my return to faith after a decade of apostasy."[30]

John May's emphasis on divine encounter is what you might expect from a leading Roman Catholic scholar in the field. For, as Andrew Greeley writes, "Catholicism has always believed in the sacramentality of creation," that it can be "a revelation of the presence of God."[31] The Catholic Church has held that God is known through the experiences, objects, and people we encounter in our lives. Catholic theologian Richard McBrien defines sacramentality, borrowing from St. Ignatius of Loyola, as a way of seeing "God in all things: other people, communities, movements, events, places, objects, the environment, the world at large, the whole cosmos. The visible, the tangible, the finite, the historical—all these are actual or potential carriers of the divine presence."[32] For Greeley, film is especially suited to the making of such sacramentals because of its "inherent power to affect the imagination." Greeley even goes so far as to posit that the filmmaker (as artist) can, at times, disclose God's presence "even more sharply and decisively" than God has chosen to do through creation itself. Be that as it may, "the pure, raw power of the film to capture the person who watches it, both by its vividness and by the tremendous power of the camera to concentrate and change perspectives, is a sacramental potential that is hard for other art forms to match."[33]

Though the sacramental in art has more typically been recognized by Catholics, Protestants have occasionally also spoken of film's transcendental possibilities. Perhaps the most influential Protestant in this regard has been screenwriter and director Paul Schrader. In his oft-quoted book *Transcendental Style in Film* (originally published in 1972), Schrader argues that filmmakers can best invite God's transcendence (can bring people closer to the Holy, who can break into one's life) through "sparse" filmmaking—that is, by long takes and slow camera movement, repeated use of silence and restrained acting and editing.[34]

One might use as an example of Schrader's thesis Terrence Malick's iconic film *The Tree of Life* (2011), which proved transcendent to Craig Detweiler. The simple story begins with a telegram conveying the tragic news of a son's death. As the family seeks to deal with this human tragedy, mother and father become iconic—in Detweiler's words, they are "elevated into type." And in the end, grace prevails. Detweiler ends his review of the movie thus:

The power of [the mother's] surrender snuck up on me. Having lost my sister in a car wreck, I am well acquainted with the grief central to the story. Yet, I did not anticipate how purgative *Tree of Life* would become. I had never encountered such purity in a movie. The film did not insist. . . . It merely offered a comforting divine possibility. How can all dross be removed from a movie frame? The mystery left our audience in stunned silence. No one moved. . . . We wanted the sacred stillness to linger.[35]

While Schrader and Detweiler concentrate on how the transcendent is often conveyed through minimalism (we need to get that human "dross" out of the way), more "abundant" means of filmmaking can also be an invitation for the inbreaking of the numinous. In addition to film's ability to convey a pregnant silence, a vibrant flowering of life can also open viewers out to the Spirit of Life.[36] A movie such as Baz Luhrmann's *Moulin Rouge!* (2001) easily comes to mind. Luhrmann's all-out assault on the senses causes for some an equal but alternate transcendence, one in which we as viewers are "silenced" by too much sight and sound. As Christian worship itself illustrates, whether one engages in "Presbyterian" or "Pentecostal" worship practices, God's presence can break in. Never coerced, it can only be invited as humankind reaches out beyond itself and is met by an Other.[37]

A Theological Parallel

Those familiar with H. Richard Niebuhr's book *Christ and Culture* will note basic similarities between the models presented above and those suggested by Niebuhr.[38] One might, in fact, see the preceding discussion as an application of Niebuhr's classic typology to the medium of film (though that was not its genesis). In his volume, Niebuhr presents five orientations that the church throughout her history has taken as she has sought to understand the relationship between Christian theology (knowing "Christ") and the culture in which it is embedded. These are (along with their contemporary American denominational equivalents): (1) "Christ against culture," the Mennonite, Pentecostal, and fundamentalist option that advises *avoidance*; (2) "Christ and culture in paradox," the Lutheran, Baptist, and conservative evangelical perspective advising *caution*; (3) "Christ the transformer of culture," an understanding of Reformed Christians and progressive evangelicals that encourages *dialogue*; (4) "Christ above culture," the Roman Catholic and more sacramental Protestant option that admits to a sacramental breaking-in to the ordinary, i.e., *divine encounter*; and (5) "the Christ of culture," the understanding of many nonsacramental mainline Protestants recognizing the *appropriation* of spirituality within the everyday experiences of life.

Critics of Niebuhr sometimes argue that the historical examples he uses to illustrate his typology are biased toward his position while being unfair to others, particularly the Anabaptists.[39] They reject Niebuhr's implicit theological position, finding in his presentation a bias in favor of the transformational paradigm (what we have called *dialogue*). It should be clear that in our use of Niebuhr, we have not followed him in this regard. Instead, though all three of the authors of this book are Protestant and though we have each written books from out of the paradigm of dialogue, we have also been deeply influenced by Catholic sacramentality. Moreover, as Protestants, as those committed to asking, "Where is it written?" we have sought to follow Scripture itself, thus finding all five approaches as useful theologically, depending on the context and the film under consideration.

The Bible makes use of all five approaches within its pages. The letter 1 John might be judged as paradigmatic of avoidance ("love not the world," 1 John 2:15–17 KJV); Paul's epistle to the Romans as expressing caution (the idea of being in the world but not of it, Rom. 12:1–2); Paul's sermon on Mars Hill, which is recorded in the book of Acts, as representing dialogue ("I see that in every way you are very religious," Acts 17:22); the wisdom sayings in Proverbs as suggesting appropriation ("The words of Agur," a non-Hebrew, Prov. 30:1); and the story of Josiah ignoring God's message to Pharaoh Neco (Josiah "did not listen to the words of Neco from the mouth of God" and was killed as a result, 2 Chron. 35:22 NRSV) as an example of divine encounter. Given these biblical examples, which support all five approaches, we believe eclecticism in our methodology is called for. Only then can we, as Christian filmgoers, be faithful to the full biblical witness.

Cultivating a Deep Focus

The above typology charts five approaches that not only have been present over the last century as Christians have responded to film, but also are representative of how Christians through the ages have attempted to respond faithfully to the culture in which they find themselves. And though at any one point in time, depending on the movie being viewed, one or another of these approaches will more strongly suggest itself to the sensitive viewer, as we have noted, all five responses to our film-going have their Christian validity. No one-size-fits-all approach can be applied to all film viewing: don't watch a snuff movie; be careful in viewing that which lingers in your imagination in harmful ways; engage in theological dialogue with those stories that reveal life in its myriad particularities; allow a film's focus to affect your spirit deeply;

be open to the Spirit of Life (the Transcendent might surprise you while at the movie theater).

To note within this typology how film can be both a medium to provoke religious experience and the occasion for greater theological understanding is rather straightforward. Movies can be theologically important, both experientially and educationally. But though it is easy to note the depth of meaning that we can experience watching movies, it is more difficult to describe what this thickness is, let alone define how we as film viewers might encounter it. Are there guidelines that can be offered to the Christian filmgoer from out of our church tradition to help us watch movies with a "deep focus"?

It has seemed to us for some time that help is available to the theology and film critic from a most unlikely source. Could the thousand-year-old practice of *lectio divina* and its scholarly companion, the medieval fourfold method of biblical interpretation (where multiple levels of meaning are uncovered from out of a single text), help chart a way forward for the theological interpretation of film? We believe the short answer is *yes*. What these interpretive resources provide is not another access to the "facts" of a movie but an entirely different way of seeing, an access into what might be called "the imagination of life." What these medievalists developed as a supplement to a close reading/viewing of the biblical text was a thick, or in-depth, response to a text that invites aesthetic, ethical, and spiritual engagement. Here, we believe, is a model for our film viewing as well.

Basil Pennington, a Cistercian father whose book *Centering Prayer* has sold over a million copies, writes of these distinct practices that Christians have used for centuries.[40] When asked to describe these practices, he uses the Latin term *lectio*, because its English translation, "reading," is too reductive. *Lectio* implies not only hearing the text (or "seeing," in reference to film) but also being willing to act on it. Pennington reminds us of the colloquial expression in English: "I read you"—which means, "I fully get you," so much so that you change your understanding and even actions in light of what you discover.[41]

For over a thousand years, Christian contemplatives and scholars have practiced *lectio*, uncovering multiple levels of meaning from a single biblical text. These medieval biblical exegetes were interested in reading Scripture in order to know God—literally, faithfully, lovingly, hopefully.[42] To facilitate their inquiry they developed a fourfold method (called the *quadraga*). They believed that a text must be understood (1) *literally* before it could be (2) *allegorically* opened up "in faith," producing greater spiritual understanding in the reader/viewer, which could lead "in love" to (3) further moral insight and action (the term that comes from the Latin is *tropologically*), and ultimately, (4) "in hope," to a *transcendent* vision that would provide a spiritual perspective helpful for life here and now (the word from Latin is *anagogically*). Though this method was used mainly with regard to Scripture, Dante took this same approach and applied it to interpreting a literary text. (The writer Flannery O'Connor has also done this.)[43]

These medievalists were concerned not just with a reader's understanding of the text (in our case, a movie), but also with the text becoming part of a reader's whole life experience—in faith, love, and hope. It was not enough simply to know what a text said; the text also invited readers to know what it meant personally, socially, and spiritually.

How might we as viewers translate this fourfold method of interpretation to the screen? We would need to first focus on the artistic/poetic meaning of the movie itself—the *literal* interpretation. (If the movie was a biopic, it would not be the "literal" history of the person that would be our initial concern but the "literal" interpretation of the story portrayed on the screen.) Second, as we open ourselves up to the movie story, we might find that story becoming by analogy "our story." This is where the *allegorical* interpretation happens. Though it remains the story of others, we sometimes also see and understand ourselves on the screen. That is, we sometimes recognize that there is a "spiritual" connection between what is experienced on the screen and what we experience in our own lives, which is precisely what Craig Detweiler experienced while watching *The Tree of Life*.

Third, it is not enough to say simply that we, as viewers, identify with the story or believe it is true. If it has really affected us, we will act on it. Our lives will be different because of this encounter. The story will stay with viewers and inform how they live and love others, which is the essence of *tropological* interpretation. Lastly, though death will cancel out life, the deeper meaning of a story can speak to that which continues even beyond life, to that which is "more" than life. Such a voice is not a mere otherworldly abstraction but a glimpse of the transcendent through the film that provides spiritual perspective and direction for life here and now.[44] In this lies the *anagogical* interpretation.

Here is the experience of filmgoers when a movie makes a deep connection with them. A thickness sometimes comes to interpretation when responding to a film's story, a depth that is plumbed. But such depth proves authentic only as the literal is first focused on. (One should be concerned with determining what a film portrays before seeking to explore what it might "mean.") Although this description of movie viewing necessarily begins with the literal, artistic sense of a film text, that literal text is not the viewer's final destination. The movie, instead, opens the viewer to an overflow of meaning as the inner meaning of the film and the viewing "self" merge, stimulating faithful belief, right practice, and even divine contemplation.[45] Two examples will help us understand what otherwise might seem too abstract.

Titanic *(1997)*

The movie *Titanic* is the second highest money-making film in history—with box-office receipts of over $2 billion. It also provides an almost textbook example of the process envisioned above. Though some might consider the movie as simply "popcorn" fare, for millions of viewers it has proven to be far more, inviting multiple re-viewings. The strength of the film lies in its multiple subplots, each opening out for the viewer onto a different level of meaning.

Titanic is, at its most basic, an adventure story about the sinking of the Titanic, one of the most written-about events of the twentieth century (here is the "what?"—the literal interpretation).[46] Viewers are captured by the verisimilitude of the re-creation. We see what it would have been like to be on that cruise. Second, the movie is also a love story that draws viewers in—its story becomes our story (here is the "so what?"—the allegorical interpretation). Told by the elderly Rose, who reflects back on her youth, the story invites viewers to identify with her. As we do, we discover the "heart" of the movie. (Here, also, is why some teenagers lined up to see the movie multiple times.) Third, the movie's story has ethical extension; it is a parable of what life is meant to be (we are asked "now what?"—the tropological interpretation). The movie challenges us to reject the prejudice of class, to fight materialism, to foster trust, and to find in community our true humanity. Even if it is only fiction, it is the "truth." As such, the story invites our active ascent. We are also to treat all people as equals; this is not just an isolated value of Jack's. Fourth, the story suggests that life has a transcendent core (analogical interpretation). We see the contrast between the hubris of the ship's invincible builders and crew, who tempt the fates, and the "innocence" of Jack, who gives his life that another might live. The movie ends with Rose reflecting on the sacrificial love of Jack (surely intended as a Christ figure by the filmmakers); she says that he "saved [her] in every way that a person can be saved." As the movie ends, viewers look at photographs on her bedstead that document her rich and full life. Her transformation is more than interior; it has been played out in a life well lived. Here is a love that has transcended all limitations. As a story, *Titanic* opens its viewers out to the Transcendent/transcendent.

Of course, *Titanic* is only one story, not four. Viewers are invited to explore all four levels of meaning simultaneously through the interaction of each of these narrative subplots as part of the larger story. But the emphasis given within each of the subplots also invites a focused gaze on one or another of the story's possible meanings. And the result has proven compelling for many viewers. The success of the movie, both theologically and in terms of the box office, is its ability to open its audience to such a spiritual viewing—one that points

Titanic (1997), © Paramount Pictures Corporation & Twentieth Century Fox Film Corporation

outward in faith, love, and hope beyond the movie's story line to a reality that transcends our finitude. *Titanic* invites viewers not only to be entertained but also to be transformed.

March of the Penguins *(2005)*

A second, and lengthier, example using the fourfold method of theological interpretation is one of the top-selling documentaries of all times, *March of the Penguins* (2005). Catching the imagination of millions, this documentary was produced for $8 million and grossed over $100 million worldwide, one of only a handful of documentaries to earn so much. The movie also spawned illustrated books both for adults and for children, caused the Gap to put penguins on its boxer shorts that were meant as Valentine's Day gifts, and sparked a new interest in travel to Antarctica.[47]

Instructive for our purposes here was the popularity of the movie with some conservative Christians. According to both the *New York Times* and the *Chicago Tribune*, this documentary about the mating ritual and rearing process of emperor penguins was considered by some religious conservatives to be "nothing short of a miraculous allegory about the universality of family values, the value of monogamy, the perversity of gay marriage and the wisdom of intelligent design."[48] Lennard Davis, in his commentary about Christian responses to the movie, rightly belittled such "theologizing," believing this to be yet another example of Judeo-Christian heavy-handedness with regard to film interpretation.[49] And surely it was. Yet the question remains, is there not a legitimate spiritual viewing of this movie, one that would take seriously what so many Christians and non-Christians alike reported as they engaged the images, music, and words of this film? Might there not be a spiritual response to this movie that follows the lead of the medieval Christian interpreters?

On the *literal* level (the poetic meaning of the film text), *March of the Penguins* is a journey into a world most of us have never seen or experienced—the world of the emperor penguin of Antarctica. In a world where the average temperature is 50 degrees below zero and winds blow with gale force, only the emperors have survived for centuries. While the film is a visual feast from the opening scenes of ice floes to the textured close-ups of the penguins' coats, it is also the poignant story of their survival (a story made all the more poignant by the ways in which Jordan Roberts infused the script with love and meaning).

Every March, the emperors march single file from the sea to their mating area up to seventy miles away. (Actually, it's more of a waddle—when they aren't belly-sliding on the ice.) There, through elaborate courtship dances and songs, couples unite, and the female subsequently lays one egg. Their communal and individual task is to protect and nurture the future generation. For almost two months the males huddle, with the eggs safely cradled on top of their feet under their warm coats. Meanwhile, the females, having lost one-third of their body weight, return to the sea for food. By the time the mothers return to feed the newly hatched babies, the fathers have endured as much as 120 days without food and have lost half of their body weight! The mothers now become the protectors, while the fathers return to the sea. These journeys are made several times as the chicks grow and become independent. Finally, with

March of the Penguins (2005), © Bonne Pioche, Alliance De Production Cinematographique, SARL, and Warner Brothers Pictures Inc.

the ice floes melting and the ocean waters coming closer, the young penguins enter the water and begin their life in the sea, until four years later, when they too will return to the place where they were born and continue the life cycle as their parents did.

What makes the film captivating, besides the natural beauty of these animals and their surroundings, is the depth of meaning that this movie embodies. It is not simply a documentary about the "facts"—eighty minutes of penguin "sex," though it is also that. The movie is for many viewers surprisingly analogous to their own lives. Somehow, these penguins open us as viewers to our own struggles for survival, our own need for family protection and care, and our own need to provide for our children. In the penguins' dance of survival, where timing is everything, we recognize our own dance. There is, in short, a spiritual resonance that *March of the Penguins* creates. The amazing truth of the movie is this: we vicariously identify with these penguins!

But for many, the movie is more than even a narrative inviting reflection on our own lives. It is also an Antarctic ballet that holds in the balance "lovers" and those they "love." *March of the Penguins* is not simply about their lives, or even our lives. It is about the lives of all creatures big and small. Despite its brutal hardships and unforgiving ways, life in the Antarctic is also wonder-filled and precious. The movie opens us as viewers to the goodness of creation and to our responsibility to somehow work as hard as these penguins do to preserve it. (We might favorably compare the moral tug of this film with that of *An Inconvenient Truth* [2004], which was also set in Antarctica.) Here is the film's unspoken but enacted "agenda"; here is the *moral* duty it embodies. We as viewers are to act out in love our commitment to life—all Life.

Finally, as religious persons, many of us will find ourselves opening up to marvel at the choreography of the Creator. Even if life as enfleshed in these penguins remains shrouded in mystery, the filmmakers imbue the story with such humor, fear, pain, suffering, joy, and love that many viewers discover life to have a transcendent dimension. *Penguins* is neither an argument for intelligent design nor propaganda for the anti–gay marriage movement. This is not what makes it theologically significant. Rather, the movie provides many viewers a *transcendent* experience.[50]

When the movie came out, I (Rob) saw it with a young married couple who were struggling with whether they could risk their future by his taking a job that would most likely mean struggle and insecurity. After reflecting on their experience in the theater, they told me the next day that they had decided to risk the unknown: "If God could take care of these 'stupid' penguins, surely God would take care of us as well." Here is the "anagogical" imagination.

In his essay "Poetry and the Christian," Karl Rahner, the Catholic theologian who was described by one writer as "a mystic of everyday life," sets forth a variation of these same four principles of interpretation—principles first meant for unpacking sacred Scripture, but principles that also invite a broader application to the interpretation of film. Rahner speaks of being open to recognizing a mystery in the word (film) that is inseparable from the word (image), but not to be confused with it; of being open to hear (see) that which reaches the heart; of being open to hear (see) that which unites and reconciles; and of being open to experience "the overbright darkness, by which all the brightness of each day is encompassed, in a word: the abiding mystery which we call God."[51]

Here is the experience of many filmgoers worldwide who, having been transfixed by what they see on the screen, are transported to a more central region where life takes on a richness and depth not ordinarily experienced. Through film, viewers may (1) see not only others but (2) themselves more fully, (3) be compelled outward to embrace others in communion, and (4) be invited into the presence of the Spirit of Life. There is a mystery here that defies codification, but the pattern is nonetheless discernible. It is what happens to many of us at the movies.

Discussion Questions

1. Out of your own experience, how would you describe the relationship between your church-going and your movie-going?
2. Has any movie caused you to change your attitudes, beliefs, or actions? How? Why?
3. Have you ever felt that going to see a particular movie was illicit or wrong? Questionable? Which movie? Why?

7

discerning mystery

a theological lens

In April 1910, the minister of South Congregational Church in New Britain, Connecticut, the Reverend Herbert A. Jump, proposed that it would be good for motion picture equipment to be purchased by his church so that the residents of the city could have movies as an adjunct to their religious education.[1] Two months later, the ex-mayor of the city, who attended the church, generously offered to underwrite thirty film screenings on Sunday evenings, including the purchase of all necessary equipment. The proposal got substantial publicity along the East Coast, and Jump spent considerable time researching the subject and choosing the movies, visiting both studios and the censorship board, and consulting with exhibitors and social workers. But ultimately his church board decided the project was too controversial (their term was "unwise") to pursue at that time. The screenings were abandoned. Moreover, Jump soon found himself needing to move on to another congregation, this time in Oakland, California.

Though it didn't work out for Jump in Connecticut, the pastor thought the information he had garnered could still be useful to other churches. Before he left, Jump published a pamphlet entitled "The Religious Possibilities of the Motion Picture."[2] In it, he not only provided information concerning how to put on such a series (complete with a sample film list), but after reminding his readers that quartet singing and Bibles printed in the vernacular were earlier also rejected as worldly, he sought to justify the use of film in the church as "a religious tool" by appealing to Jesus's use of parables in his ministry. In this way, he hoped to disarm the mood of antagonism that he no doubt had experienced at South Church and that he assumed would be present elsewhere as well.

Jump referenced Jesus's parables by telling the dramatic story of the Good Samaritan (Luke 10:30–37). He observed in the pamphlet that, just as with movies, (1) the parable was taken not from religious sources but from contemporary experience; (2) it was exciting in character and "thus interesting even to the morally sluggish"; and (3) it had realistic and morally negative features in it ("crime, accident, ignorance, sin") that made it "true to life." And yet the parable exhibited the heart of the gospel. Asked Jump, "Has it not urged more men [sic] into lives of ministry and helpfulness than any piece of literature of equal length which the race has ever known?"[3] Jump concluded his plea by saying that the movies that had value for religious education today were films like the parables of Jesus.

Film as Parable

As Jump understood it, there were three reasons for comparing film to one of Jesus's parables. Like parable, film is based in the everyday; it is exciting; and it realistically depicts life. Through the years, as our understanding of the nature of parables has sharpened, others have found additional reasons. In *Stories with Intent: A Comprehensive Guide to the Parables of Jesus* (2008), Klyne Snodgrass provides a helpful set of descriptors around which parables might be understood.[4] At their core, he argues, parables are stories and therefore are compelling to the hearer. "Discourse we tolerate: to story we attend. . . . Stories are one of the few places that allow us to see reality. . . . There, to a degree we cannot do in real life, we can discern motives, keep score, know who won, and what success and failure look like. . . . The storyteller is in control so that we are forced to see from new angles and so that the message cannot be easily evaded. . . . From this 'other world' we are invited to understand, evaluate, and, hopefully, redirect our lives."[5]

Stories should not be confused with the raw data of plot. Instead, the storyteller has a point of view—an intention, a perspective that he or she thinks important. Otherwise the narrator would not bother to tell the tale. Perhaps the agenda is to entertain; or perhaps, as with parables, it is to convince or to portray truth (or even falsehood). Nevertheless, there is always intention.

But parables are also a particular kind of story. For Snodgrass, "Parables function as a lens that allows us to see the truth and to correct distorted vision. They allow us to see what we would not otherwise see, and they presume we *should* look at and see a *specific* reality. They are not Rorschach tests; they are stories with an intent, analogies through which one is enabled to see truth."[6]

As Jesus told them, parables (1) are brief stories rooted in everyday life; (2) are compelling ("exciting") stories, arresting the attention of their audience by inviting their listeners to see reality from a new angle; (3) do not primarily convey information but, by the more indirect communication of the metaphoric process, invite their audiences to discover spiritual truth or meaning as the human condition is portrayed; and (4) function subversively, undermining certain contemporary attitudes, beliefs, and/or authority (disorienting) even while inviting, teasing, or provoking new truth and/or transcendental insight (reorienting). It is not a parable's content but its affective resonance that matters most.

Surely not all movies function as parables, but some do. Film as parable tells its narrative sparsely (usually in less than two hours). As metaphor, it has levels of meaning: the surface story being taken from everyday life but its underlying meaning opening up to symbolic and even transcendental insight. Subverting our ordinary take on reality, the depiction of our lives reveals a disparity that suggests the need for (an)other deeper meaning(s). In the process, film as parable leaves its imprint on the viewers; it provokes, enlightens, and can even transform.

Consider, for example, the award-winning movies of 2004 and 2005. The movies that won for Best Picture and Best Foreign Language Picture at the Oscars in 2004 were *Million Dollar Baby* and *The Sea Inside*. Both told stories whose plot centered on euthanasia but whose meaning actually drilled deeper, focusing on the nature of human life itself. Other movies from that year included *Eternal Sunshine of the Spotless Mind* and *Sideways*. Each captured its viewers' attention by showing reality from a new angle. And both bore down below the surface of the story, subverting regnant understandings of life's meaning in order to provoke or invite new truth in the process. In 2005, all five Academy Award Best Picture nominees—*Crash*; *Brokeback Mountain*; *Capote*; *Good Night, and Good Luck*; *Munich*—were "stories with intent," to use Snodgrass's helpful phrase. Each invited viewers to see reality from a new angle, seeking not merely to convey information but to suggest a deeper meaning concerning the human condition. To this list of parabolic movies from 2005, Woody Allen's *Match Point* and Danny Boyle's *Millions* might be added. Paul Haggis, who was the writer of *Million Dollar Baby* and the director and cowriter of *Crash* (as well as the cowriter of the 2006 Oscar-nominated *Letters from Iwo Jima*), said of his work on *Crash* that he wanted to "cause people to walk out and then argue about the film on the sidewalk. . . . I think we're all [i.e., all the directors up for an Oscar with him in 2006] seeking dissension, and we love to affect an audience."[7] Like other parables, it was not the presence of certain themes that Haggis thought was most important but rather the movie's ability to effect transformation in the audience.

In every case, these movies were stories with intent—stories that left interpretation open to the viewer, much as Jesus's parables did (and do), but also stories that invited viewers to not just be edified—to learn something—but to be transformed by what they saw. Invited into the lives of characters dealing with life's enigmas and extremities, the audiences of these movies were not merely entertained; they were also shaped by what they saw. For it was the intention of these filmic storytellers to challenge us as viewers—even to seek our transformation. These stories (1) were rooted in everyday life, (2) grabbed our attention, (3) invited a "thick" interpretation that challenged our existing understandings, and (4) opened us up to transformative and, at times, transcendent insight.

Marc Forster's *Stranger Than Fiction* (2006), starring Will Ferrell and Emma Thompson, can serve for us as an example of a film that functions as parable. Consider the film in light of the four descriptors of a parable listed above.

An Everyday Story

Life often can become lost in routine—the same route to work, the same coffee at Starbucks, even the same seat at church! Harold Crick (Will Ferrell), the main character, is simply an extreme example of the lives many of us lead. Everything has been reduced to a mathematical formula in his life, as the clever graphics that are overlaid on the images reinforce. The filmmaker has even chosen names for his characters that are associated with mathematics in real life: Crick discovered DNA; Eiffel was the architect of the Eiffel Tower; Escher is an artist known for fantastic linear designs; even Hilbert might be a reference to a mathematician, David Hilbert, whose ideas influenced quantum mechanics.[8] Crick even counts the number of strokes he takes to brush his teeth each morning and the number of steps he walks to the bus stop. His constant companion is his watch, which helps him compulsively track the minutes he spends at lunch and on coffee breaks. Harold, not surprisingly, works as an auditor for the IRS.

Grabs Audience Attention

Except for his friend Dave at work, Harold speaks to few people. He spends most of his life alone. Then one day he begins to hear a woman's voice speaking in his head and narrating his own life. The narrator turns out to be Karen

Eiffel (a superb Emma Thompson), an accomplished though reclusive mystery writer with eight novels to her credit. Her latest, *Death and Taxes* (life's two "givens"), has remained unfinished for a decade because she cannot figure out an appropriate way to kill off her main character—a plot twist that has become a trademark in each of her other stories. Desperate to overcome her writer's block, she is the perfect complement to Harold's neurosis. When we first meet her, Eiffel is balancing on the edge of her desk trying to imagine jumping off a roof. Later, she sits in the rain with Penny Escher (Queen Latifah), her personal assistant, watching cars pass over a bridge and imagining an accident.

The movie goes back and forth between the stories of these two lonely, neurotic people. But actually, it is only one story, for the main character in Eiffel's story is none other than Harold Crick. At first the voice in his head is simply a nuisance. But then he hears the woman say, "Little did he know it would lead to his imminent death." Such foreshadowing would grab anyone's attention. Is his life trajectory destined?

Invites Metaphoric Interpretation

The basic tension in the movie is thus clearly drawn: Is the story Karen's or Harold's? Who is really in control? Is the story character-driven, or is it rooted in the point of view of the narrator? Is Harold a puppet, or is he free to act? Free will or providence? Harold is desperate to know, and Karen is paralyzed to act. Harold, thus, seeks the advice of a psychiatrist (Linda Hunt) who diagnoses him as schizophrenic. He challenges her diagnosis by asking, "But what if I'm part of a story, a narrative?" to which she responds facetiously, "I don't know, I'd send you to someone who knows literature." So Harold lands at the door of Professor Jules Hilbert (Dustin Hoffman), an expert in literary theory. Hilbert gives Harold a test to narrow down the genres and archetypes of his story, and then suggests that Harold try to figure out whether his life is a tragedy or a comedy. The exchanges between Harold and the professor are filled with clever, understated humor. Viewers both laugh and groan as the teaching profession is skewered. It is a delight (even for this book's three authors, all professors by trade).

And so the movie's setup is complete. On one level, it is a story about the artistic process. Following up on his wonderful exploration of the imagination in *Finding Neverland*—a fictional account of J. M. Barrie, the creator of Peter Pan—*Stranger Than Fiction* director Marc Forster "asks" what happens when an artist comes to care about her creation so much that her affection begins to color the shape of her imaginative creation. Is there a necessary shape to a story, a narrative arc that the creator must follow? Or do a character's actions and attitudes invite the plot to develop in surprising ways? That is, is there human freedom, or does providence reign?

Opens Viewers to Transformation and Transcendent Insight

Such a question is not simply pedantic and abstract, to be left in the literature classroom. Rather, it also has to do with our own stories. Are our personal stories defined as "comedies" or "tragedies" apart from our own efforts, or do we give shape to our destinies? Or can it be both? The movie's literary conceit turns out to be the context for reflection on the narrative shape of our own lives. Free will or providence?

The surface story of *Stranger Than Fiction* is not only about the artistic process, however. It is also about love—about the compelling power of a new affection. Harold discovers love while auditing Ana Pascal (Maggie Gyllenhaal), a Harvard Law School dropout who became a baker. Even as they spar, the chemistry between Harold and Ana is delightful. When Harold finally gives in and eats one of Ana's Bavarian sugar cookies, the sensuality of the moment is palpable. We watch Harold's slow transformation as he realizes that life is not work and work is not life. Harold gives Ana an assortment of "flours" (pun intended); he asks her out on a date and plays for her (however modestly!) a two-chord song he has just learned on his guitar. Somehow schedules no longer matter and his watch no longer controls.

Stranger Than Fiction will remind many of the book of Ecclesiastes. Wisdom (Professor Hilbert), fame (Karen Eiffel), and work (Harold Crick) prove vain, ephemeral, and meaningless. Life cannot be parsed; it is more than a formula. Nevertheless, we can observe that two are better than one and that life is a gift to be savored—like freshly baked cookies with a glass of milk.

It should be clear that this Will Ferrell movie is a far cry from his portrayal of an elf (*Elf*), a race car driver (*Talladega Nights*), or an ice skater (*Blades of Glory*). Perhaps this is why the film was largely ignored when it first came out. Those expecting the broad, physical, sophomoric humor of Ferrell that was honed on *Saturday Night Live* were either disappointed or stayed away. The movie, however, has had a strong afterlife. The movie abounds in humor, but here it serves a larger purpose and remains understated and ironic (think of Bill Murray in *Lost in Translation*, Jim Carrey in *The Truman Show*, or Adam Sandler in *Punch Drunk Love*). Intelligent, poignant, heartfelt, real—this parable invites its viewers' personal introspection.

We will all die. That is a given. The only question is thus, How then should we live? And who is in charge of providing answers to this query? These are the questions that Harold Crick must face, even as they also become our questions as viewers. As the movie ends, we hear the narrator in a voice-over while previous incidents from the movie appear on the screen. Here is the filmmakers' intention for this story:

> Sometimes when we lose ourselves in fear and despair, in routine and constancy, in hopelessness and tragedy, we can thank God for Bavarian sugar cookies . . . for a familiar hand on the skin [Ana touches Harold in the hospital where he has landed after saving a young boy from being hit by a bus] . . . a kind and loving gesture [Harold sends his friend Dave to his dream—Space Camp] . . . a subtle encouragement [Karen is given no-smoking patches by her assistant, Penny], a loving embrace [the boy on the bicycle is hugged by his father], an offer of comfort [by coworkers of the bus driver who hit Harold], not to mention hospital gurneys, noseplugs [Hilbert swims with them], uneaten Danish, soft spoken secrets [Harold whispers to Ana], Fender Stratocasters [Harold plays his guitar], and maybe the occasional piece of fiction [Harold reading Eiffel's manuscript on the bus]. All these things, the nuances, the subtleties, the anomalies that we assume only accessorize our lives . . . they are here to save our lives.[9]

The movie asks, what is the meaning of Harold Crick's life? And it answers by recognizing that Someone else is providentially in charge of the story, so it is best for all of us to enjoy our portion in life with both its big and small pleasures. As Harold discovers, we need to give thanks for Bavarian sugar cookies (and for the one who baked them), for this is what gives meaning to our short lives.

Movie Watching as Spiritual Experience[10]

In 2012, the Oscars added a new component to their telecast. In addition to the jokes, the fashion, and the awards, they included a series of brief interviews with actors and actresses who responded to the question, "What is your favorite movie moment?" Christopher Plummer referenced *Snow White* (1937). Janet McTeer referenced Christopher Plummer for his role in *The Sound of Music* (1965). Several went back to their childhood when recalling their favorite movie moment—seeing a car drive off a cliff in *Chitty, Chitty, Bang, Bang* (1968), only to be surprised as it turned out to be a flying machine. Kenneth Branagh recalled, "It was a wonderful moment of cinema magic." So too was Judy Garland's singing "Over the Rainbow" in *The Wizard of Oz* (1939). Jessica Chastain confessed that while watching this movie, she "began my love affair with movies and me wanting to be a part of that wonder."[11]

Experiencing magic and wonder is something at the heart of the moviegoing experience—at least at its best. Viewers find themselves transported to another place or into the presence of another—perhaps even an Other. In the process, they explore life's possibilities and contradictions, testing out solutions and even finding themselves surprised by joy or sorrow, by love and pain, by life itself. Given such encounters with movies, it should not be surprising that writers continue to explore the spiritual dimensions of this experience. Particularly since the advent of Beta in 1979, which allowed for the re-viewing of film on demand, and the subsequent invention of the VCR, the DVD, Netflix, and now streaming, a growing number of commentators, including all three authors of this book, have continued to write about the depth and extent of film's spirituality.[12]

But as these claims have been made, questions have also been asked with increasing frequency: What exactly do we mean by "God's presence" at the movies? How is a movie's spirituality to be described? Or understood? In what way does God "show up" at the movies? (1) Is it only as a "trace" or "echo," as a reverberation of some past divine action? (2) Perhaps such claims are only human projections. Or (3) can such encounters be important, even foundational, to faith? Alternately, (4) given human sin, is such spirituality destined to be simply confused and confusing? The questions come easily. They are the same questions that are asked concerning other claims regarding encounters with God in everyday life.

So a decade ago, we began asking students in our theology and film classes to write short papers offering their testimony concerning the most personally compelling spiritual experience they had had while watching a movie and why they thought this might be the case. The numbers now exceed six hundred. In making the assignment, we did not start with a given movie—*Field of Dreams* (1989), *The Shawshank Redemption* (1994), *The Passion of the Christ* (2004), or, in more recent years, *Avatar* (2009) or perhaps *Lady Bird* (2017)—and then ask, "Was this movie spiritually significant to you and why?" Instead, we reversed the flow and asked these viewers to pick any movie they liked, but the movie should be the one they felt was most spiritually significant to them. We purposely left the meaning of the assignment ambiguous. The reason for the vagueness of the question, of course, was to allow differentiations to surface. We wanted the student viewers themselves to shape the nature of their responses according to their own perception of their experience.

As might be expected, the responses varied greatly. Nevertheless, the papers fell broadly into three groups, even as students moved freely back and forth between these differing meanings. One group of students described a divine encounter as mediated through or experienced in the cinema. A second group of students wrote about how, through their movie-going experience, they perceived something greater, or other, or whole. Their spirit was deeply affected.

And still a third group were quite sure that they had not had a direct encounter with God through film, nor had their spirits been transformed, but nonetheless they narrated a movie-watching experience in which they had garnered spiritual truth that had proven personally valuable to them. Particularly interesting about these responses was their variety. Some could remember a movie that was Spiritual (capital *S*); others chose to talk about a particular film as affecting their spirits (lowercase *s*); and still others considered their chosen film to have been instructive of spiritual truth. Not surprisingly, the results of these different experiences also varied—from transforming their lives, to offering a spiritual insight or experience, to providing theological support.

Deepening My Understanding

Of those who recalled an experience at the Cineplex that was educationally deepening, their responses most often focused on movies with explicit religious, or quasi-religious, themes—*Chariots of Fire* (1981), *The Shawshank Redemption* (1994), *A Walk to Remember* (2002), *Lord of the Rings* (2001, 2002, 2003), *Signs* (2002), *The Passion of the Christ* (2004), or *Calvary* (2014)—or movies that had clear Christ figures, like *The Green Mile* (1999) or *The Dark Knight* (2008). But not always. *Forrest Gump* (1994), *The Avengers* (2012), *X-Men: Days of Future Past* (2014), and even *Talladega Nights* (2006) also came up. A sample of the language they used to describe the connection between the movie they saw and the experience they had makes clear the intellectual nature of the spiritual connection: "whispered truth," "I learned from," "was deeply informative," "was symbolic of," "helped me to understand," "taught me," and so on. Interestingly, most of those who identified the film that was most spiritually significant to them in intellectual terms, speaking of a new understanding, were men, though there were also exceptions.

For one student whose maternal great-grandfather had escaped the pogroms of Eastern Europe in the early twentieth century, it was *Fiddler on the Roof* (1971), which taught him that God was a character who weeps, not just an idea. For another, Hugh Jackman and Ann Hathaway in *Les Misérables* (2012) helped him understand the transforming power of generosity, love, and grace; it helped him understand that God's "Yes" is more primary than his "No." For one student, Dan, "the message of forgiving and being forgiven for the past in order to move in the future" in Kevin Smith's *Chasing Amy* (1997) still resonates with him today. For Eric, the movie that gave picture and voice to something already inside him was *The Mission* (1986). The depiction of people laying down their lives for Jesus, the reminder that sin has consequences, and the scene where the native chooses not to slit the throat of Rodrego, showing the overwhelming reality of forgiveness, all helped Eric to "bring into focus Truth." Though he saw the movie only three times (twenty-five, twenty, and fifteen years prior), he wrote of drawing on these moments many times subsequently "as illustrations in discussions."

Affecting My Spirit

Others wrote of how, through their movie-going experience, they perceived something greater, or other, or whole. T. S. Eliot has called it "the still point of the turning world."[13] These viewers were not sure whether they had a divine encounter, but their experience had enhanced their own spirit. In fact, it often had proven life transforming. They spoke of a "profoundly human moment," of "tears of identification," related to a particular movie event as bringing "personal fulfillment" or change. Their experiences were often described as extraordinary and illumining. For these viewers, the world and/or their personal lives took on spiritual depth and texture because of the movie they saw. But these moviegoers were reluctant to say they had actually met God at the movies.

For Glenn, rewatching *An Officer and a Gentleman* (1982) has continued to inspire him "to believe that I could rise above my personal reality," despite his dysfunctional family. For Andrew, *Up* (2009) allowed him to understand that his present life was not practice for some future well-being but a wonderful gift to be enjoyed now. For Michelle, a woman suffering with depression from not living up to her family's expectations for her, watching *The Perks of Being a Wallflower* (2012) allowed her to wake up the next morning with the veil of depression lifted, realizing that both God and her friends loved and accepted her, messiness and all. For Vince, even his tenth viewing of *The Tree of Life* (2011) continues to affect him viscerally as the multiple parallels between his life and the O'Brien family helped him tap "into a universal well of life experiences," revealing that he is not alone.

Perhaps the most dramatic account we have read of a movie's potential for spiritual transformation was the testimony of Carol, who in her twenties was the victim of a home invasion robbery during the Christmas season. Raped, robbed, kidnapped, pistol-whipped, and shot, she was left for dead in an empty lot. Over the next five years, her life spiraled downward. Then, as it was Christmas and the anniversary of her assault once again, the Frank Capra movie *It's a Wonderful Life* (1946) came on the television. She had never seen it. As she watched, she identified with George Bailey (played by Jimmy Stewart), whose dreams had been dashed at every turn, though he had tried to help others all of his life. She too had always tried to be good, even while living in a borderline-abusive household where she could never live up to her parents'

It's a Wonderful Life (1946)

expectations. Like George, she had thought, "It would have been better if I had never been born."

However, she continued to watch as a gentle angel named Clarence showed George that all his simple acts of kindness had been important to the community where he lived, and my student's perspective on her own life also began to shift. "The gift this movie provided me with," she wrote, "was small hope." She explained, "Following this period I no longer entertained thoughts of quitting life, but [had] a desire to find meaning in what had occurred to me. If the daily decisions that George Bailey made had such a profound influence on those around him, [maybe] the decisions that I was making, even the smallest, most insignificant, [might] have a profound influence on those around me." And five years later, Carol was in seminary, sitting in class and preparing to be a counselor. Viewing *It's a Wonderful Life* had proven "life transforming."

Encountering God's Presence

Carol was not sure whether viewing *It's a Wonderful Life* had been the occasion for an encounter with the Spirit of God or simply a profoundly moving experience of the recentering and grounding of her spirit. In the words of Avery Dulles, the line between personal "discovery" and divine "revelation" was blurred beyond recognition.[14] But for a significant number of our students, there had been no doubt in their minds as they described their movie-viewing experience that God had revealed his presence to them through the truth, beauty, and goodness portrayed on the screen, or through the lack of it. They had, they said, an experience of the Holy that proved transformative in their lives. In each case, the movie's story had merged with their own stories, resulting in a divine encounter that changed their lives.

A few who wrote of their engagement with the Spirit in and through a movie said it was difficult to pick only one, for there had been "so many profound experiences." They identified themselves as "extremely easily moved" and thus experienced "God's presence in nearly every film" they saw. But more typically, most said their encounter with God at the movies had been a rare experience. Jessica wrote, for example, "I do not typically experience film in a deeply personal and spiritual way. However, last summer I was pleasantly surprised when I encountered God unexpectedly in, of all places, a children's film. Disney Pixar's *Toy Story 3* (2010) was the last place I expected to have a transcendent experience with a film, yet the unassuming packaging of a children's movie provided the perfect opportunity for an unexpected spiritual encounter."

What connected with Jessica in the film was the theme of growing up and moving on from one's childhood. She had been a fan of Woody, Buzz, and the rest of Andy's toys ever since, as an eight-year-old, she had seen the original *Toy Story* (1995). Expecting only a fun, simple little movie, she instead experienced through Andy's character "a reflection of my own childhood and transition to adulthood." As Andy handed down his toys to little Bonnie, she said she "experienced a sudden and unexpected rush of emotions, which ultimately resulted in crying." Jessica, like Andy, was about to embark on a major life transition of her own—she had just gotten engaged. "Seeing *Toy Story 3* allowed me to express and confront those bittersweet emotions associated with making a major life transition." Here, she said, was God's way of helping her process her feelings and telling her it is okay. "I learned from this experience," she wrote, "that God can speak to you and meet you in the most unexpected places, for who would have ever thought that a 23-year-old woman would have seen herself in a fictional, animated, 18-year-old boy who was giving his toys away."

The film that proved transcendent for Liz was *Moulin Rouge!* (2001). The movie is a musical romance that tells the story of Christian, a penniless writer who falls in love with the beautiful courtesan Satine, winning her heart through song, poetry, and persistence. He loves her as opposed to simply desiring her, cares for her rather than lusting after her. Even though the jealous Duke

Moulin Rouge! (2001), © Twentieth Century Fox Film Corporation

expects her to be his lover, and even though Satine is dying of consumption, the love between Christian and Satine proves undying. Each has loved and been loved in return.

Liz wrote that she is not sure why the movie continues to move her so. Perhaps it is the fact that her life history has some connection with Satine's. Given their common brokenness, was it possible to be redeemed? *Moulin Rouge!* shouted, "Yes!" When Satine was found by Christian, Liz said she was found. "I was encountering God through this movie as I was given a vision of love conquering the past and conquering human sin and brokenness." She continued: "What the movie did uniquely was provide a context and an experience, which got past my analytical study brain (the brain that often kicks in when I read the Bible), to my emotions and heart. The power of the music, the images and the theatrical experience drew me in before my usual defenses and inner critic had time to react. I encountered the love of God and it changed me."

Hearing God through Surprising Sources

As a college freshman at Stanford, Rob heard Robert McAfee Brown ask his class, "How is it possible to see the hand of God in the work of non-Christian writers?"[15] Though Brown had in mind contemporary novelists and playwrights, his question is equally applicable to screenwriters and filmmakers. If God is the source of all wisdom and beauty, how is it that unbelievers can create wonderful things and speak wisely? Brown suggests that over the centuries Christian theologians have given three different answers to this question.

The first response claims that all artists outside the Christian faith are nevertheless the unconscious inheritors of the Christian tradition. To the degree that such artists portray truth, goodness, and/or beauty, it is because they have been nurtured in a cultural milieu formed by Christian convictions that they have unintentionally absorbed. Perhaps we could use the Mexican director Guillermo del Toro and his 2006 movie *Pan's Labyrinth* as an example. While del Toro might be trying to distance himself from his grandmother's Catholic faith, the film is ultimately about a blood sacrifice to save others and a young girl who is ushered into a heavenly court where her father almost literally exclaims the words spoken by God the Father to Jesus: "Well done, my good and faithful servant."

But there are problems with this approach, particularly when engaging with filmmakers outside the West. Following this line of reasoning, we might conclude that when Yojiro Takita, the Japanese director of the award-winning film *Departures* (2008), regards humankind with reverence and portrays our significance and worth, this filmmaker is covertly affirming a Christian perspective, even if outwardly he disavows that he is a Christian. The difficulty with such an argument should be apparent. While Christianity has without doubt influenced world culture, it is disingenuous and perhaps "imperialistic" to say that such filmmakers covertly affirm what they overtly deny. Perhaps for this reason, few theologians hold to this position today.

A second theological approach that Brown describes is much more widely subscribed to by contemporary Christians. Recognizing that those outside the Christian community have produced much of value, some say, "All truth is God's truth." This argument for the general availability of truth has its roots stretching all the way back to the second century when Justin Martyr claimed, "Whatever has been well said anywhere or by anyone belongs to us Christians."[16] That is, since truth comes from God, truth is to be welcomed in whatever garb it appears. Augustine and perhaps John Calvin represent other examples of those who have given voice to this common Christian perspective toward the wider culture. Such a theological stance has much to commend itself vis-à-vis contemporary film, not the least being the humility and openness that it evidences toward both Hollywood and world cinema.

But this approach has limitations as well, which Brown recognizes. Rather than allowing film to expand our understanding of life, the critic comes to movies with the "truth" pretty well in hand. Christian affirmations of the truth contained in a movie, thus, will tend to be selective, a cut-and-paste affair. Since Christians, as they watch a film, already have the "truth," they will be tempted to concentrate only on those insights that illustrate their independently established viewpoints and to ignore the rest. The result is often a warping of a movie's larger vision or an ignoring of films that do not initially fit the viewer's theological grid. While Christians holding this perspective commend a movie like *Hacksaw Ridge* (2016), they avoid other movies like *Moonlight* (2016). But if film is to work its full charm, if it is to enrich and enliven us, then we must approach both movies as viewers with openness and humility.

Rather than holding to either of the above approaches, Brown believes Christians must recognize that "God can use *all* things for the fulfillment of the divine purposes, including the *full* message of non-Christians rather than only selected congenial portions." He reflects on the Christian's conviction that God is able to use all things for his purposes—truth and untruth. Brown turns by way of illustration to the Old Testament book of Isaiah. Just as Isaiah recognized in his day that God could speak a true word to his people, Israel, through the unbelieving, unethical Assyrians, so Christians should affirm today, argues Brown, that God in his freedom can speak not only through believers but through "Assyrians in modern dress."[17]

In the tenth chapter of Isaiah, we read that the Israelites (who believed they were "God's people") were being threatened by the Assyrians (who certainly were not "God's people"). Instead of Isaiah telling Israel that God was about to judge these pagans through his people—through *them*—in order that justice might reign, the scenario is reversed. It is the raping, pillaging Assyrians that Isaiah claims will be God's agents to make known God's way to Israel:

> Ah, Assyria, the rod of my anger—
>   the club in their hands is my fury!
> Against a godless nation I send him.
>   (Isa. 10:5–6 NRSV)

God's people ("a godless nation") will not hear, though they think they do. Thus, God will speak through the Assyrians. What makes the Assyrians such a powerful witness, moreover, is precisely their unbelief. Isaiah recognizes that they do not realize they are being used as God's mouthpiece: "But this is not what he intends, nor does he have this in mind" (Isa. 10:7 NRSV). It does not matter; pagan Assyria is to be the expression of God's revelation to "believing" Israel.

The analogy should not be overdrawn, but its point is clear. Christians need not claim that non-Christian filmmakers are covert Christians or simply appropriate from their movies what is congenial to or congruent with their understanding of the Christian faith. Rather, if viewers will join in community with a film's storyteller, letting the movie's images speak with their full integrity, they might be surprised to discover that they are hearing God as well. If we allow ourselves to be open to others, the Other might also prove to be present. If this sounds surprising, it is no more so than Assyria once being God's spokesperson to Israel.

One such experience for Rob was the viewing of the award-winning movie *American Beauty* (1999).[18] The movie is a dark comedy and not for the easily offended. It portrays the hollowness of suburbia's chase after the American dream—money, status, youth, and, of course, beauty. The story is gorgeously bleak, the filmic equivalent of a John Updike novel about a hero's midlife crisis. It is also laced with profanity and nudity, adultery and drug use.

As the story unfolds, we might think that the theme of *American Beauty* is going to be, "Eat, drink, and be merry, for tomorrow we die." But the movie is anything but sensational. Its iconoclasm mocks our media-generated illusions without resorting to either a simple fatalism or a perverse cynicism. Lester Burnham, the film's hero, is ignored by his wife, bored by his work, and unloved by his daughter. He is a shriveled soul until an infatuation with his daughter's cheerleader friend shocks him alive. He literally begins to smell the roses. Despite being a near caricature of middle-class life today, the movie's portrayal of a man who does not know what his role in life is and fears growing old is all too real. "I'll be dead in a year," Lester tells us as the movie opens. "In a way, I'm dead already."

But much like the book of Ecclesiastes, despair does not have the final word.[19] There is a hard-won serenity that Lester discovers at life's core. Lester is therefore able, even in death, to embrace his life. And through him, so do we. Ultimately, sadness does not have the last word, but compassion and joy. In the fourth century, Evagrius listed sadness as one of the eight chief sins. Under pressure to use the symbolic number seven, Pope Gregory the Great later dropped sadness from the list, which left just seven deadly sins. But Evagrius's recognition is an important one for our own day. At its core, and despite its fragility—given its mystery, its amorality, and death itself—life has a beauty that is to be cherished. *American Beauty* understands this. The movie can shock us alive to such beauty, however transient. It can overcome our sadness.

The Mystery-Discerning Business

The growing interest by Christians in spirituality and film is being triggered by larger changes occurring in Western culture, particularly around the epistemological ordering given to what are historically labeled as life's transcendentals—truth, beauty, and goodness. In the 1960s, Christianity's theological orientation circled around notions of truth; the same was true of the larger culture, which would have ordered the transcendentals as truth, then goodness, and finally beauty. By the 1970s and '80s, however, our Western culture, having lived through the Vietnam War and seen the assassinations of John and Robert

Kennedy and Martin Luther King Jr., had reordered these verities. So too had the Western church. Christians now began with the need for goodness, before moving on to truth, and finally to beauty. But as modernity came to an end in the West and as the millennium dawned, the sterility of the West's rationalism imploded, and once again the cultural ordering of the transcendentals changed. As the West is now comfortably into the new century, increasing numbers are saying that we should begin with beauty, and then move to goodness, before considering truth. All three are fundamental, but the epistemological ordering has shifted.

Such seismic shifts in the cultural plates of the West have deep implications for Christian theology. One of these is surely the ever-increasing openness to a neoromanticism in our culture. And with this comes a growing societal openness to spirituality, particularly as it is mediated through the arts. However, Christians are not fully on board. In a 2002 chapel address at Fuller Theological Seminary, Richard Mouw put the contrasting choices with regard to theology and the arts into colorful language. He identified two questions that you can ask about the cultural activity of those outside the church. You can ask of culture, "What the hell are you doing?" Or you can ask, "What in heaven's name are you doing?" Christians too often limit their focus to the former.

By concentrating, for example, on the "truth" known to the faithful, and by concluding that the good, the true, and the beautiful are permanently corrupted within the wider society, some Christians effectively screen out any new insight that the Holy Spirit might be offering through the arts, including film. To fail to ask, "What in heaven's name might be happening today outside the church and without direct reference to Jesus?" effectively muffles the Spirit, hobbling both our spiritual growth as Christians and our dialogue with those outside the church. Such a theological approach would cause us to be deaf to the humorous but telling prayer of Ricky Bobby in *Talladega Nights* (2006), for instance, and to consider it only a joke.

Throughout the Bible, there are repeated examples of the Spirit of God at work outside the believing community.[20] Unfortunately, most of these texts have been ignored or "interpreted away" by the church. Two of the most interesting of these are found in Proverbs 30 and 31, where we have written in Scripture, "The words of Agur son of Jakeh" (30:1) and "The words of King Lemuel. An oracle that his mother taught him" (31:1 NRSV). The artistic sayings (the proverbs) that follow in both of these mini-collections were recognized by God's people as inspired words from God, on par with those inspired utterances from Moses, David, and Isaiah. And yet Agur is not a Hebrew name, and Lemuel is not one of Judah's or Israel's kings. Both are outsiders. Their proverbs were part of the popular culture of the day, artistic expressions that had their origin outside of Israel. Yet they were recognized also to be God's Word. These portions of Scripture give evidence for Christians that the Spirit of God was at work outside the believing community, inspiring writers sensitive to God's Spirit to write what Jews and Christians have recognized for millennia to be God's inspired Word to us.

There are other examples as well. King Abimelech of Gerar heard the Spirit of God in a dream and, as a result, did not take advantage of Abraham's wife Sarah, even though Abraham had lied to him about who Sarah was (Gen. 20). The text makes it clear that it was someone outside the people of God—Abimelech—who spoke for God to Abraham, the father of God's people. Similarly, the biblical text makes clear that it is Melchizedek, king and priest of Salem, who is God's spokesperson to Abraham, for it is Melchizedek who prepares a sacred meal for Abraham and blesses him. And Abraham recognizes that Melchizedek is indeed God's representative by giving him a tithe, a spiritual gift.

Later, in 2 Chronicles 35:20–24 King Josiah's encounter with Pharaoh Neco of Egypt is recorded. The text makes it clear that Josiah was a man of God who had walked in God's ways for a lifetime. He had reinstituted the regular reading of the Torah, sought the prophetess Huldah's advice, celebrated the Passover once again, and restored the temple. But despite Josiah's mature faith, it is the pharaoh who the text says was sensitive to the voice of God at a critical juncture, not King Josiah ("He did not listen to the words of Neco from the mouth of God," 35:22 NRSV). As a result, King Josiah lost his life. Or again, one chapter later, 2 Chronicles ends not with an account of a faithful Israelite, but with King Cyrus of Persia's saying, "The LORD, the God of heaven, has given me all the kingdoms of the earth" (36:23 NRSV).

Behind all such biblical accounts lies the recognition that the Holy Spirit is present also in the hearts of those outside the believing community. What all Christians should gladly testify to is the continuing work of God in creation and human creativity. God is at work in the world through the Holy Spirit, including through film. Often Christians have deduced their doctrine of the Spirit's revealing presence through a process of elimination. It has been an intellectual experience, not a heartfelt one. Christians have not allowed themselves to believe they can experience God's presence at the movies (or while listening to a symphony or building a house for the homeless), for God is wrongly thought to be apart from that. Some have thought that such notions might somehow detract from the importance of hearing the full revelation of God in Christ. But is this true?

Though well intentioned, the result of such mistaken caution has been damaging on two fronts. On the one hand, a growing disconnect has developed between those in the church and those in the wider culture. On the other hand, in our postsecular age, spirituality has become more widely recognized and embraced, particularly within the arts. But Christians have too often been perceived as dismissive of the spiritual sensitivity of those around us and, as a result, have lost an opportunity for sharing about how knowing Jesus might add to and deepen others' spiritual insight (see Acts 17). Moreover, we as Christians risk stunting our own spiritual growth given our reticence to expand our theological sources to include the Spirit's ongoing gifting within conscience, creation, and creativity—through beauty, truth, and goodness wherever it is found (see Ps. 19).

In his book *He Shines in All That's Fair*, Richard Mouw concludes his reflections by quoting Thomas Weinandy concerning the nature of theology. Theology, Weinandy writes, is best understood as "a mystery discerning enterprise," not "a problem solving" one.[21] Weinandy's insight came as he reflected on the nature of divine suffering. But his insight is just as relevant when considering how we might find God in or at the movies. Too often we have approached the topics of how non-Christians contribute to our culture's expressions of truth, beauty, and goodness—as well as how we might hear God speak through such avenues—by treating such experiences as problems to be solved. Instead, we might recognize that our experience of the Spirit, our experiential pneumatology, might need to go beyond our problem-solving ability, instead inviting the discernment of mystery.

The Christian's mystery-discerning business is rooted in the Spirit, who, like the wind, blows where it will. This mystery goes far beyond how to include philosophers in our theology, or even whether Einstein might have sensed God's presence. If God spoke in biblical times through the Assyrians, or if the words of Agur are recognized as Scripture, then the mystery-discerning business is bigger and broader than most Pentecostals or Presbyterians might imagine. If this is God's world—if God has the whole world in his hands—if the Spirit of God is active throughout the world today, including through such artistic expressions as the movies (as surely the Spirit is), then we must not make limiting claims about how God might or might not choose to reveal God's presence.

God's revelation in and through creation, conscience, and culture is not a mere echo, a "residue" left over after the fall so that humankind might not go to hell in a handbasket. Rather, it is an expression of the Spirit of God's continuing revelatory presence among us. One important arena of that divine activity is the creative arts. Film might well become in God's mysterious plan the vehicle by which God speaks to those both within and outside the church. This would seem, in fact, to be the witness of increasing numbers of people as we move ever more strongly into what some call our "postsecular" age. Surely it is the witness of biblical account after biblical account. For those who have eyes to see and ears to hear, God's Spirit is indeed present. It is a mystery not to be ignored.

Discussion Questions

1. Have you seen a film that operated as a parable, such as *Crash* (2004) or *Millions* (2004)? What defining characteristics of these movies invite this comparison?
2. When has an unlikely source (a dream, nature, another person, a cultural event, etc.) revealed profound spiritual truth to you?
3. Can God speak through movies? Can you give an example of a time the Spirit spoke to you through a film? Or, alternately, can you describe a movie-watching event when your spirit was deeply moved and your life transformed?

8

expanding our
field of vision

an ethical lens

In Spike Lee's *Do the Right Thing* (1989), Da Mayor stops Mookie and tells him to "always do the right thing." Mookie asks, "That's it?" Da Mayor confirms, "That's it." It's quite a simple directive. But as the movie indicates, determining what the right thing actually is can be tricky when we're caught up within heated circumstances. How do we engage in ethical decision-making that leads to concrete actions? Movies offer a chance to observe other people's choices, to learn from their regrettable mistakes and their admirable efforts. Films also give us an ethical lens by which to evaluate our own actions. Unfortunately, if our perception is cloudy, we may draw the wrong conclusions from a given film. When Gordon Gecko proclaims that "greed is good" in *Wall Street* (1987), audiences were supposed to be horrified by his amoral vision. And yet, a new generation of filmgoers received it as license to engage in the unethical lending practices that precipitated the 2008 economic crisis. This chapter seeks to sharpen our ethical lenses to discern what filmmakers are communicating and how we as viewers are challenged to respond.

It is helpful to think of ethics as a kind of lens through which we see the world because every movie asks us to look and listen on some basic level. Film is, after all, an irreducibly audiovisual medium. But certain movies go one step further. Taking their cue from the tagline for *American Beauty* (1999), the best films invite us to "look closer"—to develop our capacity to see and hear what

155

might otherwise go unseen and unsaid. And yet, we also must wrestle with the notion that the actor communicating such truths, Kevin Spacey, might have been indulging in all kinds of ethical lapses on the set during the making of the movie. How do we work through the many ethical issues that arise both onscreen and off?

Indeed, in the wake of numerous allegations of sexual assault and the countless revelations concerning the toxic environments that were carefully guarded and cultivated by everyone from major Hollywood executives to prominent politicians to television personalities, this question is now more urgent than ever. And if the church is not willing to address these broader, more systemic ethical concerns, then someone else surely will. Case in point: a recent *Los Angeles Times* article outlined a number of films and television shows that feature as their chief antagonist a perpetrator of sexual assault. In doing so, the reviewer noted that, among numerous others, *Three Billboards Outside Ebbing, Missouri* (2017), *Big Little Lies* (2017), and *The Handmaid's Tale* (2017) all "compelled audiences to reflect on the sins of [their] characters while also exploring what motivates them. How are notions of goodness—no matter how slight—blotted out by sinister impulses and pre-meditations that are the seeds of twisted spirits?"[1]

Given the tsunami of audiovisual media that currently saturates the contemporary cultural landscape, along with various ethical questions this media raises, it has become increasingly clear that both lay and professional theologians need to consider more fully the ways in which moving pictures might expand (or in some cases constrict) the viewer's field of vision—a concern that happens to be of central importance for Christian ethics. Indeed, as Jolyon Mitchell notes in his *Media Violence and Christian Ethics*, "It is noticeable that many Christian ethicists now speak of the importance of vision, and by extension learning to see, to understand and to describe the world correctly."[2] Building on the work of Stanley Hauerwas, Mitchell goes on to suggest that "vision is deeply significant and means 'really looking' at the moral world which we inhabit, while avoiding the temptation of sliding into self-absorption, self-delusion or 'fantasy and despair.'"[3]

In many respects then, film's invitation not only to "look closer" but also to look deeper is, at its core, an ethical gesture. As such, it strikes at the heart of our larger theological project—the development of a mutually enriching, two-way dialogue between film and theology that issues forth in both robust faith and renewed action.

This ethical gesture is at least partly related to the ways in which movies so often function as one of modern society's shared narratives. As Harvard theologian Harvey Cox puts it, shared stories are what help people "locate a common vocabulary." Film stories are no different. They are important because they "speak to the inner spirit. They link the moral reasoning we do in our heads to the courage and empathy that must come from the heart."[4] Yet, for filmgoers interested in the moral discourse that can, and indeed should, issue forth from cinematic stories, a chief impediment to locating a common vocabulary is, ironically, the "ethical" watchdog system the industry itself created. The problems related to the Rating Board of the Motion Picture Association of America (MPAA) are well documented. For instance, *This Film Is Not Yet Rated*, a documentary that premiered at the Sundance Film Festival in 2006, exposes the many disparities and the lack of clarity in the ratings system, primarily by telling the story of its own encounter with the MPAA. The Rating Board originally gave the film the often-fatal NC-17 rating. However, after going through the appeal process (which of course became a part of the documentary itself), the film is now, just as its title suggests, not rated.

So before moving on to consider what might constitute a robust moral dialogue with film, it will be helpful to address the false (albeit common) assumption that a movie's moral perspective can be linked to the rating it receives from the Motion Picture Association of America.

Over-Rated!

Since the 1960s, the Motion Picture Association of America's rating system has been regarded as the moral watchdog for the industry. Every movie advertisement carries with it a rating that prospective viewers see, helping them to make their selections as to what is appropriate for them (or more importantly, for their children) to watch. Increasingly, however, the MPAA's rating system has come under attack, and not just by religious leaders. *Los Angeles Times* film critic Kenneth Turan concludes that "no one who has taken the trouble to look closely respects the system anymore."[5] For critics like Turan, the entire process seems not only arbitrary and hypocritical but also strangely unconcerned with evaluating film as an art form. And these charges seem justified. Explaining the ratings criteria, former MPAA president Jack Valenti, who administered the system through 2004, stated, "The criteria that go into the mix which becomes a Rating Board judgment are theme, violence, language, nudity, sensuality, drug abuse, and other elements. . . . The Rating Board can make its decisions only by what is seen on the screen, not by what is imagined or thought."[6] In other words, the Rating Board is only interested in one thing: the "raw" data. As a result, ratings themselves have almost nothing to do with a movie's meaning as it is communicated to and understood by the viewer. Of course, according to these criteria, unaccompanied teenagers would also be banned by the MPAA from viewing much of the Bible if it were translated to the screen, given that its stories depict, among other things, graphic sexuality (Song of Songs); adultery and voyeurism (2 Sam. 11); a disgusting murder (Judg. 3:15–24); cannibalism (2 Kings 6:24–29); ritual dismemberment (Judg. 19:22–30); the collection of one hundred foreskins (1 Sam. 18:25–27); incest (Gen. 19:30–38); rape (2 Sam. 13:8–20); and so on.[7] That the Jewish and Christian Scriptures put this "raw" data within a larger moral and religious framework would not be taken into account by the Board, or so it would seem.[8]

Somewhat ironically, when biblical stories *are* brought to life on the big screen, many Christians who are otherwise concerned with the ethics of viewing R-rated material seem largely untroubled by the content of biblical films, even when the Rating Board has deemed that content "not suitable" for certain demographics. Mel Gibson's *The Passion of the Christ* (2004) is a case in point. Almost in spite of its over-the-top violence and fetishized gore (the bulk of which is ahistorical and extracanonical), Christians not only flocked to theaters to see the film but booked entire theaters as a way of "evangelizing" viewers of all ages (with an R-rated film!). *The Passion* remains one of the highest grossing independent films of all time for this very reason. Yet, because it was presenting the "gospel" and featured (mostly) biblical material, little thought was given to the wisdom of offering a blanket invitation for others (especially younger viewers) to endure a film that, while officially rated R, could very well have been rated NC-17.

The point here is not to suggest that *The Passion* is a morally questionable film or that Christians shouldn't see it. Even with its seeming bloodlust, it remains a powerful and evocative depiction of Jesus's passion. The larger point is that the question of what is and is not "ethical" for a Christian to watch is complex and nuanced, and the ratings system is a rather blunt instrument. Children and their parents need to be given trustworthy guidance concerning a film's content in order to identify what is appropriate for children to watch. This is especially true in a time when digital technologies have not only made it possible to create onscreen violence that is (un)believably graphic but have also granted children and teenagers all-too-easy access (through online streaming) to sexually titillating, teen-oriented fluff. At the same time, a filmmaker's freedom to create needs to be preserved. And this is to say nothing of the fact that mature viewers need space to receive and judge a film's story according to its intended meaning rather than reducing it to how many breasts are bared, bloody scenes portrayed, or four-letter words uttered.

Unfortunately, the current system appears to be failing on all counts. For instance, Craig attended an event at Sony in which Joan Graves of the MPAA bemoaned the limits of her office. She finds the violence in films like *Hostel*

(2005) and *Saw* (2004) reprehensible, but the MPAA is tasked with interpreting what the average family would find objectionable. Her office is flooded with complaints regarding sexuality onscreen yet receives scant complaints regarding violence. So what she finds personally questionable does not factor into their decision-making. The MPAA ratings system is rooted in American filmgoers' values. If the MPAA seems no longer able to discriminate effectively beyond the somewhat obvious delineation of movies that are appropriate for children in the younger grades of elementary school (G) and movies that are entirely inappropriate for them (R), it is largely because American audiences are confused and confusing. In addition, the system is unable to allow full artistic freedom to those filmmakers wanting to create a genuinely mature movie without having the prurient label NC-17 attached.[9]

In other words, it's a one-size-fits-all system. And while a case could be made that MPAA ratings are helpful for those seeking guidance on which films to watch and, perhaps more importantly, which films are appropriate for their children to watch, filmgoers still have to make numerous adjustments to these criteria on a case-by-case basis depending on factors such as the geographic location of a film's production (because Canadians and Europeans seem to be less concerned about sexual content than Americans, but more concerned about violence[10]), the year in which a film was made (because ratings have shifted quite drastically over time), and even the studio's distribution strategies (because numerous companies opt out of the ratings system altogether for economically motivated reasons).

What is more, in our age of instant access via the internet, ratings have become functionally obsolete, at least when it comes to actually protecting younger viewers from seeing certain films. The mechanisms that were once in place to prevent certain films from getting into the wrong hands were never entirely flawless, but at least in theory if not in actual practice a multitiered network of theater managers, ticket-booth employees, and video-rental clerks served as a gatekeeping device for movies with "adult" ratings. However, with the rise of online streaming services like Hulu, Netflix, and Amazon Prime, both the gatekeepers and the gates have all but disappeared—which means that now more than ever viewers of all ages need to develop a moral framework that functions beyond the rigid confines of the rating system.

Put more succinctly, given the changing standards of different cultures and different time periods, the arbitrariness of nonartistic standards (i.e., sex, violence, language) being applied to an artistic medium, and the increasing accessibility of supposedly restricted movies, the rating system is at best limited in its usefulness. And while some might argue that something is better than nothing, there are perhaps better ways of conveying this information, especially given the fact that parental advisories (which contain every minute detail about a film's content) are readily available on any number of film-related internet sites.

Expanding Our Ethical Field of Vision

Beyond its lack of utility, the present system also has an actual cost. That is, by framing our ethical questions about film only in terms of the "raw" data concerning sex, violence, and vulgar language, we are operating with a truncated understanding of a movie's ethical significance. The result is an artificial (and even false) narrowing of the ethical field, one that allows other depictions with moral import to come in under the radar. Because nudity, violence, and foul language have largely co-opted ethical discussions stemming from the movies, very little energy is directed elsewhere, even by churches and educators interested in moral instruction.

This lack of depth is somewhat tragic, especially since the list of ethically important issues dealt with in films is as wide as life itself. What, for example, of the plight of immigrants? *Spanglish* (2004), *The Visitor* (2007), *Entre Nos* (2009), and *Capernaum* (2018) invite both our appreciative gaze and our critical reflection about "the stranger in our midst." Or what should we make of the stories about Native Americans that are told through the eyes of white men, films such as *Little Big Man* (1970), *Dances with Wolves* (1990), *The Last of the Mohicans* (1992), and *The New World* (2005)? Are these honest portrayals? Are they romanticized? Moreover, might these films have anything to say about current debates in the US over the historic oppression of Native American peoples and their rights to the land? Or again, what insight might the depictions of people with physical or mental disabilities—*Rain Man* (1988), *Forrest Gump* (1994), *I Am Sam* (2001), *The Sessions* (2012)—offer viewers? Can such movies help locate a common vocabulary for discussion of societal values and policies? And what might war movies—*The Thin Red Line* (1998), *The Hurt Locker* (2008), *Zero Dark Thirty* (2012), *American Sniper* (2014)—have to say about our present involvement in global military conflicts or our care for vets returning home with PTSD?

Such questions can easily be multiplied. The point here is not to seek to be comprehensive—to list the full range of ethical issues that have been given a "common language" by the cinema and thus invite our discussion. Rather, it is to point out how little moral discourse is at present actually arising from the movies, in large part because ethical discussions are almost entirely focused on the presence or absence of sex, violence, and/or foul language. And even these discussions are rarely linked to a movie's larger ethical tone or intention.

There are exceptions, of course. The courageous story of Sister Helen Prejean was made known to the world in *Dead Man Walking* (1995), which is credited by many with helping the Catholic Church more aggressively challenge the use of the death penalty. Rather than argue statistics or abstract principles, the movie concentrated on the power of a human story. Though the US bishops had voted to oppose capital punishment as early as 1974, Catholic doctrine continued to state that capital punishment could be a just penalty. It was not until the movie came out and a common moral vocabulary was made available that discussion surrounding the death penalty moved beyond a largely academic debate regarding legal loopholes. Influenced in part by Sister Helen's ability as a storyteller and the moral discourse it generated, opposition to the death penalty gained momentum in the church. In a speech in St. Louis in 1999, Pope John Paul II declared, "The dignity of human life must never be taken away even in the case of someone who has done great evil."[11] The world's lone superpower had a moral responsibility, he said, to proclaim the gospel of life by lobbying against the death penalty, which was cruel and unnecessary.

How directly Sister Helen's story influenced the pope is unknown, although he was aware of her testimony and the movie it sparked. What is clear is that Catholics in the United States were now prepared to respond to the theological discussion, in part because *Dead Man Walking* had given the dialogue an emotional center.

Should Christians View Morally Questionable Stories?

Despite the multiple problems associated with the Rating Code, many will still rightfully ask, aren't there morally objectionable movies that a Christian should simply avoid altogether? Isn't the issue about more than the effectiveness of the ratings system (or the lack thereof)? Here is one of the most frequent lines of questioning we are all asked, both by students and by the people in our faith communities. Aren't Christians instructed by Paul to think about "whatever is true, whatever is noble, whatever is right, whatever is pure, whatever is lovely, whatever is admirable" (Phil. 4:8)? Shouldn't religious viewers at least self-censor what they see?

The simple answer is, of course, *yes*. What we find personally degrading or troubling, we should avoid. Rob and Kutter do not see many horror movies, for example, because the grisly images stay too long in our imaginations and give us nightmares. But Craig is able to watch films in the horror genre without being affected in the same way. He is thus able to interact and engage constructively with films like *The Exorcism of Emily Rose* (2005), *The Conjuring*

(2013), and *The Witch* (2015), which are profound and gripping explorations of evil, spiritual realities, and the unique power of the Christian story. Indeed, as part of their work with Reel Spirituality, Craig and Kutter watched *Annabelle: Creation* (2017) with trepidation and hosted a public conversation with the film's director regarding the spiritual and theological conversation this film invites. Late at night, in an otherwise generic greater Los Angeles–area theater, three hundred people showed up to talk about why they are so compelled by stories in which religious figures confront and, ultimately, defeat evil incarnate.

In a previous chapter, we outlined numerous examples of rightful self-discipline. However, the question about what Christians "ought" to watch is usually not nuanced by consideration of the sensitivities of the viewer or by other criteria such as movie genre or theme. Nor does the questioner usually have in mind the need for many of us to understand and empathize with those unlike us. Instead, what is being asked more narrowly is the "purity" question. If the movie contains scenes of, or language about _____ , shouldn't we stay away? In this case, the answer is, "Maybe yes, but maybe no."

Consider for a moment *Birth of a Nation* (2016), a film that presents ethical quandaries both within and behind its story (which we will address more fully in chap. 9). Although all would agree that the violent images presented in the film are ghastly and thus garner for the movie a deserved R rating, few would say Christians should not see this movie, though some individuals might choose not to see it because of the intensity of the story. The courage that Nat Turner shows in the face of both systemic and individual evil is inspiring, all the more so in light of the film's unflinching depiction of the horrors of American slavery. Indeed, the movie's narrative cannot help but provoke ethical dialogue, especially for Christians.

As Turner is forced by his (Christian) slave owner to preach submission to his fellow (Christian) slaves on the basis of the biblical text, questions pour forth not only about what Jim Wallis has described as "America's original sin" but also about how such brutality is even humanly possible, much less condoned and carried out by "Bible-believing" Christians.[12] Here is a profoundly moral story about immoral events that cannot be fully "seen" unless such second-order moral reflection takes place. Here also is a movie some might not want to see for fear of being disturbed, but for that very reason, every adult Christian should see it. And the same can be said of any number of gritty but morally urgent films such as *Hotel Rwanda* (2004), *12 Years a Slave* (2013), or *Spotlight* (2015).

Daniel Defoe, the eighteenth-century author of *Moll Flanders*, wrote in the book's preface, "To give the history of a wicked life repented of, necessarily requires that the wicked part should be made as wicked as the real history of it will bear, to illustrate and give beauty to the penitent part, which is certainly the

The Birth of a Nation (2016), © Twentieth Century Fox Film Corporation & TSG Entertainment Finance, LLC

best and brightest, if related with equal spirit and life."[13] The language of men in prison should be coarse. The adulterer should be seen to be a real adulterer. A hit man should be callous. A depiction of war might well need to be horrific. To sanitize life is to falsify the story and thus to bring it stillborn into the world. Or as Cardinal John Henry Newman reflects somewhat more elegantly, "It is a contradiction in terms to attempt a sinless Literature of sinful man."[14]

Ron Reed, a playwright and actor who has run a successful theater company in Vancouver for over twenty years, has reflected on Paul's advice to Christians regarding purity.[15] Though Christians, he suggested, might at first blush think a movie like *American Beauty* (1999) is not for them (given its sexuality, nudity, violence, and drug content), this would be a mistake. The movie is actually a meditation on truth—the truth of our culture of consumption, the truth of estranged families, of things that can imprison us, of the damage we can do to one another. It is also a movie that portrays purity. Though the temptation of lust and marital infidelity is present right up to the end of the story, Carolyn's tryst is found lacking even within the movie's story line, while Lester ultimately resists and, in his simple care for Angela and his innocent recollections of family, finds peace. Above all, though, the movie is about beauty. It asks, what is actually lovely? The hybrid American Beauty rose we can nurture to near "perfection"? Or a plastic bag floating freely in the wind? Like the writer of the book of Ecclesiastes, the movie portrays much of life's vanity. But, also like this ancient sage, and like the apostle Paul, it recognizes a fragile alternative, the Spirit's gifting, which brings truth, purity, and beauty.

Given the "raw" content of many movies, should spiritually sensitive people protect their thoughts and imagination from evil? With Cardinal Newman, the apostle Paul, and Ron Reed, we respond that we need not hide from truth or flee from reality. In fact, we must ground our understanding of life in the real. Movies, by eliciting from their viewers emotional responses to the full range of life, can give us a common moral vocabulary, even while portraying that which is troubling and immoral. For just as Cecilia Gonzalez-Andrieu has suggested, the absence of beauty (i.e., "ugliness") in art is often the very thing that points us toward the beautiful, revealing how impoverished a life without beauty truly is. Beauty's opposite is therefore not ugliness, says Gonzalez-Andrieu, but rather "glamour"—a titillating but ultimately counterfeit form of the good that can only ever point inward, toward itself.[16]

Let us be clear then. Just as it is with other forms of art, it is indeed the case that certain movies are simply vacuous. To use Gonzalez-Andrieu's turn of phrase, they are concerned only with "glamour" in the worst sense of the term. And while the sheer popularity of some of these films can grant us insight into the shape and texture of the contemporary cultural imagination, there are simply too many great films now available to waste our time on those with little or no redeeming social content. So to be open to the full range of human experience is not to baptize any and all movies as worthy of viewing. Instead, what we are suggesting is that, by focusing our attention and our emotions on one possible interpretation of life's meaning, film can (and often does) help us engage in a common dialogue about the good, the true, and the beautiful—or the lack thereof.

Developing Skill in Moral Discourse

To understand the ethical import of film and film-going in this way, we are intentionally drawing from the biblical wisdom tradition and its approach toward moral discernment. Think of the way the author of Proverbs pictures wisdom as "calling out" in the public square from every street corner (Prov. 1:20), or the way Jesus taught his disciples by pointing to flowers and birds (Matt. 6:26–28) and through stories about women baking bread (Luke 13:21). In these cases, moral insight has little to do with judging culture according to an abstract set of ethical norms or categorical imperatives. Rather, wisdom emerges through a process in which one explores, discerns, and ultimately enacts the truth that is *already present* in the structures of the created order.

Indeed, wisdom is pictured in Proverbs as being present and active during the creation of the world (Prov. 8:22–31), which is why wisdom (*hokmah*) in the Hebrew Bible is often understood to be intimately connected with, and in some cases even synonymous with, the Spirit of God (*ruach*), who was "hovering over the face of the waters" in Genesis 1:2. So the Spirit, in the form of wisdom, is always already present and active in the world around us, if only we have the "eyes to see and the ears to hear." This particular phrase is repeatedly used not only by the prophets of Israel (Ezek. 12:2; Isa. 6:9–10) but by Jesus too (Matt. 13:15–17). Biblical prophets and teachers use it so frequently because our ability to know how we ought to live as the community of faith comes not by determining what is universally "moral" and then either condemning or approving everything in our purview according to this ethical absolute. Rather, Christian ethics requires learning how to see and hear well. It's about developing our eyes and ears in a way that we can discern not only what is corrupt and destructive, but also what is true and good and beautiful in the world. Indeed, this is the goal of any moral discourse, whether it takes place among friends, with family, or even with film.

Learning how to see and hear well is not always comforting or easy. It can be downright unsettling. Our critical faculties may have atrophied through lack of use. And, in fact, reality itself is often unsettling. For instance, *The Lobster* (2015) is meant to be disturbing. The film is set in an alternative present where all nonmarried people are sequestered in a hotel and forced to identify a spouse among their fellow guests in the span of forty-five days. The unlucky few that either choose to remain single or are unable to find a mate are turned into an animal of their choosing at the end of their stay. In other words, marriage is reified and single people are literally dehumanized. The film thus paints a somewhat terrifying picture of the state of singleness, marriage, and romantic love in the modern world, but not because it is so far removed from reality. It is terrifying because of how close to reality it actually is.

The Lobster is not for the faint of heart, but that is exactly the point. It invites audiences to see the world as it truly is, not as they wish it would be. And sometimes it takes a rather bald-faced depiction of reality to do so. Yet many Christians tend to reject or condemn as "immoral" any cinematic vision that threatens to disturb our puritanical sensibilities in this way, even (and perhaps especially) when a film is simply being honest. As we mentioned before, this is to elevate the "purity" section of Philippians 4:8 over and above the equally important bit about "truth." Moral "purity" thus becomes the central, if not the only, interpretive lens for assessing a film's power and meaning. From this perspective, certain images have the power not only to defile viewers but, worse yet, to desensitize them to images of sex and violence altogether. And while this concern is fine and good as far as it goes, the truth of the matter is that, by completely avoiding these difficult realities, we run the risk of becoming desensitized in another, far more significant way—that is, we eventually lose the capacity to see and hear the ways in which the Spirit of God is present and active in our world. Over time, our eyes and ears become desensitized to the wisdom that so often comes in the form of unsettling truths, to such a degree that, at some point, we become incapable of discerning whether God is up to anything in the world at all, much less how we might participate.

Practicing Ethical Patience

At this point, some may be wondering whether we are guilty of simply overcorrecting. Responding to the unthinking negative judgments of movies by certain members of the religious community, have we not swung the pendulum too far in the opposite direction and, in doing so, unwittingly adopted an attitude that is "indiscriminately celebrative"?[17] How does this do anything more than "baptize" film as a cultural product filled with wisdom and truth when in fact it rarely exhibits anything of the sort? After all, it is fine to hear and understand a movie on its own terms before critiquing it; but don't we also need to bring our own religious and ethical perspectives to bear on the story if the dialogue is truly to be a two-way conversation? The answer, once again, is *yes*. And we hope the discussion in this book has made this abundantly clear.

However, we want to stress the need for lay and professional theologians to practice "ethical patience," both with film and with our fellow filmgoers.[18] It is one thing to offer a thoughtful critique of a movie that is found to be ethically wanting, but it is quite another to judge a film entirely on the basis of a preformed set of moral preferences. Indeed, it was the Pharisees' complete lack of ethical patience that Jesus was calling into question when he said, "What goes into someone's mouth does not defile them, but what comes out of their mouth, that is what defiles them" (Matt. 15:11). In their haste to critique and condemn those practices that did not obviously align with their religious preferences, the religious leaders had become blind to their own moral culpability and, by extension, their desperate need for others to be patient with their ethical shortcomings. Much like the Pharisees then, when we fail to exhibit ethical patience, we too run the risk of immediately being offended (15:12) at just about everything we encounter in the world out of fear that it could possibly "defile" us. But if we take Jesus's words seriously, then we need to find a way to have our sensibilities offended without taking offense. Put differently, we need to learn the art of ethical patience because, more times than not, dogmatic commitments to religious or moral "purity" are just another form of self-blindness (15:14).

The Law of Proportionality

As we attempt to assess whether a movie should be seen, we would do well to follow a variation of Defoe's "law of proportionality" as an ethical rule of thumb: If there is evil presented, is there a concomitant good that shines through, or that is offered and rejected, or that suggests itself by its very absence, such that truth, beauty, or goodness may be considered? Picasso's *Guernica* is not a beautiful painting, nor is it about the good. But its very ugliness—the absence of what is good and beautiful—is what allows the painting to convey a truthfulness about the horror of war that continues to inspire all who let their spirits be touched by it. Such can also be the case with movies. They need not be pretty. *Dead Man Walking* would never be described as such. But they should, by their ability to generate in viewers an honest emotional response, open us to the truth of life in one of its many dimensions.

Appreciation before Appraisal

A number of prominent Christian thinkers in theology and film will suggest that, while watching a movie, viewers always need to be critically evaluating how a filmmaker might be trying to manipulate their emotions through film technique, script, and music.[19] In this way, they can protect themselves from any experience of evil or from unknowingly imbibing destructive ideologies. While such a strategy might accomplish its purpose, it will unfortunately also shield viewers from fully experiencing the truth, goodness, and beauty a movie conveys. Such shielding will ensure that the film experience remains stillborn. As the philosopher Mitch Avila argues effectively, felt emotion is the essence of the movie experience.[20] So we need first to appreciate before we appraise.[21] That is, we must experience the sense and taste of life that the movie opens up if we hope also to sense and taste something of the Infinite. When we go to a movie, we should not first think about what makes the movie religious or moral, or whether a movie aligns with our own religious or moral perspective, but should rather let the movie itself focus our attention. This of course might include religious and ethical dimensions, but these will be integral to and flow out of the movie itself. In other words, the process of discernment and dialogue should be inductive, not deductive.

An adequate theological ethic of movie-going will thus involve an initial, careful "seeing/hearing" before attempting a subsequent "responding," even while viewers recognize that they bring to their viewing a wider life experience and cultural knowledge that inform their initial viewing. To quote German theologian Dietrich Bonhoeffer, who wrote this while sitting in a Nazi prison awaiting his execution for his involvement in a conspiracy against Hitler: "Who is there . . . in our times, who can devote himself with an easy mind to music, friendship, games or happiness? Surely not the 'ethical' [person], but only the Christian." It is not that ethics was unimportant to Bonhoeffer. He gave his life for a just cause. But for Christians in particular, there is also a place for the aesthetic joys of "art, education, friendship, play."[22] To put it in explicitly theological terms, it is because the Spirit of God is already present and active in the world that Christians are not merely free to perceive and seek to enjoy before judging or evaluating but are actually called to do so.

What does this mean concretely though? In an effort to answer this question, we conclude with an extended example concerning the moral discourse that movies can and often do encourage.

The Wolf of Wall Street and *The Big Short*: The Love of Money and the Need for Wisdom

The rich are wise in their own eyes;
    one who is poor and discerning sees how deluded they are.

                    —Proverbs 28:11

There is no nobility in poverty. I've been a rich man and a poor man and I choose rich man every time. I want you to deal with your problems by becoming rich.

              —Jordan Belfort, *The Wolf of Wall Street*

Truth is like poetry, and most people f—— hate poetry.

                    —*The Big Short*

In 2008, the global economy imploded, triggered in part by the collapse of US securities backed almost entirely by subprime mortgages. A potent mixture of greed, stupidity, predatory lending practices, inappropriate and ineffectual regulations, and outright fraud created a massive financial crisis, the likes of which had not been seen since the Great Depression. A full decade later, the American economy has been able to slowly recover from this "Great Recession," but only because US taxpayers bailed out the so-called Big Banks, which were deemed "too big to fail." As a result, the extremely wealthy are now seeing record-setting returns on their investments once again, and the disparity between the haves and the have-nots continues to grow. Those who lost everything (whether a result of willful ignorance, greed, or simply being deceived) still have little to no recourse for preventing history from repeating itself. Adding insult to injury, the very people who gambled away the public's money either cashed out on unthinkable bonuses (from bailout funds) or made it rich on credit default swaps that banked on the economy's failure.

If the economic bankruptcy was surprising, the moral bankruptcy of it all was shocking. But it shouldn't have been. When it comes to the power that money wields over individuals and society as a whole, the story of the Great Recession is a tale as old as time. The author of Ecclesiastes noted this long before things like stock markets and collateral debt obligations (CDOs) ever existed:

> Whoever loves money never has enough;
>   whoever loves wealth is never satisfied with their income.
> This too is meaningless.
>
> As goods increase,
>   so do those who consume them.
> And what benefit are they to the owners
>   except to feast their eyes on them? . . .

> There is something else meaningless that occurs on earth: the righteous who get what the wicked deserve, and the wicked who get what the righteous deserve. (Eccles. 5:10–11; 8:14)

Given the current state of our consumer culture, it is patently obvious that American society at the dawn of the twenty-first century is in need of a deeper wisdom and a more discerning ethical vision. The collapse of the global economy in 2008 did not create the innumerable moral failures and injustices that are now so glaringly apparent to us. In truth, these gross indiscretions were always present and in operation; we just didn't have the eyes to see them. Nor did we have the capacity to recognize the many ways in which we were complicit in the problem, much less how our pursuit of material wealth was impacting our neighbors. We desperately need not only a common moral vocabulary that will allow us to see the truth of our current situation with greater clarity but also one that might help us forge a more life-giving response to the ethical dilemmas of modern life—especially those related to our undying love of money and our insatiable desire to acquire it at any cost.

Although a number of films might provide a common vocabulary of this kind, two notable examples are *The Wolf of Wall Street* and *The Big Short*. Interestingly enough, both films contain strikingly similar content in terms of their "raw" data (i.e., language, sex, and all manner of amoral/immoral behavior). But the kind of ethical dialogue that follows from each of these films is quite different. After we have taken the time to listen to these movies and have made an effort to appreciate what they have to say, the primary question we face is not which film is "more virtuous" than the other or which film more closely aligns with a "Christian ethic." Rather, the central question is whether either of these films helps viewers truly see the moral world they inhabit and, in turn, encourages them to respond in ways that are neither self-absorbed nor despairing, but wise.

In the eyes of fans and critics alike, *The Wolf of Wall Street* and *The Big Short* are excellent films. Cinephiles on Rotten Tomatoes and IMDb gave them high marks,[23] and both films were nominated for multiple Academy Awards, with Adam McKay (writer/director of *The Big Short*) winning the Oscar for Best Adapted Screenplay. Yet, as it concerns the moral discourse that these two films prompt among filmgoers, critics and theologians are far more ambivalent about *The Wolf of Wall Street* than *The Big Short*.

The Wolf of Wall Street *(2013)*

Adapted for the screen by Terence Winter and directed by Martin Scorsese, *The Wolf of Wall Street* tells the story of Jordan Belfort (Leonardo DiCaprio), a stockbroker who makes it rich trading penny stocks and, along the way, defrauds investors of massive amounts of money in a securities scam that involves widespread corruption on Wall Street and in the corporate banking world. Remaining true to its source material (Jordan Belfort's memoir), the three-hour film features wall-to-wall profanity, graphic sexuality, rampant drug use, and stomach-churning scenes of domestic violence. It is pure, unadulterated excess, and that's exactly the point. If it weren't based on an apparently true story, and if a filmmaker as revered as Martin Scorsese hadn't directed it, the film would not be "near pornographic" as some have described it; it would just be pornographic.

And that is exactly why this film presents us with such an ethical quandary. The content is crass, to be sure. It depicts a world that is not just immoral, but perhaps entirely amoral. Yet in doing so, could it actually be inviting us to consider the emptiness of such amorality/immorality? Isn't that, just as we have suggested, the entire point of telling the stories of "sinful men"—to make the "wicked part . . . as wicked as the real history of it will bear"?[24] And isn't Scorsese well regarded as the kind of daring auteur who is capable of showing us the truth—as raw and offensive as it may be—without descending into mere titillation?

Many critics (including Christian critics) interpret the film in exactly this way. It is true that the film fails to show Belfort suffering any real consequences for his debauchery (e.g., it depicts his twenty-two-month stint in a white-collar prison with a three-second scene of him playing tennis). Neither does it give much in the way of screen time to any of his victims (e.g., his wives or his children). But as one prominent critic at *IndieWire* suggested, this is because the film is dedicated to exploring the *appeal* of Belfort's lawless pursuit of wealth. And if

The Wolf of Wall Street (2013), © TWOWS, LLC

Scorsese is going to be "honest" about Belfort's life of self-centered avarice, and if he is going to make a movie that explores this life with any kind of artistic integrity, then it has to be appealing. So even though we are right to believe that "it would be nice if the movie provided a more fitting comeuppance for Jordan Belfort; it would . . . be a lie."[25]

The same critic goes on to say that, even if Scorsese had chosen to abdicate his artistic responsibility and fabricated some punishment for Belfort, it wouldn't have made any difference. "There is no ending so dark or sufficiently moralistic that it can dissuade would-be Jordan Belforts from seeing only the private jets and the prostitutes and the high-grade drugs. You can't make a movie asshole-proof. . . . [The film] won't turn people off financial crime, any more than any cautionary tale can stop people from trying drugs, but it's a frightening and clear-eyed look at why so many indulge, and why they get to keep on indulging."[26]

Interestingly, a number of Christian reviewers offered nearly identical interpretations of the film, in terms of both its artistic merit and its ethical significance.[27] In short, these critics all suggest that a robust moral dialogue can and does emerge from a viewing of *The Wolf of Wall Street* primarily because it is an aesthetically excellent film and it depicts the "truth" of sin—both its undeniable destructiveness and its genuine appeal.

But when it comes to a film's ethical import, things are never so simple, for standing behind all of these positive reviews is another shared assumption regarding authorial intention: "The self-absorbed, monstrous main character at the center of *The Wolf of Wall Street* may be the one narrating the story, but the director of the movie is Martin Scorsese, who is passionately interested in showing us how power corrupts. I think he's hoping that we'll see right through this narrator to the folly of his perspective."[28]

Here our film-critical tools are truly put to the test. A filmmaker's creative intentions can and should inform our understanding of a movie's power and meaning. But these intentions (however virtuous they may be) cannot be our only interpretive criterion. To grant too much weight to a filmmaker's intentions is another way of not letting the film speak on its own terms. So while it is important to consider a filmmaker's artistic vision and his or her larger body of work, it is equally important to keep in mind that no author is the ultimate or even final arbiter of a film's meaning. Meaning emerges from a negotiation between author, film, and audience. And when we allow any one of these players either to monopolize the conversation or to drop out altogether, our assessments are far more likely to be unhelpful or even misleading. Much like the critic quoted above, we end up "hoping" for some kind of meaning that the film itself simply does not (or cannot) supply.

So let's bracket for a moment whatever we think Scorsese's hopes and dreams for his film might be and instead approach the movie from a slightly different angle. Rather than focus on authorial intent, if we were to place *The Wolf of Wall Street* into conversation with a movie like *The Big Short* by critically analyzing their formal and structural elements, we would gain much-needed insight concerning the ways in which each film's storytelling structure gives rise to a certain kind of moral discourse.

The Big Short *(2015)*

On the surface, *The Wolf of Wall Street* and *The Big Short* share a number of similarities. Although *Wolf* is primarily about "the little guys" who were skirting the law while trading penny stocks and *The Big Short* is about "the big boys" like Lehman Brothers and Goldman Sachs, both films are telling parallel stories about a particular time in US history when our collective love of money went largely unchecked and resulted in devastating consequences. Because of this shared setting, *The Big Short* depicts a world not unlike the world of *The Wolf of Wall Street*—one in which profanity, greed, sexual promiscuity, violence, and injustice are simply the norm. Like its counterpart, it too deserves its R rating. Beyond their explicit content, though, both *The Big Short* and *The Wolf of Wall Street* have narrators who are shamelessly unscrupulous—Jared Vennett (Ryan Gosling) and Jordan Belfort, respectively. Vennett and Belfort are equally unapologetic about their crass materialism, and they demonstrate very little regard for anyone who might be harmed by their unflinching pursuit of wealth. What is more, because these narrators are also characters in their own story, both films make clear that the story we are being told is coming from a very particular (and therefore skewed) perspective. There is no "objectivity" here, moral or otherwise. Everything is open to interpretation, and everyone is being played.

Given these striking similarities, the formal differences between the two films are all the more revealing. This is especially the case when it comes to the particular ways in which their narrators break the fourth wall—the imaginary boundary separating the audience from the film's narrative world. In *The Big Short*, Jared Vennett tells us the story of three different groups of individuals who not only predicted the collapse of mortgage-backed securities but also made a fortune betting on that very collapse. His opening monologue, which frames the entire film, is spoken directly to the audience: "A few outsiders and weirdos saw what no one else could see. . . . These outsiders saw the giant lie at the heart of the economy and they saw it by doing something the rest of us suckers never thought to do. They looked."

This opening narration serves as an interpretive key to the heart of the film. As it subverts narrative conventions, *The Big Short* invites us not simply to look, but to look closer. In the midst of all the excesses the film shows us, it prompts us to stop for a moment and open our eyes—to think critically and, hopefully, to respond with wisdom and discernment. Indeed, throughout the movie, every time Vennett breaks the fourth wall, the narration is functioning not to give us an increasingly narrow take on what we are seeing but to open our eyes so that we can evaluate what we see. Thus, when important details about the economic collapse are at risk of being lost in a sea of jargon, Vennett speaks directly to us in layman's terms, clarifying what would otherwise remain befuddling. And in those moments when we might be distracted by something shiny and thus tempted to ignore the true horror of what we are witnessing, he appoints a pop-culture celebrity to take over the narration.

In doing so, *The Big Short* acknowledges that the acquisition of massive amounts of wealth by any and every means is truly appealing. But in turning toward the audience and addressing us directly, Vennett prevents us from becoming lazy and uncritical viewers. He never allows us to forget that the story he is narrating, although genuinely alluring, is leading us toward a collective bankruptcy. In this way, Vennett becomes the voice of wisdom and moral insight. In no uncertain terms, he lets us know that, while this story is indeed about gaining the whole world, it's first and foremost about losing our soul (Matt. 16:26).

And so, even after netting huge profit margins on behalf of his investment fund by betting that the Big Banks' securities would fail, Michael Burry (played by Christian Bale) writes to his investors: "Making money is not like what I thought it would be. This business kills the part of life that is essential." Whether intentional or not, Burry's words echo Proverbs 1:19: "Such are the paths of all who go after ill-gotten gain; it takes away the life of those who get it." Or as Mark Baum (Steve Carrell) says in his closing speech, "We live in an era of fraud in America. Not just in banking but in government, education, religion, food, even baseball. What bothers me isn't that fraud is not nice or that fraud is mean; it's that, for 15,000 years, fraud and shortsighted thinking have never ever worked. Not once. Eventually, we get caught. Things go south. When the hell did we forget all that? I thought we were better than that."

This seeming resonance between the film and the Jewish wisdom tradition may not be entirely accidental. The real-life Mark Baum not only studied Torah as a child but, if the film is accurate in this regard, approached Scripture looking for inconsistencies. In other words, his moral compass, his critical insight, and his consequent pursuit of justice were all born from the religious tradition that he inherited. And this leads him to deliver another line in the film that is at once utterly obvious and profoundly true: "Nobody's acting responsible."

Here then is the moral center of *The Big Short*. Look closer. Seek Wisdom. Be responsible. Especially when it comes to money. To do otherwise is not simply to wade into murky ethical waters. It is to destroy life—both our own life and the lives of others. The film thus invites us to see and describe well the moral structure of the world we inhabit, but it also challenges us to respond with wisdom and discernment—to be responsible rather than reckless. And it offers this invitation not because it is beholden to some puritanical form of moralism but because it recognizes that this is simply a better way to live.

It remains unclear if the same can be said about *The Wolf of Wall Street*, and one of the primary reasons for the film's lack of moral clarity has to do with the fact that we don't see the victims of Belfort's schemes. As one critic put it, "Jordan's the one telling this story, and he couldn't care less about them."[29] But plenty of narrators show little concern for others. Much like Belfort, Jared Vennett also doesn't care about anything other than making money. Yet *The Big Short* still manages to show (often through documentary footage) many of the victims of Wall Street corruption. So the moral ambiguity in *The Wolf of Wall Street* cannot so easily be written off as the product of a self-centered narrator. By way of comparison, when Vennett speaks directly to the camera in *The Big Short*, it serves to jolt the audience out of the film's narrative so they might reflect critically on what they are seeing. Belfort, however, breaks the fourth wall at the very moment when the audience is on the verge of becoming uncomfortably self-conscious. And rather than prodding viewers to "look closer" at the reckless debauchery before them, he diverts their attention with what amounts to a slick sales technique.

For instance, just after SEC officers set up shop in the Stratton Oakmont offices to investigate suspicions of the firm's illegal trading practices, Belfort walks through the chaos of the trading floor while speaking directly to the audience. Much like Jared Vennett's narrative asides, it seems at first blush that Belfort intends to explain to the viewer what an "IPO" is (it's the initial public offering of a private company's stock) and why he and his partners were in fact guilty of insider trading when his firm managed the Steve Madden IPO. But he doesn't. Instead, he stops in the middle of his explanation and simply says to the camera with a wink and a smile: "I know you're not following what I'm saying. Was all of this legal? No, but we were making more money than we knew what to do with."

In stark contrast to the ways in which *The Big Short* breaks the fourth wall, Belfort's narration doesn't enhance our critical capacities but instead renders them impotent. To borrow again from Cecilia Gonzalez-Andrieu, at the very moment when the audience is waking up to the true ugliness of Belfort's crass materialism (i.e., its complete lack of beauty), he holds up something glamorous (i.e., money), not only to distract us, but also to convince us that the glamorous is actually beautiful. We need not worry about the consequences of these actions because, well, just look at all that money! And like all good cons, though we know it's a lie, we no longer care. We love our wolves, even as they devour us, because ultimately we want nothing more than to be a wolf too. This is why, in the final scene, when Jordan and the audience should have learned from his wicked ways, we find him going back to sales, seizing on the allure of the profit to be made from selling a simple pen. Scorsese turns his camera's gaze on those in Jordan's audience, leaning in, eager to learn from his "wisdom" regarding how to get rich quick. The implication is clear—we all have sinned and lusted after Jordan's wealth.

And this is also why, even for those who believe Scorsese is actually attempting to encourage his audience to see the folly of Belfort's perspective, the primary problem concerning *The Wolf of Wall Street* is not the immorality it depicts but "the fact that the viewer's response to [these depictions] will vary based on whether or not he or she finds the lifestyle shown attractive, or despicable. In other words . . . a viewer's desire for Belfort's money and the lifestyle it brings could be a factor in making some viewers more or less tone deaf to the moral judgments buried in the film."[30]

If film is at its best when it opens our eyes and ears—when it invites us to listen closely and look deeper—then a movie is missing something both aesthetically and ethically when it causes audiences to become tone deaf to its own moral intentions. This is not to suggest that *The Wolf of Wall Street* is entirely without value (as we have noted, there is a great diversity of opinion among film critics and theologians concerning the kind of moral discourse this film occasions). It is rather to point out that, as it concerns the development of an adequate theological ethic of movie-going, our assessment of a film must emerge from what the film itself offers up, not from whatever it is we hope it might be saying. This is no easy task, especially because the best films will likely generate a wide array of legitimate interpretations. So it may be that *The Wolf of Wall Street* actually succeeds in generating a conversation about the ethics of wealth generation that American society so desperately needs. After all, it is certainly possible to read the film "against the grain," and this might be exactly what Scorsese intended all along.

But even if this is true, we would do well to keep in mind that the bulk of the critical discourse surrounding *The Wolf of Wall Street* has not been focused on the ethics of amassing wealth in a late-capitalist society—a conversation that should emerge quite naturally from a film of this kind. Rather, the focus of these conversations has been on the ethical merits of the film itself and, even more specifically, the ways in which the film affects its audience. Rather than ushering us back into the world with a clarified moral vision and a renewed sense of action regarding our collective love of money, the film keeps our gaze fixed firmly on itself. It forcibly narrows rather than expands our ethical field of view.

Ultimately then, as much as we might want the film to be a savvy critique of consumer culture and capitalism gone amok, the formal structures of the movie place viewers in the same position as the audience in the final scene—leaning in, desperate to hear the con man's secrets for getting rich. As David Edelstein wrote for *Vulture,*

> Scorsese seems to think that by blowing Belfort's book up to three hours he's making an epic statement. But it's not as if he shows you the consequences of Belfort's actions. The movie has no scope; there's barely enough content for a short. *The Wolf of Wall Street* is three hours of horrible people doing horrible things and admitting to being horrible. But you're supposed to envy them anyway, because the alternative is working at McDonald's and riding the subway alongside wage slaves. What are a few years in a minimum-security prison—practically a country club—when you can have the best of everything?[31]

Even if Edelstein slightly overstates things to make his point, it is safe to say that *The Big Short* seems to move in another, perhaps more promising direction. To be sure, both films have their merits, and both are well crafted. But in the final analysis, one might be more worth our time. As it concerns the law of proportionality, our ethical patience quite clearly pays off at the end of one film, but we remain forever uncertain about the other. And at least part of the reason is because one seems to mistake glamour for beauty, whereas the other invites us to stare in horror at the ugliness of our relentless pursuit of wealth in the hopes that an encounter with a world entirely devoid of beauty might nudge us toward goodness—toward wisdom even. After all, as the ancient book of wisdom reminds us, "Blessed are those who find wisdom, those who gain understanding, for she is more profitable than silver and yields better returns than gold" (Prov. 3:13–14).

In a world of IPOs, CDOs, and subprime mortgages, this kind of wisdom is profoundly countercultural—scandalous even—but that doesn't make it any less true. Both of these films, to greater or lesser degrees of effectiveness, remind us of this basic truth and urge us to respond accordingly. But as a wise man once said, "Truth is like poetry, and people f—— hate poetry."

Discussion Questions

1. How would you describe your personal sensitivities when it comes to the content of certain films?
2. What does "ethical patience" look like in your own context? What practices (communal or personal) do you take up to ensure you are actually being "ethically patient" and not simply "unethical" in your movie-going?
3. At what point is a cautionary tale (e.g., *The Wolf of Wall Street* or *The Big Short*) just an opportunity to revel in moral bankruptcy? How do you know when a story (film or otherwise) is functioning in one way or the other?

act iii

dialogue

9

encountering
the other

a cultural lens

Memorable films have been made about some of our most atrocious acts. Type "films about genocide" into a search engine, and a long and powerful list emerges: *The Killing Fields* (1984), *Schindler's List* (1993), *No Man's Land* (2001), *Hotel Rwanda* (2004), *Lebanon* (2009), *The Promise* (2016). The tangled histories depicted in these films remain so raw that *The Promise*, a movie about the Armenian genocide, was being actively undermined by the Turkish government even before its release. *The Act of Killing* (2012) explored atrocities in Indonesia by casting those who committed mass killings in re-creations of their own crimes. Perhaps only with the critical distance of drama can we confront and begin to understand our barbaric tendencies. By watching "foreign films" about events that happened far away from our time and place, we may begin to see our own cultural blind spots a little more clearly. This chapter will take up a cultural lens to wrestle with our own prejudices. Why watch films that require us to read subtitles or that take us beyond our comfort zones? The goal is to broaden our understanding and embrace of those we may consider as other. By transporting us to cultures beyond our immediate experience, movies can open our eyes and broaden our hearts toward our neighbors around the globe, as well as those back at home. Indeed, as the history of film (and history itself) reminds us, failure to embrace the other—choosing to demonize rather than empathize—can be deadly.

In the mid-1990s, Miroslav Volf, who was at Fuller Seminary at the time, wrote an award-winning book titled *Exclusion and Embrace: A Theological Exploration of Identity, Otherness, and Reconciliation*. A native Croatian himself, Volf's text was both a response to and a theological reflection on the war in his former Yugoslavia. But in much broader terms, Volf dared to suggest that, for the Christian, the most appropriate (and faithful) response to the hate-filled and fear-based demonization of otherness that marks so much of the modern world is not to exclude but to embrace the other—just as Christ embraces us through his self-giving love.

Much has changed in the three decades that have passed since Volf first penned his seminal work. But the renewed sense of tribalism, nationalism, and xenophobia that has emerged in response to our increasingly globalized world (and, by extension, our encounters with an even wider array of "others") is nothing new. Thus, Volf's central claim remains as timely and urgent as ever:

> Various kinds of cultural "cleansings" demand of us *to place identity and otherness at the center of theological reflection* on social realities. . . . The growing awareness of cultural heterogeneity brought about by economic and technological developments of planetary proportions explains why "tribal" identity today is asserting itself as a powerful force, especially in cases where cultural heterogeneity is combined with extreme imbalances of power and wealth. . . . [So] theologians should concentrate less on social arrangements and more on *fostering the kind of social agents capable of envisioning and creating just, truthful, and peaceful societies, and on shaping a cultural climate in which such agents will thrive.*[1]

In times such as these, says Volf, grappling with "otherness" is central to the theological task. Both lay and professional theologians should focus not only on fostering social agents who "act justly, and love mercy, and walk humbly" (Mic. 6:8) but also on creating generative spaces in which the outsider, the alien, and the oppressed encounter both a human and a divine embrace.

To be sure, this all sounds wonderful, but it might simply be too good to be true. When it comes to the real world—one in which radical otherness is seen by many as the primary source of society's ills—how exactly do we create the kind of environment that would accomplish what Volf is describing here, much less bring about the kind of others-oriented agents he envisions?

According to theologian and communications theorist Gaye Williams Ortiz, movies (especially world cinema) provide us with a unique and perhaps even unparalleled vehicle for addressing these seemingly intractable questions. Borrowing from Volf's work, Ortiz also underscores the human propensity to exclude and reject the other. On a very basic level, "*anything* that 'blurs our accepted boundaries, disturbs our identities, and disarranges our symbolic cultural maps' is a threat to our domination of the world as we see it."[2] As a result, we will even go so far as to "persecute others because we are uncomfortable with strangeness in ourselves."[3]

From Ortiz's perspective, the core Christian conviction encapsulated by Jesus's command to "love your neighbor as yourself" (Mark 12:31; Matt. 22:39) stands in stark contrast to this all-too-human tendency to exclude otherness through passive avoidance or active persecution. Just as the apostle Paul makes clear in his letter to the Galatians, God ultimately overcame divine/human otherness in the person and work of Jesus Christ, which is why there is now "neither Jew nor Gentile, neither slave nor free, nor is there male and female, for you are all one in Christ Jesus" (Gal. 3:28). So Christians are called not only to overcome otherness within their own ranks, but also to take the much more radical step of self-identifying with the cultural, religious, and sociopolitical other.

Ortiz suggests that members of the Christian community must seize every opportunity for being taken out of their "from here" perspective and immersed in a "from there" viewpoint. They need to pursue experiences in which they can glimpse different ways of life yet, at the same time, recognize their common humanity.[4] And film, says Ortiz, opens up exactly this kind of opportunity: "The challenge of embracing different cultures and the Other through world cinema is one that American educators, writers, and church leaders can issue to society. It may be a small step toward tolerance, but nonetheless an important one, in that the viewing of films from around the world could offset the post-9/11 perception of cultural isolation felt by many Americans."[5]

Following Ortiz, we suggest not that movies are some kind of silver bullet for solving the radicalization of otherness that currently threatens the global human village. Rather, we simply want to conceive of the cinematic encounter as a theologically expansive space (if cultivated properly) in which viewers are able to experience the world "from there" and through which they might develop a more empathetic posture toward any and all others in their midst. Again, just as Ortiz says, it is a small step, but a necessary one.

Ultimately, we intend to locate this empathetic encounter with (human) otherness within a larger theological framework. In fact, we will go so far as to suggest that our ability to identify with the other in and through film-going is intimately related to the presence and activity of the divine Other who is always already pervading these cinematic encounters. So we begin somewhat globally with a consideration of the cultural and religious other embodied by world cinema. We then turn our attention toward a more local phenomenon by exploring representations of racial(ized) otherness in films about slavery and race relations in the United States. Finally, we narrow our focus even further by asking how divergent interpretations of recent biblical films might reveal pathways for overcoming the otherness that threatens to divide the Christian community from within.

Encountering the Cultural and Religious Other

To paraphrase something Craig once said, one of the greatest gifts of cinema is that it allows us to walk in others' shoes. That is, it provides us with an opportunity to see the world through a different set of eyes and to feel it out with a different set of sensibilities. As Margaret R. Miles and Brent S. Plate have put it, "How we see the other affects the way we treat the other. Film, as a medium of mass reception, promotes, negates, and generally alters our perception of identities, especially with regard to gender, race, ethnicity, and religion."[6]

In doing so, film can take us to new places that we might never have encountered otherwise (e.g., the planet Scarif in *Rogue One: A Star Wars Story*, the bustling city of Mumbai in *The Lunchbox*, or even a *completely* alien landscape like . . . Montana in *Arrival*). But it's also more than that. As a movie ushers us back into the "real" world, it prods us to look at our own context with eyes that are no longer our own. In other words, film (like any good piece of art) is able not only to make the strange familiar but also to make the familiar strange.[7]

It is important for us to point out cinema's capacity to make the commonplace seem odd. In our effort to facilitate a dialogue with film that might cultivate a sense of empathetic engagement with otherness, the goal is not to develop some kind of intellectual "mastery" over another culture, context, or people group. We aren't after a comprehensive understanding of the other, as if that were even possible. Rather, the goal is to listen empathetically to the other so that we might better understand *ourselves*.

This was my (Kutter's) hope for the opening-night session of a men's retreat at my church that I co-led with Ralph Winter (producer of *X-Men*, *X-Men 2*, and *Planet of the Apes*). Of particular interest to us that year was Guillermo del Toro's *The Shape of Water* (2017), which won Oscars for Best Picture, Best Director, Best Original Music Score, and Best Production Design. The majority of the attendees appreciated our conversation that night, which focused on the need for the Christian community to develop a greater sense of empathy for the other, the outsider, the marginalized. However, a few couldn't get past the sexual content of the film, describing it as "nearly pornographic" and thus inappropriate for such a setting. Initially, Ralph and I thought that some of the discomfort these individuals were voicing might have been rooted in the film's depiction of interspecies love. Some may have been understandably approaching this R-rated film from a position of avoidance or caution. But as the conversation unfolded, we soon discovered that their primary concern actually was the film's depiction of the heroine, Elisa Esposito (played beautifully by Sally Hawkins). Apparently, it was one thing to imagine a mythical sea creature having sex with a human, but to see a woman "like her" (i.e., a woman unable to speak) express her fully orbed sexuality was just too much.

To be sure, *The Shape of Water* is a kind of fairy tale or fable—but like the best fairy tales, it exposes the "real" world for what it truly is. It makes the familiar strange and the strange familiar by telling a story in which the others are the heroes (the protagonists are a mute woman, a woman of color, a gay man, and an amphibious nonhuman). Even though such a film can be deeply unsettling, it has the potential to reveal something about how we are prone to treat others—whether the racial, the cultural, or the religious other—not simply as different but as less than fully human. By revealing this innate tendency, it prompts us to change. It urges us not simply to be better humans but to be more deeply human.

In film as in life, we overcome otherness by identifying differences and commonalities between two groups and by becoming people who are able to embrace the other as a fellow human being. It's about taking up difference as an integral part of our own identity. One of the best ways of fostering this kind of sensibility is to allow the gaze of the other to fall on our own life and circumstances, exposing us to hard truths we might otherwise ignore or overlook.

Spring, Summer, Fall, Winter . . . and Spring *(2003)*

A film that opens up such possibilities is Korean filmmaker Kim Ki-Duk's *Spring, Summer, Fall, Winter . . . and Spring*. The movie charts the journey of a young boy who stumbles upon a Buddhist monk living in a kind of premodern Zen utopia. The monk raises the boy in the ways of a contemplative life, but when a young woman and her mother enter the picture, the now teenage boy chooses to abandon his master's ascetic ways in pursuit of his more sensual impulses. Some time later, the young man returns, having murdered his wife in a crime of passion, thus fulfilling his master's prophetic words: "Lust leads to desire for possession, and possession leads to murder." In an act of repentance, the apprentice commits once again to his master's meditative practices until he is taken into custody by the authorities. Many years pass. The master ends his life by burning himself on a pyre, and the apprentice returns to the monastery after serving his sentence for murder. The cycle comes full circle as the aging apprentice takes up the mantle left by his deceased master and as

Spring, Summer, Fall, Winter . . . and Spring (2003), © Korea Pictures, LJ Film Company Ltd. and Pandora Filmproduktion

another mother abandons her baby at the monastery, leaving the monk to raise the boy just as he was raised.

To describe the basic trajectory of the plot in this way, however, is to miss one of the most significant aspects of this film: it is visually stunning. The entire narrative takes place in an idyllic setting—a monastery that floats on a lake at the base of a Korean mountainside. That the monastery itself is a literal island only heightens the sense that what takes place here is one step removed from the goings-on of everyday life. At various points throughout the film, scenes are framed through freestanding doorways, wooden frames, and open gateways, a visual nod to the Buddhist concepts of emptiness and illusion.[8] Kim's camera is never too quick to move, always willing to linger a few extra moments on the smallest details of animal and plant life. Here a young boy prays before a statue of the Buddha; there a young girl observes fish swimming in the lake; and here a monk meditates in the center of a blindingly white frozen lake. All of these interactions seem mundane at first, but in Kim's vision they are actually sacred. At the same time, there is no question that they are also fleeting.

Although a Protestant Christian himself, it is Kim's Korean imagination that most discernibly shapes his depiction of Buddhism, in terms of both its religious and its cultural significance. To Western eyes and ears that are more accustomed to the frenetic, digitally mediated sights and sounds of Hollywood blockbusters, the stillness, silence, and sheer naturalness of Kim's vision demand an adjustment of sorts. The film invites Western audiences into a contemplative mode of film-going with which they are hardly familiar. In doing so, it forces filmgoers to slow down, to take stock of when and where their passions have perhaps become misdirected.

While North American viewers may never be able fully to inhabit the conceptual space of an Asian character or filmmaker, it is likely that they have all experienced a moment when, like the young apprentice, their unchecked desires got the better of them. It may not be a universal human experience, but it surely comes close. Indeed, one would be hard-pressed to find anyone who had never made the mistake of disregarding the voice of wisdom to pursue something far less substantive or enduring. In this way, *Spring, Summer, Fall, Winter . . . and Spring* lays bare the world with which we are familiar, exposing the emptiness of so many of our desires.

If only things were so simple. One of the challenges we face while engaging world cinema is the tendency to "exoticize" the other by valorizing certain cinematic depictions of a culture or religion simply because they are radically different from our own. Especially in Western contexts, audiences are prone (and often prompted) to uncritically embrace films that reinforce their preconceived (i.e., Western) notions about the cultural or religious other while, at the very same time, making generalizations about the whole of a culture or society based solely on these (often narrowly conceived) representations. In doing so, we as filmgoers run the risk of grossly misunderstanding the other (even enacting a kind of symbolic violence on them) and of foreclosing any possibility that the other could grant us new eyes to see and be seen.

Indeed, in her *Silver Screen Buddha*, Sharon Suh suggests that, in spite of its critical acclaim, *Spring, Summer, Fall, Winter . . . and Spring* is a prime example of a movie that (perhaps unknowingly) contributes "to the perpetuation of a narrowly conceived Buddhism characterized by the male monastic virtuoso as primary religious specialist, and meditation as the primary practice at the expense of other vibrant forms. As a result, popular perceptions of Buddhism give undue primacy to ascetic forms of Buddhism that come to be identified with 'proper' Buddhism."[9] Suh goes on to suggest that the problem with Kim's film is not that the movie itself is poorly executed—in terms of aesthetics, it is simply beautiful, which is partly why so many viewers fail (according to Suh) to recognize the narrowness of its vision. Rather, the problems with the film have as much if not more to do with the ways in which American audiences receive and internalize the movie's depictions of Buddhism:

> The Oriental Monk as a signifier of otherness, exoticism, nurturing, and femininity is also implicated in current American struggles to both contain and reframe Asian religions in ways that appease the desire for difference while rendering this difference tolerable for the viewer. In so doing, it is the viewer, and not the

viewed, that remains in the position of power through the act of looking as the Oriental Monk soon comes to symbolize a virile white male Euro-American identity constructed over and against Asian and Asian American difference.[10]

According to Suh, the film domesticates "Asian-ness" in order to make it more palatable for American audiences; even more problematically, however, it deals uncritically with the Buddhist treatment of women. Because the Buddhist disciplines found in the ancient monastic codes of the *Vinaya* conceive of sexual desire as one of the main reasons why (male) monks remain trapped in the cycle of rebirth known as *samsara*, women's bodies often function as both the primary source of (male) spiritual struggle and a crucial hurdle one must overcome on the journey toward enlightenment. Suh is quick to point out that Kim's film is a rather antiquated and uncharitable depiction of Buddhist teachings—one that might be easily dismissed as "vintage sexism"—but that is exactly why, in her estimation, it is so important to call out such a restricted vision of the religious other. Even in a film as lauded and laudable as *Spring, Summer, Fall, Winter . . . and Spring*, what we actually witness is a young man achieving enlightenment only when he realizes that his sexual desire is the very source of suffering that has kept him tethered to this ephemeral world. But, we might ask, at what cost? Or, perhaps better, at *whose* cost?

From Suh's perspective, it is clearly women who pay the ultimate price for this vision of Buddhism, both in the film and in the broader society:

> The film reaffirms the textual perspective that women bind men to samsara and yet, unlike the canonical texts [i.e., the *Vinaya Pitaka*], Kim's film holds up the possibility that were it not for the women's seductive powers, the monks might never reach enlightenment and liberation. . . . The men are driven to murder, experience desire and remorse, and therefore mature on the path to liberation, while women in the Buddhist world seduce with their duplicitous bodies and minds, trap their men, and are ultimately killed off.[11]

Suh is right to name the "orientalizing" and "exoticizing" tendencies in Kim's work, especially as it concerns the ways in which women are conceptualized and depicted onscreen. And her overarching critique is one that we would do well to remember: that is, just because a film exposes us to otherness does not automatically mean that the vision it provides is good or true or beautiful. Likewise, to strictly equate "foreign" with "insightful" or "visionary" is to traffic in the very ethnocentric reductions we want to avoid.[12]

That being said, we also want to be careful not to overstate the matter, in large part because, as we have mentioned before, our methodological priority is to appreciate before we appraise. Maintaining this kind of appreciative posture is perhaps even more important when we are attempting to unpack the power and meaning of a film that originates from a context radically different from our own. Given that there is so much potential for cross-cultural *mis*understanding, we want to acknowledge genuine critiques of a film like *Spring, Summer, Fall, Winter . . . and Spring*. Nevertheless, we also want to remain open and sensitive to ways in which it might serve as a means for us to experience the world "from there," even if imperfectly and only for a moment.

Departures *(2008)*

Needless to say, no interaction with such diverse cinematic representations is ever going to be "pure" or "simple," so it makes little sense to throw the baby out with the bathwater. Still, some films present us with a different sort of encounter that seems to expand rather than constrict our imagination, even while offering us a rich and compelling (i.e., complex) depiction of otherness. Yôjirô Takita's *Departures* (original Japanese title: *Okuribito*) is a prime example. Winner of the Oscar for Best Foreign Language Film in 2009, *Departures* is the story of Daigo Kobayashi, an erstwhile cellist who, after his symphony dissolves, moves back to his hometown with his wife to start their lives over. He responds to a classified ad for the NK Agency with the title "assisting departures," believing it to be a travel agency of some kind. Much to Daigo's surprise, it turns out that "NK" actually stands for *nōkan*, a person who prepares bodies for passage into the next life. Before he fully realizes what has transpired, Daigo is hired on the spot to work as an encoffiner.

Much about *Departures* is quite endearing—from the various awkward yet comical situations Daigo encounters with families of the deceased, to his growing awareness of his true vocation in spite of the stigma it carries, to the poignant moment when he prepares his estranged father's body for cremation. But it is the film's celebration of the mundane that infuses Daigo's story with such life—a story that is, somewhat paradoxically, about death and dying. This affirmation of the everyday resonates far more with the religious vision of Shin Buddhism · than the Theravada Buddhism that orients *Spring, Summer, Fall, Winter . . . and Spring*. According to Shin Buddhist scholar Taitetsu Unno, the stream of Buddhist thought depicted in *Departures* is one that encourages viewers to form a "deep appreciation for the preciousness of this fragile life on earth, prompted by an awareness that death can instantly end this human life, a life that can never be repeated in eternity. . . . [Shin] Buddhism does not negate life but affirms life, including everything within it—despair, frustration, and anger."[13]

In one of the film's key scenes, Daigo's mentor, Mr. Sasaki, invites Daigo to the top floor of the NK Agency for lunch. At this point in the narrative, Daigo's

Departures (2008), © Departures Film Partners

wife has left him because of his job's poor reputation within Japanese culture, so he is struggling to reconcile both his failing marriage and his own conflicted sense of self-worth. As he makes his way to the lunch table, Daigo navigates a lush and verdant room filled with all manner of plant life. In the midst of this office-garden sits a picture of Mr. Sasaki's deceased wife, his first client as a *nōkan*. While the mentor and his apprentice grill and eat puffer fish together, Mr. Sasaki reflects on the fragile beauty of life: "Even this [fish] is a corpse. The living eat the dead. Unless you want to die, you eat. And if you eat, eat well."

Even without this dialogue, the soundtrack makes Mr. Sasaki's point re-soundingly clear. The crackle of fish sizzling on an open grill, the slurping of hot fish into their mouths, and the thickness of teeth chewing on the corpses of puffer fish all work together to emphasize a single point with visceral clarity: not only is death a natural part of life, but it creates the very conditions for the living to flourish. This fact means that the choice before these two men is not whether to live or to die, but whether they will enjoy life while it's still here.

The notion that life is fundamentally impermanent is thoroughly Buddhist, but it also shares similarities with the Wisdom literature in the Hebrew Bible. The book of Ecclesiastes, for example, offers what could easily serve as a tagline for *Departures*: "It is better to go to a house of mourning than to go to a house of feasting, for death is the destiny of everyone; the living should take this to heart" (Eccles. 7:2).

What is actually gained by contemplating the unsettling reality that life is short and we are all on a slow and painful march toward death? Mr. Sasaki and the author of Ecclesiastes would likely offer a similar response. It is only when we accept the universality and inevitability of death that we are able to receive life as the gift that it is. Life is unexpected. It is breathtaking. And it doesn't last long. So eat well. Or, to put it a bit differently, "I commend the enjoyment of life, because there is nothing better for a person under the sun than to eat and drink and be glad. Then joy will accompany them in their toil all the days of the life God has given them under the sun" (Eccles. 8:15).

The contrast between *Departures* and *Spring, Summer, Fall, Winter . . . and Spring* now appears even more striking. Rather than commending the enjoyment of life's sensual pleasures given the inevitability of death, Kim's film seems to extol detachment from life and the uprooting of desire. As a consequence, if we understand Kim's film to be a normative depiction of Buddhism, we are left with a somewhat truncated vision of the cultural and religious other. It certainly provides viewers with a unique opportunity to envision the world through a different set of eyes, but in doing so, it elevates a detached kind of asceticism over and against an empathetic engagement with other flesh-and-blood human beings.

Departures, however, assumes a different posture. It leans toward rather than away from the concrete difficulties that otherness entails. On a purely narrative level, by treating the bodies of those who have "departed" with dignity and honor, Daigo creates a ritual space for family members of the deceased to encounter each other as the utterly complicated human beings that they truly are. The scene in which he carefully attends both to the body of a transgendered woman and to the family members who loved her serves as a prime example of this dynamic. After her grief-stricken father and mother instruct Mr. Sasaki and Daigo to prepare the body with women's makeup, the father states aloud: "Once he went like he did, we did nothing but fight. After that I was not seeing him. But when I saw him smile I remembered him. He may dress like a girl, but he is still my son." It is thus in and through Daigo's ritual preparations that the father and, indeed, the entire family are finally able to mourn the loss of this precious child. In doing so, they are able to overcome the differences that set them apart, not by ignoring complexity or brushing it aside, but by embracing each other, perhaps for the very first time.

Daigo's interaction with bereaved families also corresponds to the ways in which the film engages the viewer. According to Suh, "*Departures* can be seen as devotional in and of itself. Each ritual ceremony creates that moment of nowness whereby viewers come to appreciate the oneness that characterizes the relationship between all beings—the living and the dead."[14] By opening up a space in which filmgoers are encouraged to reflect on death and dying through the eyes of the cultural and religious other, *Departures* invites audience members to assume a more empathetic posture toward the outsider and alien in their midst. It is an invitation neither to exoticize nor to romanticize otherness, but to see the other as beautifully mundane, which is to say, just like us.

If space allowed, we could expand our engagement with world cinema far beyond the confines of Korea and Japan. Thankfully, entire volumes now exist that do exactly this. Some scholars have focused on the oeuvre of a single auteur, such as Mathew P. John's insightful book on the work of Indo-Canadian filmmaker Deepa Mehta (*Film as Cultural Artifact: Religious Criticism of World Cinema*).[15] Others have examined a wider array of films that contribute to our theological understanding of both the divine and the human other. For instance, in *World Cinema, Theology, and the Human*, Antonio Sison explores the cultural and anthropological richness of an incredibly diverse set of movies like *Babette's Feast* (1986), *Be with Me* (2005), *Billy Elliot* (2000), *The Son* (2002), *Lagaan* (2001), and *Whale Rider* (2002).[16] But whether one casts the net wide or deep, the goal remains the same. We are seeking to take a small step toward embracing the cultural and religious other in and through our engagement with the cinematic other. In doing so, we hope to cultivate a generative space in which we find, in the words of Sison, an "alternative spiritual path to possibility by way of cinematic language."[17]

Encountering the Racial(ized) Other

In an increasingly globalized world, identifying constructive possibilities for encountering the cultural and religious other is an important endeavor. But the human tendency to magnify the differences that distinguish one "tribe" from another is not simply the result of globalization. It is also, and perhaps most often, an intensely local phenomenon. And in an American context, it's a phenomenon that is decidedly racial(ized).

One of our operating assumptions is that lay and professional theologians have a unique opportunity to respond to the demonization of otherness that characterizes the contemporary cultural context by "fostering the kind of social agents capable of envisioning and creating just, truthful, and peaceful societies, and [by] shaping a cultural climate in which such agents will thrive."[18] Film can potentially foster these kinds of empathetic agents and cultivate these kinds of generative spaces because, on a very basic level, movies allow viewers to see the world from a different perspective—to catch a glimpse of the world "from there." To quote filmmaker Matt Ruskin, in a real-world context in which encounters with the racial(ized) other are so often marred by violence, injustice, and death, "any story that makes people think about that [reality]—that makes people think about the human beings involved—is a good thing."[19]

One might expect that the Christian community would be leading the way in telling the types of stories Ruskin is describing—stories that envision the racial other not as an "other" but as a fellow human being. Tragically, though, this is often not the case. Although individual Christians and faith-based organizations have been key players in nearly every civil rights movement throughout US history, all too often the people of God as a whole have remained silent or simply apathetic in the face of the systemic injustices that continue to plague American society. Indeed, if recent polling data is any indication, white evangelical Christians in particular are unwilling to acknowledge that a racial problem even exists, much less consider how the good news of God's kingdom might compel the community of faith to respond.[20] But as Jesus reminded the Pharisees, when his followers are silent, Scripture says that "the stones will cry out" (Luke 19:40).

Perhaps for this very reason filmmakers are increasingly telling stories of racial injustice, crying out to a seemingly deaf culture. Yet these stories rarely generate the kind of audience or the box-office receipts that most Hollywood blockbusters do. Part of the problem has to do with audience expectations. Viewers pining for the next installment of the *Avengers* franchise are typically unwilling to commit their time and financial resources to a film that might challenge their understanding of racial dynamics and, in doing so, force them to reflect on certain harsh realities.

But this view may treat the movie-going public a bit too critically. A more straightforward explanation would simply be that most filmgoers come to the Cineplex to experience, first and foremost, an entertaining story. If an engrossing film also contains critical commentary about societal problems, then audiences are more than willing to be challenged. But even the most important movie on racial injustice will likely never be able to generate a broad audience if it is not, in some way, also entertaining.

Additional forces come into play here as well, though, and they too reflect the profoundly racialized nature of the film industry (and American culture more broadly). Many major studios are often less than willing to produce and distribute certain films because they continue to operate with the illusion (delusion?) that movies featuring diverse casts and diverse topics are less profitable than movies framed along the lines of white, male, heteronormativity. As the data on top-grossing movies continues to grow, however, "the numbers suggest a more diverse cast brings a more diverse audience, which brings in more money."[21]

Hollywood is producing an increasing number of major films featuring a greater amount of onscreen diversity (e.g., *Star Wars: The Force Awakens* [2016], *Get Out* [2017], *Crazy Rich Asians* [2018]). This is of course something to be celebrated. But it also means that studios and filmmakers who once hid behind the convenient excuse that diverse films simply did not make any money can no longer do so. Somewhat ironically, what had once been seen as an impediment to creating racially diverse casts (i.e., economics) may ultimately be the very thing that prompts Hollywood to take its own product seriously as a potentially constructive encounter with the racial other.

As the #OscarsSoWhite boycott of the 2016 Academy Awards suggests, however, Hollywood still has a long way to go. Indeed, as it currently stands, movies that directly address racial injustice often gain a wider audience only after they have emerged as darlings of the film festival circuit (e.g., *12 Years a Slave* [2013] and *Moonlight* [2016]). And while exceptions certainly exist (e.g., *Selma* [2014] and *Hidden Figures* [2016]), these independently financed "festival films" have become not only a helpful barometer for measuring the current state of the contemporary cultural imagination but also the de facto moral conscience of US culture.[22]

Consider the recent slate of movies coming out of the Sundance Film Festival—the largest and best-known independent film festival in the US. Before she directed *Selma* (2014), *13th* (2016), and *A Wrinkle in Time* (2018) for studios, Ava DuVernay won the directing award for US Dramatic Film for *Middle of Nowhere* (2012), a film about how the incarceration of an African American man affects his spouse. In 2013, the Grand Jury Prize and Audience Award went to Ryan Coogler's *Fruitvale Station* (2013), a dramatic retelling of the transit-officer shooting of Oscar Grant. In 2016, Nate Parker's *Birth of a Nation* (2016) also captured the Grand Jury Prize and the Audience Award, setting a record along the way when Twentieth Century Fox purchased the film for $17 million.

Shortly after it was purchased, however, *Birth of a Nation* met a fate similar to that of its protagonist, the slave-turned-preacher and revolt leader Nat Turner. Fox quietly abandoned *Birth of a Nation* when it was revealed that Nate Parker had been accused but then acquitted of sexual assault as a college student. Yet that very same Oscar season, Casey Affleck, who had recently settled two different sexual harassment lawsuits, garnered the award for Best Actor for his role in *Manchester by the Sea*. One film critic noted,

> The [Parker/Affleck] parallel is an important one. Of course, Parker was accused of a different, more serious crime—raping a female college student. [But] Parker was acquitted, while Affleck settled. Then there's the fact that Nate Parker is a black man. Like Affleck, the actor and director had been fast-tracked for critical acclaim and stardom. Considering the fact that Parker's career has taken a fatal hit, we have to ask why Affleck's history continues to be hidden paragraphs deep, or swept under the rug entirely.[23]

In other words, in a cruel twist of racial(ized) irony, both *Birth of a Nation* and its writer/director/star became victims of a rigged system that continues to privilege one skin color over another.

In spite of their limited commercial and critical success outside the festival circuit, *Middle of Nowhere, Fruitvale Station*, and *Birth of a Nation* nonetheless set the stage for an influx of films about racial injustice at the 2017 festival. Matt Ruskin's *Crown Heights* (2017), which took home the Audience Award for the US dramatic film competition, tells the true story of Colin Warner, an African American man who was wrongfully imprisoned for over twenty years. The award for US documentary directing went to Peter Nicks for *The Force* (2017), a film that details the work of Oakland police chief Sean Whent. Yance Ford's *Strong Island* (2017), a cinematic memoir about the killing of Ford's older brother, won a special Jury Award for storytelling. And a trio of African American film-makers, Sabaah Folayan, Sabaah Jordan, and Damon Davis, premiered *Whose Streets?*, a *vérité*-style documentary about the aftermath of the fatal shooting by a police officer of eighteen-year-old Michael Brown in Ferguson, Missouri, in August 2014.

None of these films were "successful" at the box office, at least not by *Avengers* standards. But they do give voice to the racial tensions that continue to percolate just under the surface of our cultural consciousness, even if the larger film-going public hesitates to acknowledge them—which brings us back to an important question: Can a film actually prompt viewers to become agents of racial justice if it cannot (or does not) capture their imagination, that is, if it isn't on some level entertaining? *Los Angeles Times* film critic Steven Zeitchik has raised a similar question, not only about Sundance films, but about audiovisual narratives in general:

> Taking a serious social issue and crafting it into screen narrative means either diluting it for mass consumption or retaining its seriousness and reaching far fewer people. It's the difference between "The Butler" and "The Black Panthers: Vanguard of the Revolution." This poses an ethical problem, since it means that, to sway a larger number of minds, one must turn mistreatment into entertainment. And it poses a practical challenge, since it means that writers on a television series [or a movie] need take a topic of deep seriousness and embroider into it some of the shinier tricks of an "Empire" or "Scandal."[24]

In other words, there is an inherent tension built into the medium of film-making between commercial viability and social conscientiousness. One of the few exceptions is *BlacKkKlansman* (2018), Spike Lee's entertaining and confrontational film, which manages to find a healthy balance between the two.

Along similar lines, Ryan Coogler followed up *Fruitvale Station* by reinvigorating the Rocky franchise with *Creed* (2015) and by directing *Black Panther* (2018) for Marvel. Coogler didn't sell out; he sold in. To borrow the words of Reggie Rock Bythewood, creator of *Shots Fired*, Fox's ten-hour series about two racially charged shootings in a small Southern town that premiered its first two episodes at the 2017 Sundance Film Festival, "Our creed was to get the audience on the edge of their seats and when they're leaning forward hit them with the truth."[25]

In our "post-truth" world, we are in desperate need of prophetic voices from DuVernay, Coogler, and Rock Bythewood to deliver heavy doses of truth in equally engrossing packages. But even when a filmmaker strikes the perfect balance between truth telling and entertainment, waking people up to the truth of racial injustice will only ever be a pyrrhic victory unless this truth lands in a generative space—one in which individuals and communities are given the opportunity to be and become agents who pursue a just and peaceful society. Put differently, films can provide us with a unique and powerful occasion for encountering the racial other, but in the absence of a broader collective discourse motivated by a desire to overcome that otherness, movies are by themselves incapable of shaping a cultural climate in which such agents will thrive. Like so much great art, films help us see our problems with a clarity we never knew possible. But they stop short of providing us with clear-cut answers. Instead, they offer up an invitation that calls for our response.

It is this "respond-ability" that best defines the theological task as it relates to the ways in which the cinema imagines racial injustice and otherness. Certain films are able to generate a shared experience and a common vocabulary in the midst of an otherwise racially dis-integrated context. But lay and professional theologians alike are responsible for creating the kind of space that might foster and sustain the viewer's capacity to embrace the racial(ized) other rather than violently exclude them. And if this is indeed the case, then, as Zeitchik suggests, perhaps the work of engaging film theologically is more "like the work of improving the criminal justice system—incremental, difficult, and not always productive. Maybe the idea is not to change a culture or system wholesale but to chip away at individuals, one streamed episode or movie ticket at a time."[26]

Encountering the Other

We have been making some rather bold claims in this chapter about the ways in which film opens up possibilities for encountering both the human other and the divine Other. But as we have suggested all along, these claims are conditional. That is, they hinge on a rather big "if." *If cultivated properly*, the cinema *can* serve as a theologically expansive space in which viewers are able to experience the world "from there" and through which these viewers *might* develop a more empathetic posture toward any and all others in their midst. This, of course, is not to say that individual films are entirely incapable of bringing about a real shift in public consciousness. Among others, we could point to *To Kill a Mockingbird* (1962), *Do the Right Thing* (1989), *Philadelphia* (1993), *Schindler's List* (1993), *An Inconvenient Truth* (2006), *Blackfish* (2013), or *Moonlight* (2016) as prominent examples of films that seared themselves into the contemporary cultural imagination in significant ways. Individual viewers may have chosen not to accept the vision of otherness that each of these films portrayed, but in terms of the effect they had on broader cultural conversations, there simply was no going back.

But these are notable exceptions that seem to prove the rule, for if it is to bring about meaningful change in how viewers understand and encounter otherness, even the best of world cinema and the most racially "woke" films still need to land in a generative space that can foster and sustain a movie's invitation to embrace the other in love. Theologically speaking, this has both external and internal implications. Internally, the Christian community in the United States at the dawn of the twenty-first century has, more times than not, failed to cultivate these kinds of spaces within the church, much less in contexts populated by those who do not identify with the Christian tradition. As a result, if lay and professional theologians have any hope for creating public (i.e., external) spaces for encountering the cultural, religious, and racial(ized) other in and through film, we need first to cultivate this kind of space for members of our own tribe. After all, as Volf reminds us, when it comes to otherness, the real source of our fear and anxiety is not some radically unknowable other "out there" but the strangeness that always already resides in ourselves.

A prime example of the problem that currently threatens the community of faith from within can be found in the divergent responses to recent "biblical" films that have been released in the past decade, including *Son of God* (2014), *Noah* (2014), *Exodus: Gods and Kings* (2014), *Last Days in the Desert* (2015), *The Young Messiah* (2016), and *Paul, Apostle of Christ* (2018). It often seems that Christian filmgoers, theologians, and film critics are fundamentally at odds concerning how best to understand the power and meaning of these films. For instance, as Rob points out in his article on viewer responses to Darren Aronofsky's *Noah*, certain Christian reviewers denounced the film as a heretical "distortion" of the biblical narrative, while others praised it for its imaginative faithfulness to the tradition of Jewish Midrash, and still others acknowledged that, whether "good" or "bad," the film had a dramatic effect in terms of leading people to consult the biblical text after seeing the film version.[27]

This wide range of responses by Christian viewers is significant given that the source material for *Noah* serves as an authoritative text for numerous religious traditions. But it isn't the lack of interpretive consensus that should trouble us. This kind of plurality should be expected. The best, most enduring narratives almost always produce a range of valid yet divergent interpretations. The biblical story is no different. However, what should be troubling is the utter lack of basic conversational skills that Christian critics demonstrate, not only toward a given film, but also toward other Christians (and representatives of other religious traditions) whose interpretations differ from their own. In the current climate, one's take on a film has become emblematic of something much more than a personal construal of a cultural product. Rather than a starting point for a collaborative conversation, individual interpretations are now functioning absolutely—as if they were the universal criteria by which we might identify and permanently excise alternative (i.e., "heretical") interpretations from the community of faith.[28]

When this kind of absolutizing takes place, there is no longer any space for establishing a middle ground, or engaging in an interpretive to-and-fro, or acknowledging multiple understandings of a film that are equally valid, for the gospel itself is under threat. Or, as one Christian critic put it,

> Let me tell you what the real scandal in all of this is. It isn't that he [i.e., Aronofsky] made a film that departed from the biblical story. It isn't that disappointed and overheated Christian critics had expectations set too high. The scandal is this: of all the Christian leaders who went to great lengths to endorse this movie (for whatever reasons: "it's a conversation starter," "at least Hollywood is doing something on the Bible," etc.), and [of all] the Christian leaders who panned it for "not following the Bible" . . . *not one of them could identify a blatantly Gnostic subversion of the biblical story when it was right in front of their faces.* I believe Aronofsky did it as an experiment to make fools of us. . . . He's having quite the laugh. And shame on everyone who bought it.[29]

What we often fail to see in the midst of these intratribal squabbles about who is the greater "fool" and who should bear the most "shame" is that our collective rush to offer critical condemnation or effusive praise of a film (and by extension, each other) tends to shut down rather than open up spaces in which we might listen to and learn from others who might see the world differently than we do. And the church's seeming inability to cultivate these kinds of generative spaces has led to an increasingly fragmented and tribalized notion of Christian community—one comprising isolated echo chambers filled with people who cannot communicate, much less commune, with those who do not think, talk, and act exactly as they do. The question then is whether the church will simply continue to echo the wider culture and its politics or whether she will lead the way by modeling a more constructive form of public dialogue.

In an important sense, the core issue in play here is not even about film, but about theological hermeneutics. We have suggested in previous chapters that the hermeneutic we have chosen to adopt is an expression of a prior theological framework that takes seriously God's wider presence in the world. From this theological starting point we have suggested that, if the Spirit of God is indeed present and active in the cinema and culture more broadly, then we would do well to listen to and learn from what God has to say. Unlike King Josiah, we do not wish to oppose God by refusing to acknowledge either the medium or the mediator that God has chosen (2 Chron. 35:21). As it pertains to cinematic renderings of the biblical text in particular, it is God's presence in culture that allows us to "reverse the hermeneutical flow" without fear or anxiety. If all truth is God's truth, then we can trust the ways in which a film might crack open our reading of the biblical text.

Discernment is always needed, and for this reason maintaining an interpretive community is so important. We need the perspective of the "other" to help us see beyond our own limited vision. But our first step must always be to appreciate before we appraise. That appreciation takes film seriously as a potential source for revelatory insight before we too quickly condemn it (and each other) either as a subversion of the gospel, as heretical, or worst of all(!), as "unbiblical."

This leads us directly to a final if/then statement. *If* our theology of the Spirit's wider presence allows us to assume this kind of open and generous posture toward even the most profane of messengers, *then* surely it demands that we do the same with our fellow Christians. Indeed, as Paul reminds us: "There are different kinds of gifts, but the same Spirit distributes them. There are different kinds of service, but the same Lord. There are different kinds of working, but in all of them and in everyone it is the same God at work. Now to each one the manifestation of the Spirit is given for the common good. . . . For we were all baptized by one Spirit so as to form one body—whether Jews or Gentiles, slave or free—and we were all given the one Spirit to drink" (1 Cor. 12:4–7, 13).

Our pneumatology matters. Because the Spirit who confronts us in the cinema is the very same Spirit who draws together the people of God, our willingness to encounter the cultural, religious, and racial other in and through film must also apply to the other we encounter within the body of Christ. The three of us (Rob, Craig, and Kutter) admit that this is far easier said than done because it forces us to stay engaged with this dysfunctional family known as the church. We all know family members can be obnoxious at times (ourselves included). But in a cultural climate that is increasingly polarized, partisan, and wont to radicalize every kind of otherness, the people of God need to double down on our Spirit-infused commitment to each other—even and perhaps especially when we disagree.

For this reason one of our central theological tasks in this chapter has been to identify films that can help us generate spaces in which agents who envision a just and peaceful society might thrive. By doing so, we aren't suggesting that the Spirit merely supports or comes alongside our feeble (and ultimately futile) attempts to embrace the other. Something much more radical is taking place. To borrow from the eighteenth-century theologian Friedrich Schleiermacher, it is only when our hearts are "lovingly directed towards the other" that "something still higher" emerges.[30] Our embrace of the human other creates the necessary conditions for an encounter with the divine Other. In this divine-human exchange, we are not the subject but the object. In an ultimate sense, agency is taken out of our hands. The Other happens to us. Whether in film or in the body of Christ, we only ever overcome otherness when the Other overcomes us.

Discussion Questions

1. Have you ever watched a foreign film? What did you learn about the culture portrayed? How did it broaden your understanding of God's world?
2. How would you describe your "from here" perspective? What would it look like for you to take up a "from there" viewpoint?
3. In our attempt to embrace the cultural and religious other, is film-going enough? Or does the overcoming of otherness require something more? If so, what?
4. What role might faith communities in particular play in addressing our tendency to radicalize and demonize the other? How can watching a movie like *The Shape of Water* help in this regard?

10

the trauma of love in the films of christopher nolan

converging lenses

At a time in cinematic history when sequels, reboots, and franchise films seem to be the norm, a small handful of filmmakers have been able to maintain a certain level of creative control over their productions. Among others, Wes Anderson (*The Grand Budapest Hotel*), Terrence Malick (*Tree of Life*), Sofia Coppola (*Lost in Translation*), the Wachowskis (*The Matrix* trilogy), Denis Villeneuve (*Arrival*), Paul Thomas Anderson (*There Will Be Blood*), Darren Aronofsky (*Black Swan*), and Martin Scorsese (*The Wolf of Wall Street*) have each made indelible films that resonate with the zeitgeist of the new millennium.

Yet none of these modern-day auteurs have matched the critical acclaim and box-office success of Christopher Nolan. Not everyone is a fan of Nolan's work (or of his more passionate fan base), but since the year 2000, every single film that Christopher Nolan has both written and directed has appeared at some point in the IMDb's all-time top 250 list.[1] At the time of this writing, only three are outside the top 100, and five are in the top 50: *Dunkirk* is tied for number 250 and *Batman Begins* (2005) is ranked at number 116, followed by *The Dark Knight Rises* (2012) at number 66, *The Prestige* (2006) at number 49, *Memento* (2000) at number 50, *Interstellar* (2014) at number 32, and *Inception* (2010) at number 14. Indeed, there are only three movies in the entire history of film that the users of the IMDb have rated higher than *The Dark Knight* (2008): *The Shawshank Redemption*, *The Godfather*, and *The Godfather: Part II*.

In addition, Nolan's films have collectively earned over $4.7 billion (and counting) at the global box office, and four are among the one hundred highest grossing movies of all time.[2] His movies feature some of the most acclaimed actors in Hollywood: Leonardo DiCaprio, Jessica Chastain, Matthew McConaughey, Anne Hathaway, Christian Bale, Maggie Gyllenhall, Heath Ledger, Marion Cotillard, Morgan Freeman, Joseph Gordon-Levitt, Ellen Page, Michael Caine, Tom Hardy, Hugh Jackman, and Scarlett Johansson—it's a veritable "who's who" of A-list talent.

Regardless of the metrics we use to evaluate his work, Christopher Nolan's movies have captivated the contemporary cultural imagination. Given his commercial and critical success, Nolan is almost singular among his generation of filmmakers. He manages to merge the brains of Stanley Kubrick with the popular (populist?) instincts of Steven Spielberg. As a result, Nolan's oeuvre functions as a kind of genre unto itself. His films are often heady, philosophical puzzles that reward multiple viewings among die-hard fans. They also work for the more casual filmgoer, even (and perhaps especially) when they upset audience expectations. But even more importantly (at least as it relates to our purposes), Nolan's films routinely confront filmgoers with expressly theological questions.

To say that Nolan's movies are "theological" is not to say that God makes any cameos. Indeed, God is notably absent from these narrative worlds. Nevertheless, at seemingly every turn, Nolan's films explore the fundamental nature of what it means to be human, how we relate to the broader society in which we live, and what, if anything, exists "beyond" the horizon of our humanity. The consistency of Nolan's creative vision may have something to do with the integral contribution of Emma Thomas, who has produced all of Nolan's feature-length films. As his wife and co-producer, she has been a constant who may only get the credit she is due long afterward as his "silent partner" in all things—art and life. Regardless, when combined with the sheer popularity of their movies, the recurring themes this dynamic duo explores in their films do more than invite theological dialogue. They demand it.

At the end of the day, "deep focus" is about our respond-ability in the face of this cinematic invitation (or in the case of Nolan's films, this demand). Placing film and theology into dialogue is, at its most basic, the practice of seeing and responding, encountering stories that both interpret us and are interpreted by us. This dynamic to-and-fro, however, cannot remain dispassionate if it is to be appropriate to the invitation of the movie story itself. Like all great stories, films provide an interpretation of life, inviting viewers to respond from their own perspective concerning life's power and meaning. It is a response that requires the whole of our selves. The very artistic shape of a movie invites more than mere conversation. It prods us toward communion. Thus, our response to a movie (and its governing convictions) needs to be completed from a definite theological perspective.

With this particular aim in mind, the previous chapters have presented a series of interpretive lenses (narrative, audiovisual, critical, ecclesial, theological, ethical, cultural), each of which helps us unpack the power and meaning of a movie on its own terms. In this final chapter, as our study of the inter-relationship of Christian theology and contemporary movies draws to a close, we offer an extended example designed to illustrate what it looks like when these lenses converge in practice. For all the reasons listed above, we have chosen to focus our gaze on the films of Christopher Nolan, which means that we are applying these multiple lenses to the study of an auteur (otherwise known as "auteur theory"). In doing so, we hope to demonstrate not only the utility of our approach, but also our conviction that the interpretive clarity and depth of understanding we seek (i.e., a "deep focus") can only ever emerge from the kind of creative convergence that stands at the heart of our project.

Narrative Lens: *Following* and *Memento*

> Memories are an interpretation not a record, and they're irrelevant if you want the truth.
>
> —Leonard, *Memento*

Although less known than his recent blockbusters, Nolan's first feature-length film, *Following* (1998), bears many of the same narrative markers emblematic of his unique cinematic style. Chief among others is his use of nonlinear narratives and unreliable narrators. A narrative lens is particularly helpful in unpacking the power and meaning of Nolan's work. For example, the principal character in *Following* is a man sometimes called Bill who gets caught up in an elaborate scheme that eventually lands him in police custody as the primary suspect of a murder. At first blush, the movie has all the makings of a classic film noir: it's shot in black and white; its characters are defined by action; it explores the dark, seedy, and often violent underbelly of criminal life; and the deeply flawed protagonist is even seduced by a femme fatale. But for Nolan, the generic conventions of noir are simply the starting point for his larger project of deconstruction and reconstruction. Rather than play according to the rules of the genre, he intentionally subverts the story's narrative form by splicing together four different phases of what is otherwise a fairly linear tale.

Nolan distinguishes between the chronologically distinct segments in *Following* primarily through visual cues. From one scene to the next, Bill, the writer-turned-petty thief, is depicted as either disheveled, or well groomed, or battered and bruised. But there is no indication as to whether one phase precedes or follows the others. By upending the traditional three-part structure of film narrative that depends on a clear beginning, middle, and end, the causal chain linking one event to the next simply evaporates, forcing the viewer to find coherence through some other means.

It isn't until the final moments of the film, when we discover that Bill is narrating the story while under police interrogation, that we are able to piece together the "real" order of events. The result is that both Bill and the audience become aware at one and the same time that they have been duped. While Bill is taken into custody for a murder he didn't commit, we come to realize our omniscient narrator was not so omniscient after all. Everything we've seen and heard emerged from the highly subjective perspective of a morally questionable narrator who was himself being double-crossed (or more accurately, triple-crossed) by a man (Cobb) who constructed the entire ruse to entrap us all.

Realizing the whole thing is a con is certainly an eye-opening moment to say the least. For perhaps the first time, we as the audience are able to see the narrative world with a degree of clarity because our field of view has at last expanded beyond the subjectivity of a single character. But this renewed vision comes at a cost, for what it reveals is the true depths of our blindness. That is, just like Bill, the whole of our reality is always already subjective, limited, and perspectival. Interpretation goes all the way down.

Nolan's penchant for creating noir-like narrative worlds that audiences experience through the subjective gaze of an unreliable narrator is clearly on display in *Memento* (2000), the film that effectively put him on the map. Like *Following*, *Memento* also features a fractured narrative recounted by a protagonist who is about as far from omniscient as one could possibly imagine.[3] But in Nolan's second film, the fractured narrative becomes an explicit part of the plot itself. Leonard Shelby, the main character, suffers from anterograde amnesia, which means that he cannot create new memories. Leonard's short-term memory loss is especially problematic given that he is attempting to find the person who murdered his wife. After all, detective work is hard enough as it is, let alone for a vigilante with a faulty memory. As a consequence, Leonard takes up the practice of tattooing clues onto his body and writing notes to himself on Polaroids in order to make up for his frequent cognitive lapses.

But Leonard's memory loss is more than a part of his characterization. In Nolan's hands, it becomes an element of the storytelling apparatus itself. As Craig Detweiler notes in his insightful analysis of *Memento*, "[Nolan's] most important artistic decision was to put the viewers into Leonard's situation so we feel just as lost as our lead. The film doesn't analyze Leonard: it puts you literally inside his head."[4] To enhance the viewer's subjective experience of the story, it is Leonard who provides constant voice-over narration, as if we were located within his mind, hearing his internal monologue. But even more importantly, Nolan tells the story entirely backward. Mimicking something of what it must be like to suffer from short-term memory loss, each of the film's subsequent scenes begins without any of the narrative information we would normally have at our disposal to make sense of the events unfolding before us. So in one sequence we wake up with Leonard on the toilet of a hotel room with a bottle of vodka in our hand, not knowing how we got there or what we ought to do next. In the next we come to conscious awareness as we are sprinting through the middle of a parking lot, without any way of knowing whether we are chasing or being chased by the gun-wielding man who is in hot pursuit (note to self: we are being chased).

Interspersed throughout these reverse-order segments are scenes shot in black and white (another nod to the film noir genre), which we eventually recognize are organized chronologically. Once again, much like *Following*, the climax of *Memento* doesn't arrive until these forward-moving sequences converge with Leonard's quickly fading memory and our ever-accumulating knowledge of the narrative whole (or at least what we perceive to be the whole). And when this happens, an all-too-familiar realization dawns on those who have encountered Nolan's narrative worlds before: not only has our virtuous "hero" been manipulated and deceived by opportunists disguised as friends, but he's also been lying to himself. In the process, Leonard has deceived us, the audience, and betrayed our trust. Or is it rather that we are the ones who have misplaced our trust?

Leonard's righteous quest for vengeance turns out to be nothing more than a convenient fiction to justify his own existence. What's worse, we've been implicated in his self-serving deception. As Detweiler points out, it's possible to interpret this narrative move as a slide "into the worst kind of postmodern relativism." But if we let Nolan's work speak on its own terms, a far better take on the film is that "*Memento* reveals our endless capacity for self-deception."[5] For Detweiler, the heart of this film and Nolan's filmmaking in general is captured not in the denial of objective truth but rather in the human propensity for self-deception.

> To overcome the limits of our perception, we need frames of reference beyond ourselves. In his concluding speech, Lenny says, "I have to believe in a world outside my own mind. I have to believe actions still have meaning, even if I can't remember them. . . . We all need mirrors to remind ourselves who we are. I'm

no different." . . . *Memento* raises core questions of epistemology. It forces us to examine our receptors, our mirrors, lenses, and recording devices—basically our entire mental capacity. How do we know what we know? What kind of information do we trust? Are there objective facts or only subjective experiences?[6]

The inherent subjectivity (and thus limitations) of all knowledge, the infinitely interpretive nature of reality, and even the relativity of time itself—Nolan explores each of these themes time and again in his films. And when we consider the ways in which he is intentionally subverting narrative expectations in movies like *Following* and *Memento*, these epistemological concerns become all the more apparent.

But Nolan's films share another commonality—one that often precedes the formal structure of the narratives themselves and in many ways creates the very conditions for them to exist in the form they do. Simply put, his movies are all post-traumatic. The reason they are nonlinear, highly subjective, and told by unreliable narrators with incomplete or false knowledge is because, in every instance, the event that precedes the narrative proper (and continually pushes it forward) is itself a fracturing, dis-integrating, destabilizing experience of personal trauma. In other words, these stories have their origin in the catastrophic—literally a *kata-strophe* (from the Greek), an "over-turning." Nolan is interested not simply in the limits of human knowledge (i.e., epistemology) but in why (and how) we would dare to go on living in light of the deep and abiding trauma that constitutes the human condition.

Audiovisual Lens: *The Prestige* and *Inception*

Now you're looking for the secret, but you don't really want to work it out. You want to be fooled.

—Cutter, *The Prestige*

In nearly every one of Nolan's films, the originating trauma that haunts his narratives takes place prior (in story time) to the drama we see onscreen. In *Following*, it's two shockingly brutal murders that initiate both the primary narrative and its retelling. In *Memento*, it's the murder of Leonard's wife (possibly at his own hands) that serves as the impetus for the entire film. We might say the same is true for *The Prestige* (and it probably is), but we can never be entirely certain. In true Nolan form, it all might be an illusion—a *trompe l'oeil*. "Are you watching closely?" These are the first words uttered in the film, and they hide as much as they reveal, for the corresponding visuals we see—images of top hats on a forest floor—belong to a different time and place than that of the narrator's voice. So from the very start, we cannot trust what our eyes see or our ears hear. But that's the whole point, isn't it? We watch a magician (or movies about magicians) not to discover the truth—to know "how he does it"—but because we find pleasure in being deceived. As Cutter reminds us, we want to be fooled. Indeed, we yearn for it.

Beyond the obvious fact that *The Prestige* is a film about two ambitious illusionists trying to outclass one another (Christian Bale as Alfred Borden and Hugh Jackman as Robert Angier), the reason we are never entirely sure "when" a particular narrative event takes place in the film (or whether it even took place at all) is because of the formal techniques Nolan employs—namely, a deft combination of crosscutting and narrative "embedding" (which has everything to do with masterful editing). Like *Memento* and *Following* before it, *The Prestige* also features a nonlinear story, but Nolan adds an additional level of narrative complexity by incorporating what is actually a rather classic storytelling convention—the "discovered manuscript." More specifically, it's the personal journals of Borden and Angier. To further muddy the waters, the events these stolen journals recount turn out to be neither straightforward nor simple. As both Borden and Angier read to the end of their enemy's manuscript, the voice-over narration (and author of the journal) directly addresses the reader (which is made possible by the film's sound design), revealing that both diaries are fabrications created for the sole purpose of misdirection and gamesmanship.

Insofar as we allow an audiovisual lens to focus our gaze on the film's editing and sound design, we are able to see that the story fractures into at least four (or maybe more) discrete phases that overlap but actually take place at different times. As David Bordwell has noted,

> In presenting these four phases, Nolan pursues a fresh strategy. *The Prestige* treats its time zones not as if they run parallel to the present action, but as if they are embedded stories. This is partly because we have two protagonists and a split point-of-view pattern. It's also because of the crucial role of each magician's journal, in which he recounts and conceals his exploits. . . . In *The Prestige*, embedded stories permit Nolan's crosscutting to become more audacious. Crosscutting juxtaposes the two men's life stories, at the same time keeping us focused on the trial taking place in the present. Moreover, the discovered-manuscript convention motivates not only trips into the past but a brisk alternation of past and present.[7]

By embedding stories within stories, crosscutting between and among various narrative times, and then calling into question the truthfulness of the events that are chronicled by the magicians in their journals, Nolan is doing more

The Prestige (2006), © Touchstone Pictures and Warner Brothers Pictures

than simply restricting the spectator's view to the subjectivity of a character or characters. Like Borden and Angier, he is intentionally obfuscating and misdirecting his audience. And it would all be too much to follow if not for the clear visual cues Nolan provides that orient us to these various levels of storytelling. Whenever one or both of the principal characters are involved in an illusion, Nolan places them on the left-hand side of the frame, looking toward an off-screen performance on the right—whether as young apprentices pretending to be audience members in their own act or, later in time, as each magician furtively observes his competitor's show. However, during scenes in which they are playing no active role in the illusion (e.g., when they attend a performance of the wizard Chung Ling Soo), Angier and Borden are positioned on the right-hand side of the frame, looking toward the left.[8]

Nolan is meticulously consistent with this framing device (some might say repetitive), and that is what makes it a highly effective means for orienting the audience toward the various levels of an otherwise (purposefully) convoluted story. Depending on which way the scene is framed, viewers are able to tell not only whether Borden or Angier are involved in a given performance, but also, depending on the presence or absence of their faux facial hair, the approximate period of narrative time in which the performance is taking place.[9] Nolan is able to develop a compelling narrative world that confounds viewers and presses them to question how much they can trust their own eyes and ears, but without completely alienating them. Like any master illusionist, he knows full well that we all love a good magic trick, but we have very little patience for that which is simply confused and confusing.

Nolan makes a strikingly similar move in Inception. Rather than the somewhat subtle framing techniques he uses in The Prestige, he distinguishes the various narrative levels in *Inception* by designing and adhering to a series of clearly demarcated mise-en-scènes. The whole plot turns on the characters' ability to navigate a series of dreams set within dreams set within dreams. And it would be nearly impossible for the audience to keep all of the embedded stories straight if not for the clear visual differences between each of the various dreamscapes. On the first dream level Nolan gives us a rain-drenched metropolis, whereas the next level down takes place inside a posh hotel, and the third is set on a snow-covered mountainside. The deepest level—limbo—is even more distinct. It's a kind of surreal wasteland ever on the verge of collapsing in on itself. All told, these visually distinct layers work together to keep viewers from becoming lost in their own kind of narrative limbo.

In addition to these visual cues, the question of how and whether we can distinguish between reality "as it is" and reality as we have imagined it to be is so central to the film that the construction of believable but illusory dream worlds becomes an integral part of the plot as well. The protagonist, Cobb (Leonardo DiCaprio), is an architect of dreams, and he uses this particular skill set to extract information hidden in the unconscious minds of victims who are unaware that they are sleeping. When he is hired by a powerful corporate executive named Saito (Ken Watanabe) to plant a thought in a subject's mind (aka "inception") rather than simply steal it, Cobb is forced to involve a young and talented architect named Ariadne (Ellen Page) to design the dream worlds within which his team will operate. The only reason he is unable to design the dream worlds himself is because the subconscious "projection" of his deceased wife, Mal (Marion Cotillard), is threatening to undermine his work and leave him suspended in a perpetual dream state. Herself a victim of inception (Cobb planted in her mind the simple idea that "her world wasn't real, and that death was the only escape"), Mal framed Cobb for her suicide in an effort to convince him that they were still living in a self-constructed reality. On the run from the authorities ever since, Cobb accepts the job when Saito promises to clear his name, thus allowing him to return home to be with his children.

The plot is definitely complicated. We should expect nothing less from a film designed to blur the boundaries between the dream world and the "real" world, between the world we subjectively construct in the inner recesses of our mind and the world as it exists "out there" (if there even is such a thing as a world "out there"). Still, critics of Nolan's filmmaking are quick to point out that his embedded plot structures are not just complex but convoluted. They note that complex visual effects can't cover up the lack of character development. One of the more frequent complaints about Nolan's films is that we simply never get to know enough about his characters to care much about them. They are too abstract, too philosophically oriented, too unconcerned with being fully orbed human persons.

The critics aren't wrong. As Bordwell has noted, "With an elaborate premise framed as both a heist that Cobb must pull off and a mystery that Ariadne must solve, *Inception* would seem to confirm the frequent complaint that big-budget summer films have lost interest in human beings. Storytelling, we're told, has traded psychology and character traits for special effects and slam-bang action. . . . In fact, *Inception* takes this lack of characterization much farther than normal."[10]

But as Bordwell goes on to suggest, to become overly concerned about character development or plot holes is to fundamentally misunderstand Nolan's work as a filmmaker. Nolan's primary goal isn't to convey narrative information. It's to present us with a particular narrative experience—one in which we don't learn *about* the film's characters so much as we experience reality *alongside* them. Thus, "our relationships with the characters (apart from Cobb) come through learning new information along with them and being attached so closely to them while they execute the plan and react to its unfolding."[11]

Given these storytelling sensibilities, we suggest that Nolan's movies are functioning as modern-day parables. Indeed, to repeat our earlier description of film as parable (chap. 7), his movies (1) are brief stories rooted in everyday life; (2) are compelling ("exciting") stories, arresting the attention of their audience by inviting their listeners to see reality from a new angle; (3) do not primarily convey information but, by the more indirect communication of the metaphoric process, invite their audiences to discover spiritual truth or meaning as the human condition is portrayed; and (4) function subversively, undermining certain contemporary attitudes, beliefs, and/or authority (disorienting) even while inviting, teasing, or provoking new truth and/or transcendental insight (reorienting). It is not a parable's content but its affective resonance that matters most.

Nolan's preferred mode of storytelling bears striking similarities to an ancient (and profoundly religious) narrative form—one that is primarily concerned with listeners and viewers encountering life through a new set of storied experiences. Much like a parable, his movies lead us toward deeper insights by subverting our previously held expectations.

Nolan's goal of providing filmgoers with a cinematic encounter that approximates the disorienting/reorienting experience of his characters becomes even more evident when we consider how music functions in *Inception*. Music initially serves as a plot device that signals the countdown to the "kick"—the sync point when all the characters must ascend through the various levels of their shared dream and return to full consciousness. The music of choice for

Cobb's final inception job is Edith Piaf's "Non, je ne regrette rien" ("No, I don't regret anything"). Although the song plays at full speed in the "real" world where all the characters are resting peacefully in the first-class cabin of a 747, its pace slows at each of the lower dream levels to such a degree that what the characters and the audience both hear is more of a droning, pulsating sound effect than music. Sound, it would seem, remains the only clear link between our dreams and our conscious awareness of the world.

This use of music would be somewhat unremarkable if not for the opening credits. Here, prior to delivering any other single piece of narrative information, Nolan shows his hand. The elongated chords of the Piaf song ring out from underneath the corporate titles, with a hard stop triggered by the first image we see—a washed-up Cobb on the shores of Limbo looking at his children. It becomes clear later on that this sound is the musical countdown to the kick, but to hear it in this context can only mean one thing: we are already dreaming. It also means (or at least suggests) that someone, somewhere is signaling to us that we need to wake up.

When viewed through an audiovisual lens, *Inception* isn't simply a film about shared dreaming. It is itself a shared dream—one in which the audience experiences the narrative world just as Cobb does. It also happens to be another of Nolan's worlds haunted by a prior trauma—the catastrophic death of Cobb's wife that has separated him from his children. So deep is this trauma that neither we nor Cobb can ever really be sure if we have fully woken up, or if we have chosen an endless cycle of self-delusion in order to protect ourselves from further harm. As the film fades to black while Cobb's totem spins on the table, we realize that we too have been incepted just like Mal. This world may not be real. Worse yet, it may very well be an illusion/delusion that we have not only constructed but have designed with the express purpose of deceiving ourselves.

The same is true of *The Prestige*, *Memento*, and *Following*. In each of these films, Nolan is drawing on a common repertoire of sights, sounds, and narrative structures to explore humanity's seemingly infinite capacity for self-deception. But he is doing something both more and different than that. To be sure, Nolan's films highlight the fundamental limitations of what we can "know" with certainty, but in addition, we are actively deceiving others and asking to be deceived ourselves. As Cutter says, "We want to be fooled." Nolan's films urge us to adopt a greater degree of epistemic humility. On another level, though, because these narratives all take place in the aftermath of an originating trauma, they are also about the fundamental woundedness we have all been born into and cannot seem to move beyond. They invite us to reflect on our shared sense of grief and the pang of guilt that seem to constitute our lived experience even as we delude ourselves into thinking that we have nothing to regret ("Non, je ne regrette rien").

To classify Christopher Nolan's films as "post-traumatic" is also to acknowledge a distinct countermovement that emerges from the immanent structures of these narratives. While it might be somewhat unexpected given the thematic material in many of his stories (not to mention the borderline nihilism of some of his most memorable characters), what pervades Nolan's entire body of work is a certain kind of hopeful optimism. It is without question a hard-won hope, and often fractured and fleeting, but it is still clearly hope. It's a kind of wistful discontent captured both when Leonard asks, "How am I supposed to heal if I can't feel time?" and when Ariadne asks Cobb, "Why can't you go home?"

Because it functions as a narrative countermovement, this persistent longing for restoration, for wholeness, and for finding a way back "home" leaves Nolan's characters with little choice but to posit a reality untouched by humanity's innumerable foibles. Whether it's our deceiving others (*Following*), our faulty memories (*Memento*), our self-serving sleights of hand (*The Prestige*), or our fabricated dreams (*Inception*), this vision of flourishing—of healing our memories—is itself only understood through the lens of our flawed and disintegrating faculties. But as we encounter the true depth of our self-delusions right alongside Leonard, Mal, Cobb, Angier, and Borden, a simple thought cannot help but creep into our minds: things aren't how they are supposed to be.[12] And it hasn't always been this way. It's like a truth that we once knew but have chosen to forget. Somehow, deep within us, we begin to sense that there must be a way of being human that is pre-traumatic.

Cultural-Critical Lens: The Dark Knight Trilogy

> Their morals, their code, are a bad joke, dropped at the first sign of trouble. They are only as good as the world allows them to be. I'll show you. When the chips are down, these civilized people—they'll eat each other.
>
> —Joker, *The Dark Knight*

If there were a poster boy for characters haunted by the demons of their traumatic past, it would be Bruce Wayne. In more ways than one, his alter ego, Batman, is a kicking, punching, glowering embodiment of the fundamental catastrophe that precedes every telling of his story. True to form, in his Dark Knight trilogy, which includes *Batman Begins* (2005), *The Dark Knight* (2008), and *The Dark Knight Rises* (2012), Nolan explores this archetypal superhero by focusing not only on the individual fears that often emerge from Bruce Wayne's/

The Dark Knight (2008), © Warner Bros. Entertainment Inc.

Batman's originating trauma but also on our collective fears and on how each of us, in ways both big and small, leverage the fear residing in ourselves and others as a means for exerting our own will to power. As with his other films, the only real difference between the "superheroes" and the "super-villains" (and everyone in between) is not their intrinsic virtue but the degree to which they are honest about their self-interested intentions. In other words, no one gets to claim the moral high ground here.

But in the process of rebooting the Batman mythology, Nolan departs in some key ways from his previous movies. Namely, the primary point of view in these narratives is omniscient rather than subjective, and the plots unfold sequentially rather than out of order, which tends to make them less about the trauma of an individual character and more about society at large. In contrast to a film like *Memento*, in which viewers are placed entirely within Leonard's subjectivity, Nolan's Dark Knight trilogy provides us with a view of the system as a whole. So while narrative analyses and formal considerations remain important tools for understanding the way Nolan constructs these story worlds, a cultural-critical framework proves particularly helpful for these three films.

One of the primary reasons that a cultural-critical lens helpfully illuminates the power and meaning of these films is because the trauma they depict is personal but also embedded in the very structures of power that make modern life possible. This is especially the case with the Batman story, as his primary beef is not with an individual criminal (although at times it is) but with the injustice of an entire system that would allow his parents to be murdered so senselessly in the first place. Indeed, in Nolan's telling of Bruce Wayne's backstory, the man who murdered Wayne's parents is later gunned down by the mob to keep him from testifying against Carmine Falcone, Gotham's most notorious syndicated crime boss. So while his parents' murder serves as the key motivation for his training with the League of Shadows, he lives with the knowledge that he will never be able to enact any kind of personal justice. In many ways then, his desire to bring about systemic justice is the displacement of a desire for personal justice that can never be fully realized.

For instance, Wayne constantly speaks about his goal to "save Gotham" (i.e., "the people") from the corrupt system that feeds off their suffering. The only problem is that Batman is himself a product of this inequitable system. Tellingly, most superheroes (e.g., Superman and Wonder Woman) possess some kind of supernatural power—a gift that transcends our humanity and thus lies outside or beyond our reach. But not Batman. His power is tangible and concrete. It's his material wealth. But in truth, this "superpower" isn't any less fantastic or any more within our reach than laser vision or the ability to fly. For the countless other orphans in Gotham whose parents also became victims of systemic injustice, this way of being in the world is quite literally inaccessible to them—an impossibility bordering on the absurd. Regardless of how pure their quest for justice, or how much their anger motivates them, or how many hours they spend at the gym training with mysterious ninjas, they simply cannot become Batman. He is a billionaire whose crime fighting is made possible only by the inordinate amount of wealth his family has amassed, which means that he can never fully untangle himself or his endeavors from the very systemic trauma he is seeking to remedy. As Batman, Bruce Wayne seeks justice, but the question remains: Whose justice?

It is not insignificant, then, that Nolan goes out of his way to depict Bruce Wayne's parents as philanthropic martyr-saints—benevolent patrons of "the people of Gotham" whose wealth is only outmatched by their compassion for others. But knowing something of Nolan's larger body of work and his predilection for interesting inversions, it might be that we should read this depiction of the Waynes "against the grain," so to speak. In other words, to gain deeper insight into the film's (and Nolan's) understanding of wealth, we need to view it through a cultural-critical lens. Consider for a moment what Peter Buffet (son of Warren) had to say about philanthropy among the uber-rich, or what he calls "Philanthropic Colonialism":

> Inside any important philanthropy meeting, you witness heads of state meeting with investment managers and corporate leaders. All are searching for answers with their right hand to problems that others in the room created with their left. . . . As more lives and communities are destroyed by the system that creates vast amounts of wealth for the few, the more heroic it sounds to "give back." It's what I would call "conscience laundering"—feeling better about accumulating more than any one person could possibly need to live on by sprinkling a little

around as an act of charity. But this just keeps the existing structure of inequality in place. The rich sleep better at night, while others get just enough to keep the pot from boiling over. Nearly every time someone feels better by doing good, on the other side of the world (or street), someone else is further locked into a system that will not allow the true flourishing of his or her nature or the opportunity to live a joyful and fulfilled life.[13]

Picking up on Buffett's biting critique of the systemic nature of economic inequality, cultural critic and political philosopher Slavoj Žižek identifies Nolan's Dark Knight trilogy as a particularly helpful conversation partner. In *Trouble in Paradise*, Žižek suggests that the trilogy follows an immanent logic that can be charted according to the ways in which each installment develops its overarching narrative.[14]

First, in *Batman Begins*, the hero works within the bounds of society as it is presently ordered, even though his operations are not officially legitimated by that order. In this case, "the system can be defended with morally acceptable methods."[15]

Second, in *The Dark Knight*, the narrative presses the limits of this moral ordering by revealing that the maintenance of society has to be grounded on a lie:

> One has to break the rules in order to defend the system. Or, to put it another way, in *Batman Begins*, the hero is simply a classic urban vigilante. . . . *The Dark Knight* changes these coordinates: Batman's true rival is not the Joker, his opponent, but Harvey Dent, the "white knight." . . . It is as if Dent is the reply of the legal order to Batman's threat: against Batman's vigilante struggle, the system generates its own legal excess, its own vigilante, who—much more violent than Batman—directly violates the law.[16]

Finally, in *The Dark Knight Rises*, the character of Bane takes the narrative to its logical end: the complete destruction of an unjust system in the name of justice. This final development returns us, full circle, to the central mission of the League of Shadows, which, as Ra's Al Ghul tells us in *Batman Begins*, is to liberate corrupt societies by burning them to the ground. Bane, who is working on behalf of Ra's al Ghul's daughter (Miranda/Talia al Ghul), is the embodiment of this "emancipatory" vision. As Žižek notes, "The rise of such a figure [i.e., Bane] changes the entire constellation: for all participants, Batman included, morality is relativized, it becomes a matter of convenience, something determined by circumstances."[17]

At first blush, it seems that these three movements are simply setting the stage for the triumphant return of the hero—a superhuman intercessor who is able to descend from on high and rescue both the system and the people in it because he is unmarred by their mundane realities. But that's not what we get, because that's not who Batman is, at least not Christopher Nolan's Batman. What we get instead is a hero who saves Gotham from its imminent destruction but then flees the scene of the crime, never to be seen again. He leaves the Batcave to Blake (Joseph Gordon-Levitt), the city's new hero who is tasked with succeeding where Wayne/Batman clearly failed—defending the system through morally acceptable means.

The trilogy concludes with Alfred reading from Charles Dickens's *Tale of Two Cities* at the wake of Bruce Wayne, who is presumed to have died in the violent riots: "It is a far, far better thing that I do, than I have ever done; it is a far, far better rest that I go to, than I have ever known." Some have suggested this final quote encourages us to understand Batman as an "ultimate Christ-figure, Batman sacrifices himself to save others."[18] But as Žižek points out, this interpretation is problematic given the final scene in which Alfred sees Bruce Wayne and Selina in a Florence café. As it turns out, Bruce Wayne/Batman has faked his own death. He doesn't "lose his life" to save Gotham. Instead, he goes along his merry way as the billionaire that he is, unshackled by the system of commerce and exchange he is able to leave behind only because he amassed more capital than any human being could ever need. This can be no Christ story. If anything, it's the inversion of the Christ story. In Nolan's telling, Batman is not a Christ figure but a faux Christ.

But if Batman isn't the true hero of this story, who or what is? Interestingly enough, in contrast to Batman, Bane is the only character who displays genuine, unconditional love (although Alfred comes in a close second). Indeed, Bane's undying commitment to Miranda is sincere, demonstrated by the fact that he sacrifices his life for hers. But even this is too simple of an inversion, for although he loves Miranda, it's a love that has become distorted and misdirected. No one, it would seem, is above the fray.

Nevertheless, by allowing a cultural-critical lens to inform our take on the film, what we can see is that Bane's authenticity, however misdirected, leaves a trace in the film's texture—an "absent center" that is best expressed when he invokes the idea of "the people's republic of Gotham City."[19] In other words, the film issues a call for emancipation from an unjust system, but it does so only in its failure to realize this liberation. From this perspective, the problem with the character of Bane is not simply that he is the "bad guy" or that he is a terrorist. As Žižek points out, the critique is that he translates the violence of the emancipatory impulse in the film into murderous terror.[20] But the core "event" to which he is responding continues to linger. Even after Bane, Miranda, Selina, and Bruce Wayne have all departed the scene, the faint but elemental call to systemic justice remains.

It's important to note that we never actually see this event; it is only a specter. Nolan places the final showdown with Bane and Batman in front of civic structures—either City Hall or Gotham's version of Wall Street. Regardless, it evokes the backdrop for struggles against the 1 percent. In certain respects, Nolan the filmmaker becomes a kind of Bruce Wayne figure, a wealthy multi-millionaire aiming to alleviate suffering but ultimately revealing that as a fool's mission. How amazing that the masses still liked it!

And yet the prospect of a "people's power" exerts a strange kind of attraction, even though the film never depicts its proper functioning. Hidden behind the trauma(s) of the Dark Knight trilogy is a vision of future hope that comments on the existential now. This hope calls to us, unbidden, in and through the absent center of these films. It's the presence of a profound absence that whispers to us: *this isn't all there is.* This post-traumatic reality, this economic disparity, this rigged system—things haven't always been this way. Indeed, they don't always have to be this way.

Theological Lens: Original Sin, *Interstellar*, and the Trauma of Love

> Love isn't something we invented. It's observable, powerful. It has to mean something. . . . Maybe it means something more, something we can't yet understand. . . . Love is the one thing we're capable of perceiving that transcends dimensions of time and space. Maybe we should trust that even if we can't understand it yet.
>
> —Dr. Brand, *Interstellar*

In *Suspicion and Faith: The Religious Uses of Modern Atheism*, Merold Westphal makes a somewhat counterintuitive claim: Marx, Freud, and Nietzsche—three of the most militant atheists in modern times—are, in fact, the "great modern theologians of original sin."[21] Their basic diagnosis of our existential state is that humans respond to our prior, unseen (and often repressed) traumas through various forms of self-deception (Freud), self-interested moralism (Nietzsche), and the politicization of instrumental religion (Marx). In other words, both humans and the societal structures they inhabit are "rotten to their core."[22] Worse yet, we don't even know it.

Given their take on the human condition, these three thinkers, says Westphal, were "masters of suspicion." Needless to say, Christopher Nolan is cut from the same cloth. As we have seen, his characters, his narratives, and indeed, even his filmmaking techniques all reflect a fundamental suspicion about the reliability of knowledge, the convenient fictions we so often construct, and even the institutional structures that organize our shared lives. For Nolan, it's hermeneutics all the way down. Caught in the infinite abyss of our own subjectivity, we can't trust anyone, least of all ourselves. In fact, taking a page from Westphal's book, we might even go so far as to say that Nolan is one of the great modern filmmakers of original sin.[23]

Of course, to invoke "original sin" is to shift the conversation into an explicitly theological register. More specifically, in terms of the fourfold method of medieval interpretation we outlined in chapter 6, it is to move from the literal to the allegorical level, which presses us to consider how Nolan's films might lead us to further moral insight and possibly even a transcendent vision. Up to now, we have described the origin of Nolan's films in terms of a core trauma—a prior and more fundamental catastrophe that animates all of his story worlds. But when we allow this multifaceted theological lens to converge with the critical, audiovisual, and narrative lenses we have already employed, it becomes clear that Nolan is borrowing from a stream of thought that actually precedes Marx, Nietzsche, and Freud—one that is not only rooted in but is in fact parasitic upon the Christian theological tradition.

As far as doctrines go, original sin has a bit of a bad rap. After all, the notion that we are "rotten to our core" is a bit unsettling to modern ears. But as Tommy Givens, New Testament scholar at Fuller Theological Seminary, notes, part of the problem is that original sin is often misunderstood, even within the theological tradition. For instance, according to Givens's read of Romans 5:12–21, the apostle Paul's interest in human sinfulness entering the world through Adam is not about naming "what's wrong with us," but about pointing out that "it hasn't always been this way."[24] In other words, Paul is suggesting that there is both a prehuman reality to sin and a way to be human without sin. If Givens is correct, then the concept is perhaps better understood not as "original sin" but as "originating sin"—an order of knowing that is indeed limited by the existential state of the human condition. That is, we can only imagine pre-sin humanity (or anything else for that matter) in and through our sin. Thus, to name what plagues human persons and human society as "original sin" is to comment on the here and now, to underscore that *this* isn't all there is.

The concept of originating sin strikes at the heart of the cinematic stories Nolan is creating. Thus, Marx, Freud, and Nietzsche move us in the right direction, but if we only go as far as their critical frameworks allow, we miss the other half of the equation embedded in so many of Nolan's movies—the "absent center" of the human condition that posits another way of being in the world. This is why it is vital that, once we have unpacked a film according to its literal meaning (to return to the terminology of the fourfold method), we move to the allegorical level. By doing so, we are able not only to offer thicker interpretations of a given film but also to consider how a movie's story might become *our* story—that is, the story of our common humanity.

For instance, in the context of Nolan's narrative worlds, human beings are limited in their ability to know anything (*Memento*), prone to self-deception (*Inception*), and, when it suits them, willing to deceive others to maintain their illusions/delusions (*The Prestige* and *Following*). His characters (and by extension his audience) accept this arrangement not because it is ideal but because the only alternative would be to face the reality of their traumatic origins. And let's be honest, none of us are prepared for that. We haven't the resources to handle it. All we can do in the face of these limitations is acknowledge them as part and parcel of what it means to be human. In other words, Nolan's films don't provide us with any solutions to the dilemma of original sin, nor should we expect them to. But when it comes to the nature of our beliefs—or what we could possibly know with any kind of certainty—these movies do urge us to be a bit more humble. And we would do well to listen, lest we end up like Leonard in *Memento*, endlessly pursuing "justice" for a crime that we ourselves committed.

Yet this brokenness is not merely personal. As Nolan underscores in the Dark Knight trilogy (at times literally through the force of Hans Zimmer's scores), it pervades the structures of society as well. And it is here that we need to augment Žižek's ideological reading of the Dark Knight trilogy with a theological interpretation (specifically a "moral" one), especially as it concerns the "authentic event" that multiple signs in these films point toward but that is never fully realized. To borrow from John Caputo, the event of the "people's power" that Žižek identifies is, in theological terms, the event otherwise known as "God." For Caputo, God is the name that harbors the event of a call—an unconditional call to systemic justice, wholeness, and, indeed, shalom, a call that exerts an influence on the world, not from a transcendent or superhuman point of reference, but from within its immanent structures.[25]

Thus, Žižek is right to suggest that something is hidden within the narrative of Nolan's Dark Knight trilogy—something that, when seen from a theological perspective, can be understood as the event that takes place in the name of God. It's the disruptive call of the kingdom of God that speaks truth to power (or rather, whispers like the "sound of sheer silence"—1 Kings 19:12 NRSV) by challenging unjust systems. But more importantly, it is a call that demands our response, for it is only in and through our concrete response that this unconditional demand for justice becomes a substantive reality in the world. The system is broken, yes. And we too are broken. But the justice of God's kingdom still calls. And we are respond-able.

According to Caputo, the unconditional call of the kingdom of God goes by various names, depending on the context: justice, democracy, friendship, mercy, and even life. But if we approach this kingdom call in terms of the transcendent vision it entails (i.e., anagogically), we are granted a future perspective that informs the here and now—a significant point to bear in mind as we turn to *Interstellar* (2014).

Interstellar has all the trademarks of a Christopher Nolan film: a trauma that precedes the narrative, characters driven by guilt, and the deception of self and others. In true Nolan fashion, it even plays with time, but in this case, time is literally relative, folding in on itself under the gravitational force of a black hole. Very basically, the film follows a farmer and former NASA pilot named Cooper (Matthew McConaughey) as he joins a team of scientists searching for a planet that could potentially sustain human life. Cooper's wife died prior to the beginning of the formal narrative, so he leaves behind a son and a daughter (Murph, played by Jessica Chastain) to be raised by their grandfather on an increasingly uninhabitable Earth.

Because of the nature of space travel, time passes much more quickly for Murph and everyone else on Earth than it does for Cooper and the members of his expedition. Years pass without any word from those aboard the spacecraft. Thus, for the majority of her life (and the movie), Murph believes that her father knowingly abandoned her. It is not until the climax of the film, as Cooper manipulates gravity to communicate with his daughter from a five-dimensional structure inside a black hole, that Murph realizes the "ghost" in her bedroom was, is, and always has been her father.

It's equal parts *2001: A Space Odyssey* (1968) and *The Martian* (2015). It's also quite polarizing. Not everyone buys the science or the plot, much less the characters. But what is compelling about *Interstellar* is that, even though it follows a trajectory similar to Nolan's previous films (which also have their fair share of critics), it features a new and rather striking development. As we suggested earlier, the undercurrent that stirs beneath Nolan's larger body of work is a sense of hard-won hope, even if we sense its presence only by its absence. But in *Interstellar*, this hope becomes explicit. It's a hope grounded in love—an unconditional, familial love that calls to us through time, space, and even gravity.

Dr. Brand (Anne Hathaway) says as much in her soliloquy on love as a quantifiable reality that we don't fully understand. And Cooper echoes her sentiment when he discovers the solution to escaping the black hole and saving Earth's inhabitants: "They didn't choose me; they chose her. To save the world. I'm going to find a way to tell Murph just like I found this moment. With love . . . with love. Brand was right. My connection with Murph, it is quantifiable. It's the key."

Interstellar (2014), © Paramount Pictures Corporation and Warner Bros. Entertainment Inc.

Here, expressed clearly and explicitly for perhaps the first time in Nolan's body of work, is the hope that has always been present in his films as an "absent center." Theologian Miroslav Volf has remarked that hope, "in a Christian sense, is love stretching itself into the future."[26] But *Interstellar* shifts the possibilities of this hope into an entirely different register. According to Nolan's cinematic vision, hope is not simply love stretching itself into the future, but love calling to us both within time and beyond time. Indeed, in every concrete moment of her life, Murph is in the infinite presence of her father's love—a love that is neither purely "in" her time nor absolutely "above" or "outside" it. In other words, it is a love that encounters her as an immanent transcendence. She doesn't fully understand the mechanics of it all, but just as Dr. Brand suggests, that doesn't mean it is any less real.

What then can we say is Nolan's response to our post-traumatic reality—the fundamental givenness of originating sin? Is there any hope at all beyond our infinitely interpretive and thus incomplete/subjective/delusional awareness of reality? In a word, yes. Nolan's vision of the postmodern moment is certainly sobering, but it has no room for nihilistic despair. Rather, his films are responding to an unconditional call—the call of hope that issues in and through each everyday experience of our broken (i.e., "sin-filled") lives. Like the "ghost" of Murph's father who is personally present even in his absence, this is a hope that haunts reality, making itself known most often through subtleties like the unique gravitational forces in a young girl's bedroom.

And while the theological analogue of a father's timeless love is hard to miss, *Interstellar* does more than merely illustrate a theological concept. It actually has the potential for expanding and clarifying our vision. Of course, for it to function in this way, both lay and professional theologians would first have to admit that our own confusion about how best to understand and respond to the existential state of the human person is exacerbated by a truncated imagination. We have focused so much energy on "what's wrong with us" that we have failed to remember that "this isn't all there is." As a result, we struggle to take Paul seriously when he says, "And now these three remain: faith, hope, and love. But the greatest of these is love" (1 Cor. 13:13). Does he really mean to suggest that love endures—that it is the one thing that is not and cannot be bound by time? Surely this is figurative, flowery language. We all know that reality doesn't work this way. Nothing can traverse time and space, not even love . . . but is that true?

Maybe our theological imaginations have been taken captive by the wrong picture, one that lends itself more to the empirical "proofs" of modern science than to the poetic insights of science fiction. And maybe we need Nolan's vision to point us in a better direction. His films don't offer solutions or answers to the problem of human brokenness. Rather, they simply comment on the existential now, and in doing so, they urge us to respond to trauma with a transcendent love. For just as Dr. Brand says, "[Love] means something more, something we can't yet understand. . . . Love is the one thing we're capable of perceiving that transcends dimensions of time and space. Maybe we should trust that even if we can't understand it yet."

Deep Focus: Finding Our Way Back Home with PTSD

As a war movie dramatizing the true story of the defense and evacuation of Allied troops from the beaches of Dunkirk, France, during World War II, the subject matter of *Dunkirk* (2017) represents something of a departure from Nolan's larger body of work. Nevertheless, by operating within the generic constraints of a historical war film, Nolan manages to bring his unique cinematic vision to bear on a well-worn genre while, at the same time, producing what is perhaps one of his most restrained and, indeed, affecting films to date. .

To be sure, *Dunkirk* bears all the markings of a Christopher Nolan film—an all-star cast, the collapsing of narrative time, a taut Hans Zimmer score, and, of course, an originating trauma. In this case, the catastrophe that upends the narrative world is war itself. But beyond the sheer horror of war, one of the more striking parallels between *Dunkirk* and the rest of Nolan's oeuvre has to do with the larger theme of "going/being home." Much like Cooper in *Interstellar*, Bruce Wayne in the Dark Knight trilogy, and Cobb in *Inception*, the troops on the beaches of Dunkirk are caught in the midst of a seemingly hopeless scenario that has a good chance of ending in their untimely death (Churchill thought they might be able to save 30,000 of the 400,000 troops trapped on the beach). Yet, like so many of Nolan's characters, the animating vision that allows these soldiers to muster enough courage to press forward is the simple prospect of returning home. At various points in the film, a number of British soldiers openly reflect on the fact that the shores of France and England are so very close to one another, and yet the soldiers remain so very far from actually being home. When countless civilian vessels from their native land arrive to take them home, Commander Bolton (Kenneth Branagh) clearly identifies the events that transpire for what they truly are: a miracle.

Thus, a basic sense of homelessness captures the way many of us experience our life in the world. But it's only because we operate with some notion of "home" in the first place. We have been thrown into the wake of an originating sin from which we cannot escape—a moment of deceit and self-deception that we repeat time and time again. We are much like the traumatized soldier (played by Cillian Murphy) who ends up killing an innocent boy who is trying to help him, which seems to reveal how sin works. We simply do not do what we want to do (Rom. 7:15). As a result, nothing short of a miracle will break us out of this cycle of violence and allow us to return to our place of origin. And as it turns out, this is exactly what takes place. We cannot get home, so home comes to us.

This then is the Christian narrative writ large. Without our being fully aware of what has transpired or how to overcome our alienation, God comes looking for us: "Where are you?" (Gen. 3:9). We are being called. We are being actively pursued. And there are no limits to the love of the One who chases after us. Just ask Cooper and Murph. The Father's love knows no bounds. Indeed, "neither death nor life, neither angels nor demons, neither the present nor the future, nor any powers, neither height nor depth, nor anything else in all creation, will be able to separate us from the love of God" (Rom. 8:38–39). It's a love beyond space and time that nevertheless calls out to us from within space and time. It's a love that constitutes the only reality that is more catastrophic (i.e., *katastrophe*, over-turning) than the originating trauma itself. We, with Commander Bolton, might even call it a miracle. And rather than explain it or control it or try to figure out how it works, maybe, just maybe, we should trust this love, even if we can't understand it yet.

Discussion Questions

1. Recall the first time you watched a Christopher Nolan film. What was your original response? Did you love it, hate it, leave the theater confused? Why do you think you had this initial response?

2. How do you account for the success of Nolan's films? Is it the pacing, the high-octane action, the puzzling (sometimes confusing) plots? Or is it something else? In your own words, what might that "something else" be?

3. Beyond what this chapter mentions, in what other ways might a theological lens help us discern some of the deeper movements in Nolan's work, whether individual films or his entire body of work?

epilogue

a deeper focus

Do you stick around for the closing credits? Marvel Studios has done a great job of teasing viewers with previews of upcoming sequels embedded within the end credits. These tasty little hints of what's next give filmgoers even more to ponder and discuss as they exit the theater. This epilogue will function in a similar way—as an invitation to consider the future of film and your place within it.

Hopefully, this book has deepened your appreciation for the work and the craftspeople involved in creating a movie. You may find yourself studying the names scrolling by in an effort to further unpack the meaning. Who wrote the screenplay? Who directed the film? What kinds of themes do their stories almost always explore? The final song over the end credits may also deepen our understanding of the story. John Legend and Common connected the historic resistance in *Selma* (2014) to "why Rosa sat on the bus" and "why we walk through Ferguson with our hands up." In their Academy Award–winning original song, they welcomed viewers "to the story we call victory / The comin' of the Lord, my eyes have seen the glory."[1] Staying through the end credits gives us time to ponder the implications of what we've seen, to sit with the characters and their choices just a bit longer. It is an invitation to let the full gravity of the journey sink in deeper.

While the big screen theatrical experience will continue to offer an opportunity to venture into the dark, many of us will increasingly be watching movies in the comfort of our homes. We will start and pause a film at our convenience. We may view these stories on the go, on portable devices, in settings far from the directors' idealized, original intentions.

Some wonder if movie-going itself will fall out of favor. Will a generation raised on the bite-sized portions of YouTube have the patience to sit through a two-hour movie? In *Film Comment*, Paul Schrader praises motion pictures as the dominant art for the twentieth century but concludes, "It will not be so in the 21st century." He writes, "Cultural and technological forces are at work that will change the concept of 'movies' as we have known them."[2] The 2017 Sundance Grand Prize winner for the US dramatic film competition, *I Don't Feel at Home in This World Anymore*, never received a theatrical release; it went straight to Netflix. *Icarus*, the 2017 Sundance U.S. Documentary Special Jury Award winner, was purchased by Netflix and subsequently received the 2018 Academy Award for Best Documentary Feature for its investigation of Russia's doping of Olympic athletes. With Alfonso Cuarón's semiautobiographical recollection of growing up in Mexico City, *Roma* (2018), Netflix simultaneously released an Oscar contender to viewers in theaters, at home, and on mobile devices. The rise of streaming services has closed the gap between film and television, long form and short form. The epic documentary *O. J. Simpson: Made in America* (2016) premiered as an eight-hour theatrical feature at the Sundance Film Festival but later played as a five-part television miniseries on ESPN. Director Ezra Edelman won both an Oscar and an Emmy, revealing how quickly the lines are blurring even between the film and television academies.[3]

Streaming services like Netflix, Amazon Prime, and Hulu, and nascent original programming from YouTube, Facebook, and Apple, will continue to collapse the gap between features, miniseries, webisodes, and television shows. We have stories that fit within whatever time slot we seek to fill. To many viewers, a two-hour story might come across as too small, not meaty enough compared to whole seasons of character arcs available in a television format. A six-episode miniseries like *The Night Manager* (2016) allows the complexities of a John Le Carré novel to unspool at a more leisurely pace (or in this case, in a more fascinating way) than ever before. The overlapping Marvel Universe or the multiple spin-offs of the Star Wars franchise are remarkable efforts to draw viewers into a larger shaping story that expands beyond a two-hour window. Our attention spans seem to be contracting and expanding at the same time.

We want to encourage more active viewing and conscientious reflection on all forms of entertainment. The lenses we've applied to feature films still apply to YouTube videos. They can be judged according to craft, authorial intent, viewer response, cultural impact, and theological center. Thanks to the mobiquity (mobile ubiquity) of smartphones, we all have the ability to create and distribute our own stories. The collapse and consolidation of the studio system has made entertainment both more affordable and more diverse, on the one hand, but also more costly than ever before. How great that we have such unprecedented storytelling power in our hands. We've found that thoughtful reflection on the craft and possibilities of film (and TV and videos) expands our range and potential as storytellers. A deeper focus leads to more active discipleship.

Our efforts to place theology and film into dialogue have proven more impactful and widespread than we ever imagined. For instance, Reel Spirituality and Fuller Seminary have been honored to host Martin Scorsese for a screening and conversation about his underappreciated *Silence* (2016) and Paul Schrader for a series of conversations about his masterful *First Reformed* (2017).[4] The Windrider Film Forum teamed up with the Sundance Film Festival to showcase the underappreciated and highly redemptive award winner *Burden* (2018). Churches are incorporating the power of film and media into their worship experiences and ministries, including movies about worship such as *Hillsong: Let Hope Rise* (2016). As we screen more electronic entertainment as individuals and families, our need for a deeper focus has expanded. Given that we now invest fifty or even one hundred hours of our lives into a single series, we must think further about the themes, issues, and potential theological import of such shaping stories.[5] Despite our enthusiasm for films and television shows, we may end up encouraging the next generation to spend less time in front of screens and more time reading and reflecting on the original shaping story for Christians found in the Bible. Time away from electronic inputs and endless entertainment may prove more fruitful than ever in an age of constant connection. Perhaps a new generation introduced to films via iPads and iPhones will find solace and warmth in the analogue entertainment of books and LPs. Formats will rise and fall, but the power and potential of story to reveal meaning will remain, as will the need for lenses to interpret our experiences. As distractions expand, those who practice a deep focus will develop rare and valuable skills. We will always need those who can discern the true, the just, the pure, the lovely, the commendable, the excellent, the praiseworthy. Focus on these things.

Discussion Questions

1. What kinds and lengths of stories do you prefer? What formats do you turn to most frequently—theaters, home viewing, mobile devices?
2. How much time do you spend away from electronic inputs? What kind of practices can help you reflect on your experiences and acquire a deeper focus?

notes

Introduction

1. George Nolfi, quoted in Dylan Callaghan, interview for Writers Guild of America, April 23, 2013.

2. Josh Rottenberg, "Jordan Peele on How 'Get Out' Defied the Odds to Become a Full-Blown Cultural Phenomenon," *Los Angeles Times*, March 22, 2017, http://www.latimes.com/entertainment /movies/la-et-mn-get-out-box-office-phenomenon-20170321-story.html.

3. Ross A. Lincoln, "'Get Out' Director Jordan Peele Explains 'The Sunken Place,'" The Wrap, March 17, 2017, https://www.thewrap.com/get-out-director-jordan-peele-explains-the-sunken-place.

Chapter 1: The Power of Film

1. Rose Pacatte, FSP, conversation at the Luce consultation on theology and film, Fuller Theological Seminary, Pasadena, CA, December 8, 2005.

2. Robert McKee, *Story: Substance, Structure, Style, and the Principles of Screenwriting* (New York: Harper Entertainment, 1997), 12.

3. McKee, *Story*, 12.

4. See "Frequency of Going to the Movies in the US," Statista, accessed August 4, 2017, https:// www.statista.com/statistics/264396/frequency-of-going-to-the-movies-in-the-us; "Box Office Revenue in North America from 2001 to 2016 (in Billion US Dollars)," Statista, accessed August 4, 2017, https://www.statista.com/statistics/187061/north-american-box-office-gross-since-2001.

5. Mary McNamara, "The Bigger Picture: Going to the Movies Remains a Timeless Experience," *Los Angeles Times*, June 4, 2017, https://www.yorkdispatch.com/story/entertainment/2017/06/08 /bigger-picture-going-movies-remains-timeless-experience/102616124.

6. Writing in the first edition of the *New Yorker* after 9/11, Anthony Lane pointed out that

   you could argue that last Tuesday was an instant dismissal of the fantastic—that people gazed up into the sky and immediately told themselves that this was the real thing. Yet all the evidence suggests the contrary; it was the television commentators as well as those on the ground who resorted to a phrase book culled from cinema: "It was like a movie." "It was like 'Independence Day.'" "It was like 'Die Hard.'" "No, 'Die Hard 2.'" "'Armageddon.'" And the exclamations from below, from the watchers of the skies caught on video, as they see the aircraft slice into the side of the tower: where have you heard those expressions most recently—the wows, the whoohs, the holy shits—if not in movie theatres, and even on your own blaspheming tongue? (Anthony Lane, "This Is Not a Movie," *New Yorker*, September 24, 2001)

7. Of course, the downside of this phenomenon is that any preceding history is often lost, as if the whole of human history was birthed along with the advent of film technology. So while movies are the repository for our historical consciousness, they also reflect our historical amnesia.

8. Elizabeth Van Ness, "Is a Cinema Studies Degree the New M.B.A.?," *New York Times*, March 6, 2005, https://www.nytimes.com/2005/03/06/movies/is-a-cinema-studies-degree-the-new-mba.html.

9. David Thomson, *The Whole Equation: A History of Hollywood* (New York: Alfred A. Knopf, 2005), 136.

10. Jerry Sittser, *A Grace Disguised: How the Soul Grows through Loss* (Grand Rapids: Zondervan, 1996), 173. Not all responses by children to the movie *Bambi* are as positive. Stephen King, for example, recalls: "Yet 50 years later I can still remember the sense of dismay I felt when Bambi's mother was killed, leaving the poor little feller alone. I was a single-parent child myself, and I spent many long nights after lights-out thinking about Bambi and wondering what would happen to me if something happened to my mother. I still remember the simple power of the film's most potent line: 'Man was in the forest.'" Stephen King, "Do Movies Matter? (Part 1)," *Entertainment Weekly*, November 14, 2003, 136.

11. Mark Olsen, "On 'A League of Their Own's' 25th Anniversary, Geena Davis Still Isn't Afraid to Say 'Feminist,'" *Los Angeles Times*, July 4, 2017, http://www.latimes.com/entertainment/movies/la-et-mn-geena-davis-a-league-of-their-own-25th-anniversary-interview-20170701-htmlstory.html.

12. Ted Baehr notes the same event but reports alternate figures—a drop from $9.5 million to $4.1 million. Ted Baehr, *What Can We Watch Tonight? A Family Guide to Movies* (Grand Rapids: Zondervan, 2003), 15.

13. David Van Biema, "Life Is Sweet for Jack Dowd as Spielberg's Hit Film Has E.T. Lovers Picking Up the (Reese's) Pieces," *People*, July 26, 1982, https://people.com/archive/life-is-sweet-for-jack-dowd-as-spielbergs-hit-film-has-e-t-lovers-picking-up-the-reeses-pieces-vol-18-no-4; Leslie Earnest, "Oakley Proves Sales Mission Possible," *Los Angeles Times*, July 20, 2000, http://articles.latimes.com/2000/jul/20/business/fi-55633; Steven S. Cuellar, "The 'Sideways' Effect: A Test for Changes in the Demand for Merlot and Pinot Noir Wines," *Wines & Vines*, January 2009, https://www.winesandvines.com/features/article/61265/The-Sideways-Effect.

14. Nick Thompson, "When Do Moviegoers Become Pilgrims?," *The Conversation*, July 31, 2017, https://theconversation.com/when-do-moviegoers-become-pilgrims-81016.

15. See Carol Pinchefsky, "The Impact (Economic and Otherwise) of Lord of the Rings/The Hobbit on New Zealand," *Forbes*, December 14, 2012, https://www.forbes.com/sites/carolpinchefsky/2012/12/14/the-impact-economic-and-otherwise-of-lord-of-the-ringsthe-hobbit-on-new-zealand/#40145ef331b6.

16. "Preventing Tobacco Use among Youth and Young Adults: A Report of the Surgeon General," US Department of Health and Human Services, 2012, https://www.surgeongeneral.gov/library/reports/preventing-youth-tobacco-use/exec-summary.pdf.

17. Victoria Knight, "Tobacco Use Jumps 80% in Top-Grossing Movies," CNN, July 10, 2017, http://www.cnn.com/2017/07/10/health/tobacco-movies-teen-smoking-study/index.html.

18. Craig Detweiler, quoted in Knight, "Tobacco Use."

19. Amy Wallace, "'Ryan' Ends Vets' Years of Silence," *Los Angeles Times*, August 6, 1998, sec. A, 1.

20. Neal Gabler, *Life: The Movie: How Entertainment Conquered Reality* (New York: Knopf, 1998), 9. Of course, years earlier, Neil Postman predicted exactly what Gabler describes. See *Amusing Ourselves to Death: Public Discourse in the Age of Show Business* (New York: Penguin Books, 1985).

21. Elia Kazan, *Elia Kazan: A Life* (New York: Knopf, 1988), 381.

22. Clive Marsh and Gaye Ortiz, eds., *Explorations in Theology and Film: Movies and Meaning* (Oxford: Blackwell, 1997), 1.

23. Martin Scorsese, "Duel in the Sun," in *Private Screenings: Insiders Share a Century of Great Movie Moments*, by American Film Institute with Duane Byrge (Atlanta: Turner, 1995), 141.

24. Quoted in Guy Bedouelle, "Eric Rohmer: The Cinema's Spiritual Destiny," *Communio* 6, no. 2 (1979): 280.

25. Margaret Miles, quoted in Christopher Deacy, *Screen Christologies: Redemption and the Medium of Film* (Cardiff: University of Wales Press, 2001), 1.

26. Read Mercer Schuchardt, "Cinema—The New Cathedral of Hollyworld: How Films Are Replacing Religion in Our Cinematic Age," Metaphilm, November 9, 2001, http://www.allhotels illinois.com/metaphilmcom/index/detail/cinema-the-new-cathedral/. Cf. David Lodge, *The Picturegoers* (1960; repr., Harmondsworth, UK: Penguin Books, 1993), 108–9, quoted in Gerard Loughlin, "Looking: The Ethics of Seeing in Church and Cinema," in *Faithfulness and Fortitude: In Conversation with the Theological Ethics of Stanley Hauerwas*, ed. Mark Thiessen Nation and Samuel Wells (Edinburgh: T&T Clark, 2000): One of the characters muses, "Going to church was like going to the cinema: you sat in rows, the notices were like trailers, the supporting sermon was changed weekly. And people went because they always went. You paid at the plate instead of the box-office, and sometimes they played the organ. There was only one big difference: the main feature was always the same" (281).

27. George Miller, quoted in Michael Frost, *Eyes Wide Open: Seeing God in the Ordinary* (Sutherland, NSW, Australia: Albatross Books, 1998), 100.

28. Robert K. Johnston and Catherine M. Barsotti, "The Year of Living Dangerously," in *Finding God in the Movies: 33 Films of Reel Faith* (Grand Rapids: Baker Books, 2004), 262–63.

29. This section was originally published in a slightly different form in Craig Detweiler, *Into the Dark: Seeing the Sacred in the Top Films of the 21st Century* (Grand Rapids: Baker Academic, 2008), 13–14.

30. Lawrence S. Friedman, quoted in Christopher Deasy, *Screen Christologies: Redemption and the Medium of Film* (Cardiff: University of Wales Press, 2001), 121.

31. Michael Blowen, quoted in Deasy, *Screen Christologies*, 122.

32. This section was originally published in a slightly different form in Kutter Callaway, *Scoring Transcendence: Contemporary Film Music as Religious Experience* (Waco: Baylor University Press, 2013), 1–4.

33. This section was originally published in a slightly different form in Robert K. Johnston, *Reel Spirituality: Theology and Film in Dialogue*, 2nd ed. (Grand Rapids: Baker Academic, 2006), 39–40.

Chapter 2: The Church and Hollywood

1. For an excellent introduction to the history of cinema, view (or read) the Jefferson Award Lecture for 2013 by Martin Scorsese, "Persistence of Vision: Reading the Language of Cinema," on the National Endowment for the Humanities website, https://www.neh.gov/about/awards /jefferson-lecture/martin-scorsese-lecture.

2. Craig Detweiler was in Paris on the hundred-year anniversary of the Lumière brothers' screening and passed by the Grand Café; a small plaque commemorating the event hangs on the wall outside the venue. But alas, no one seemed to notice or care.

3. Terry Lindvall, *The Silents of God: Selected Issues and Documents in Silent American Film and Religion, 1908–1925* (Lanham, MD: Scarecrow, 2001), xi.

4. André Gaudreault and Tom Gunning, quoted in Lindvall, *Silents of God*, xi.

5. For helpful discussions of early religious cinema, see John Baxter, *The Australian Cinema* (Sydney: Angus & Robertson, Pacific Books, 1970), 7–8; Ronald Holloway, *Beyond the Image: Approaches to the Religious Dimension in the Cinema* (Geneva: World Council of Churches, 1977), 45–59. We are dependent on Holloway for much of our discussion of the rise of cinema.

6. "On August 18, 1900, Booth explained in the Salvation Army pamphlet, *War Cry*, that 'these means are employed by the worldling; they form a source of attraction in the theaters and music halls. Why should they be usurped by the enemy of the souls?'" Lindvall, *Silents of God*, 3.

7. Barton W. Currie, "The Nickel Madness," *Harper's Weekly*, August 24, 1907, quoted in F. Miguel Valenti, *More Than a Movie: Ethics in Entertainment* (Boulder, CO: Westview, 2000), 49.

8. Herbert Jump, *The Religious Possibilities of the Motion Picture* (New Britain, CT: South Congregational Church Private Distribution, 1911), reprinted in Lindvall, *Silents of God*, 54–78 (esp. 58).

9. Holloway, *Beyond the Image*, 52.

10. Holloway, *Beyond the Image*, 53.

11. D. W. Griffith, quoted in Les Keyser and Barbara Keyser, *Hollywood and the Catholic Church: The Image of Roman Catholicism in American Movies* (Chicago: Loyola University Press, 1984), 20.

12. Keyser and Keyser, *Hollywood and the Catholic Church*, 24.

13. James Skinner, *The Cross and the Cinema: The Legion of Decency and the National Office for Motion Pictures, 1933–1970* (Westport, CT: Greenwood, 1993), 18.

14. Quoted in Holloway, *Beyond the Image*, 118.

15. Quoted in Skinner, *Cross and the Cinema*, 35.

16. Skinner, *Cross and the Cinema*, 37.

17. Quoted in John R. May, "Close Encounters: Hollywood and Religion after a Century," *Image: A Journal of the Arts & Religion* 20 (Summer 1998): 88.

18. For a fuller discussion of this period, see Gregory Black, *Hollywood Censored: Morality Codes, Catholics, and the Movies* (New York: Cambridge University Press, 1994); Black, *The Catholic Crusade against the Movies, 1940–1975* (New York: Cambridge University Press, 1997); and Frank Walsh, *Sin and Censorship: The Catholic Church and the Motion Picture Industry* (New Haven: Yale University Press, 1996).

19. Pauline Kael, quoted in Ronald Austin, "Sacrificing Images: Violence and the Movies," *Image: A Journal of the Arts & Religion* 20 (Summer 1998): 27.

20. Michael Medved, *Hollywood vs. America: Popular Culture and the War on Traditional Values* (New York: HarperCollins, 1992).

21. Rodney Clapp, quoted in "Pop Goes Theology," *Publishers Weekly*, November 17, 2003, S10.

22. Sally Morgenthaler, "Film and Worship: Windows in Caves and Other Things We Do with Perfectly Good Prisms," *Theology, News & Notes* 52, no. 2 (Spring 2005): 13–15, 25.

23. However, Sally Morgenthaler, a consultant to the Emerging Church movement, also complained that worship pragmatism was too often undermining the quality of the worship service in churches. Although movies were increasingly being used, they were being used poorly. See Morgenthaler, "Film and Worship." Congregants were seeking the Light but were instead being treated to worship lite. For Morgenthaler, there was no doubt that the quality of dialogue and usage needed to improve in the years ahead. But there was also this new reality: the astounding proliferation of film usage by churches as they entered the twenty-first century.

24. Pope John Paul II, quoted in Peter Malone with Rose Pacatte, *Lights Camera . . . Faith! A Movie Lover's Guide to Scripture, A Movie Lectionary—Cycle A* (Boston: Pauline Books & Media, 2001), xi.

25. Pope John Paul II, "Address of John Paul II to the Participants in the Ninth Public Meeting of the Pontifical Academies," November 9, 2004, http://w2.vatican.va/content/john-paul-ii /en/speeches/2004/november/documents/hf_jp-ii_spe_20041109_pontifical-academies.html. Cf. also Pope John Paul II's 1999 letter to artists about their gifts and responsibilities. He begins, "To all who are passionately dedicated to the search for new 'epiphanies' of beauty so that through their creative work as artists they may offer these gifts to the world" ("Letter of His Holiness Pope John Paul II to Artists," April 4, 1999, http://w2.vatican.va/content/john-paul-ii/en/letters/1999 /documents/hf_jp-ii_let_23041999_artists.html). Cf. also the pamphlet by Cardinal Roger M. Mahony, archbishop of Los Angeles, *Film Makers, Film Viewers: Their Challenges and Opportunities, A Pastoral Letter* (Boston: St. Paul Books & Media, 1992).

26. Bishop T. D. Jakes, quoted in Rebecca Winters, "Q&A: T. D. Jakes," *Time*, October 4, 2004, 95, http://content.time.com/time/magazine/article/0,9171,995294,00.html.

27. Richard Corliss, "The Gospel according to Spider-Man," *Time*, August 9, 2004, http:// content.time.com/time/magazine/article/0,9171,678640,00.html.

28. Terry Lindvall, "Religion and Film, Part I: History and Criticism," *Communication Research Trends* 23, no. 4 (2004): 3–44; Lindvall, "Religion and Film, Part II," *Communication Research Trends* 24, no. 1 (2005): 2–40.

29. Several books use film to unpack the Apostles' Creed. See, e.g., Bryan Stone, *Faith and Film: Theological Themes at the Cinema* (St. Louis: Chalice, 2000); David Cunningham, *Reading Is Believing: The Christian Faith through Literature and Film* (Grand Rapids: Brazos, 2002); and John May, *Nourishing Faith through Fiction: Reflections of the Apostles' Creed in Literature and Film* (Franklin, WI: Sheed & Ward, 2001).

30. Cf. Robert Jewett, *Saint Paul at the Movies: The Apostle's Dialogue with American Culture* (Louisville: Westminster John Knox, 1993); Jewett, *Saint Paul Returns to the Movies: Triumph over Shame* (Grand Rapids: Eerdmans, 1999); Larry Kreitzer, *The New Testament in Fiction and Film: On Reversing the Hermeneutical Flow* (Sheffield, UK: JSOT Press, 1993); Kreitzer, *Gospel Images in Fiction and Film: On Reversing the Hermeneutical Flow* (London: Sheffield Academic, 2002); and Robert K. Johnston, *Useless Beauty: Ecclesiastes through the Lens of Contemporary Film* (Grand Rapids: Baker Academic, 2004).

31. Peter Malone and Rose Pacatte have compiled three large volumes providing movie suggestions that correlate with lectionary texts for all three cycles of the church's lectionary (*Lights Camera . . . Faith! A Movie Lover's Guide to Scripture, A Movie Lectionary—Cycle A, Cycle B, Cycle C* [Boston: Pauline Books & Media, 2001, 2002, 2003]), while Craig Brian Larson has cowritten two books titled *Movie-Based Illustrations for Preaching & Teaching: 101 Clips to Show and Tell* (with Andrew Zahn) and *More Movie-Based Illustrations for Preaching & Teaching: 101 Clips to Show & Tell* (with Lori Quicke) (Grand Rapids: Zondervan, 2003, 2004).

32. Doug Fields and Eddie James's two volumes, *Videos That Teach* and *Videos That Teach 2* (Grand Rapids: Zondervan, 1999, 2002), and Bryan Belknap's two books, *Group's Blockbuster Movie Illustrations* and *Group's Blockbuster Movie Illustrations: The Sequel* (Loveland, CO: Group Publishing, 2001, 2003).

33. Cf. Edward McNulty, *Films and Faith: Forty Discussion Guides* (Topeka, KS: Viaticum, 1999); Bob Smithouser, *Movie Nights: 25 Movies to Spark Spiritual Discussions with Your Teen* (Wheaton: Tyndale, 2002); Robert K. Johnston and Catherine M. Barsotti, *Finding God in the Movies: 33 Films of Reel Faith* (Grand Rapids: Baker Books, 2004). Web-based resources include Reel Issues, study guides from The Bible Society of Great Britain, http://www.reelissues.org.uk; Cinema in Focus, http://www.cinemainfocus.com; Reel Spirituality, http://www.reelspirituality.org; and Damaris Media, http://filmblog.damaris.org.

34. Cf. Edward McNulty, *Praying the Movies: Daily Meditations from Classic Films* (Louisville: Geneva Press, 2001) and *Praying the Movies II: More Daily Meditations from Classic Films* (Louisville: Westminster John Knox, 2003); Sara Anson Vaux, *Finding Meaning at the Movies* (Nashville: Abingdon, 1999); Richard A. Burridge, *Faith Odyssey: A Journey through Life* (Grand Rapids: Eerdmans, 2003).

35. Alissa Wilkinson, "How 2016's Movies and TV Reflected Americans' Changing Relationship with Religion," Vox, December 15, 2016, www.vox.com/culture/2016/12/14/13899722/religion-tv-movies-2016-sausage-party-silence-innocents-americans-rectify.

36. It is worth noting that all three of these faith-focused movies that were successful in the wider market were produced by Rich Peluso and his team at Sony Affirmed.

37. Cf. "Multiple-Choice God," editorial, *Los Angeles Times*, September 17, 2006, http://articles.latimes.com/2006/sep/17/opinion/ed-god17.

38. Cf. Steven Felix-Jager, *Spirit of the Arts* (New York: Palgrave Macmillan, 2017), 170–73.

39. Kyle Smith, "'Logan' Is a Return to Science Fiction's Glory Days," *New York Post*, February 28, 2017, http://nypost.com/2017/02/28/logan-is-a-return-to-science-fictions-glory-days.

40. Paul Asay, "Logan Is a Christian Fable Disguised as a Superhero Story," Watching God, March 31, 2017, http://sixseeds.patheos.com/watchinggod/2017/03/logan-is-a-christian-fable-disguised-as-a-superhero-story/2.

41. We are dependent in what follows on the excellent article by Elijah Davidson on the influences of the western in *Logan*: Elijah Davidson, "Beating Claws into Plowshares: Logan at the End of All Things," Brehm Center, Reel Spirituality webpage, March 6, 2017, http://www.brehmcenter.com/initiatives/reelspirituality/film/articles/beating-claws-into-plowshares-logan-at-the-end-of-all-things.

42. Davidson, "Beating Claws into Plowshares."

43. Cf. Dave Urbanski, "The Man Came Around," *Christianity Today*, December 19, 2005, www.christianitytoday.com/ct/2005/decemberweb-only/johnnycash-1205.html.

44. "The Man Comes Around," on Johnny Cash, *American IV: The Man Comes Around*, compact disc, American Recordings, 2002.

45. Wade Bearden, "In 'Logan', Wolverine Confronts the Wages of Sin," *Christianity Today*, March 2, 2017, www.christianitytoday.com/ct/channel/utilities/print.html?type=article&id=137914.

Chapter 3: Fade In

1. *Stranger Than Fiction*, directed by Marc Forster, screenplay by Zach Helm (Culver City, CA: Sony Pictures Home Entertainment, 2007).

2. First published in 1979, Syd Field's *Screenplay: The Foundations of Screenwriting*, rev. ed. (New York: Delta Books, 2005), revealed Hollywood trade secrets in unprecedented ways.

3. Robert McKee, *Story: Substance, Structure, Style, and the Principles of Screenwriting* (New York: HarperCollins, 1997), 4.

4. McKee, *Story*, 11.

5. McKee, *Story*, 12.

6. See everything from the postliberal narrative theology of George Lindbeck and Stanley Hauerwas to the popular Storyline and StoryBrand Conferences of Donald Miller, inspired by his experience of Robert McKee's "Story" seminars.

7. Robert Newman, quoted in Patrick Goldstein, "Sequels Are Fish Food," *Los Angeles Times*, July 8, 2003, sec. E, 4.

8. David Thomson, *The Whole Equation: A History of Hollywood* (New York: Alfred A. Knopf, 2004).

9. From Roger Ebert's remarks as he was awarded a star on the Hollywood Walk of Fame on June 23, 2005—the first critic to be so recognized. Transcript on RogerEbert.com, June 24, 2005, http://www.rogerebert.com/rogers-journal/eberts-walk-of-fame-remarks.

10. Wesley Kort, *Narrative Elements and Religious Meaning* (Philadelphia: Fortress, 1975).

11. Frederick Buechner, *Listening to Your Life* (San Francisco: HarperSanFrancisco, 1992), 10.

12. Shirley Li, "Reese Witherspoon Makes Plea for Women to Tell Their Own Stories after *Big Little Lies* Win," *Entertainment Weekly*, September 17, 2017, http://ew.com/awards/2017/09/17/big-little-lies-limited-emmy-win.

13. Barry Jenkins, "'Moonlight's' Barry Jenkins: Here's the Oscar Speech I Would Have Given," *The Hollywood Reporter*, March 1, 2017, http://www.hollywoodreporter.com/news/moonlights-barry-jenkins-heres-oscar-speech-i-would-have-given-981581.

14. Jon Boorstin, *Making Movies Work: Thinking Like a Filmmaker* (Los Angeles: Silman-James, 1995), 154.

15. Linda Seger, *Making a Good Script Great* (Hollywood, CA: Samuel French, 1987), 4.

16. Louis Giannetti, *Understanding Movies*, 5th ed. (Englewood Cliffs, NJ: Prentice Hall, 1990), 300.

17. Ramona Zacharias, "Barry Jenkins on Moonlight," *Creative Screenwriting*, February 9, 2017, https://creativescreenwriting.com/moonlight.

18. Zacharias, "Barry Jenkins on Moonlight."

19. Meredith Woerner, "The Making of *Mad Max: Fury Road*: 'We Shot One Scene for 138 Days,'" io9, May 12, 2015, https://io9.gizmodo.com/the-making-of-mad-max-fury-road-we-shot-one-scene-fo-1704025550.

20. Russ Fischer, "*Mad Max: Fury Road*—Eight Awesome Facts about the Making of the Film," SlashFilm, May 22, 2015, http://www.slashfilm.com/fury-road-trivia/2/.

21. Terry Gross, "'Mad Max' Director George Miller—The Audience Tells You 'What Your Film Is,'" National Public Radio, February 8, 2016, http://www.npr.org/templates/transcript/transcript.php?storyId=465989808.

22. Nathan Scott Jr., *The Broken Center* (New Haven: Yale University Press, 1966), 4.

23. Paul Woolf, "Turning Towards Home," *Image: A Journal of the Arts & Religion* 20 (Summer 1998): 123.

24. Frederick Buechner, *Telling the Truth: The Gospel as Tragedy, Comedy, and Fairy Tale* (San Francisco: HarperCollins, 1977).

Chapter 4: Sights and Sounds

1. Alfonso Cuarón, director, *Gravity* (Burbank, CA: Warner Brothers Pictures, 2013).

2. Christopher Doyle, quoted in Robert Mackey, "Cracking the Color Code of 'Hero,'" *New York Times*, August 15, 2004, https://www.nytimes.com/2004/08/15/movies/15MACK.html.

3. Toby Skinner, "20 Ways Harry Potter Changed the World," *American Way*, October 2017, 63.

4. While teaching a summer program in London, Craig took all the students on "The Making of Harry Potter" tour, https://www.wbstudiotour.co.uk/home.

5. Jon Boorstin, *Making Movies Work: Thinking Like a Filmmaker* (Los Angeles: Silman-James, 1995), 75.

6. See the Hobbiton movie set website: http://www.hobbitontours.com/en/our-tours/hobbiton-movie-set-tour.

7. There are countless examples of Pixar's process documented online, including the credits, "From Storyboard to Animation: See How Pixar Created *Toy Story 2*," Motion Picture Association of America, October 17, 2016, https://www.mpaa.org/2016/10/storyboard-animation-see-how-pixar-created-toy-story-2.

8. The process of "Previsualizing Gravity" is among the special features on the Blu-ray of *Gravity* (Burbank, CA: Warner Brothers Pictures, 2013).

9. Boorstin, *Making Movies Work*, 77.

10. The most comprehensive introduction to the art of cinematography is the DVD *Visions of Light*, produced in association with the American Society of Cinematographers (ASC).

11. Rodrigo Prieto, quoted in Bob Fisher, "Uneasy Street," *ICG Magazine* 73, no. 12 (December 2002): 49.

12. John Alton, *Painting with Light* (Berkeley: University of California Press, 1995), xli.

13. Susan Doll posted film stills illustrating Alton's work in "John Alton: Painting with Light in *The Big Combo*," at Filmstruck.com, June 6, 2016, http://streamline.filmstruck.com/2016/06/06/john-alton-painting-with-light-in-the-big-combo.

14. Anita Busch, "Rachel Morrison Is First Woman Nominated for Cinematography in 90-Year History of Oscars," Deadline.com, January 23, 2018, https://deadline.com/2018/01/rachel-morrison-first-woman-nominated-cinematography-90-year-history-oscars-2018-1202267107.

15. Alfonso Cuarón discusses how these scenes were created, in the "extras" section of the DVD for *Children of Men* (New York: Universal Pictures, 2006).

16. Secrets for how the filmmakers solved these "Initial Challenges: Long Shots and Zero G" are available on the Blu-ray for *Gravity*.

17. On the Blu-ray for *Gravity*, Lubezki discusses how "the hues of space" factored into their cinematography and lighting.

18. The most thorough explanation of this concept comes from Bruce Block, *The Visual Story: Seeing the Structure of Film, TV, and New Media* (Boston: Focal Press, 2001).

19. Sidney Gottlieb, ed., *Hitchcock on Hitchcock: Selected Writings and Interviews* (Berkeley: University of California Press, 1995), 15.

20. Boorstin, *Making Movies Work*, 65–66.

21. Sergei Eisenstein, *The Film Sense*, trans. and ed. Jay Leyday (New York: Harcourt, Brace & World, 1947), 4.

22. Boorstin, *Making Movies Work*, 110.

23. See Philip J. Skerry's book-length study: *The Shower Scene in Hitchcock's Psycho: Creating Cinematic Suspense and Terror* (Lewiston, NY: Edwin Mellen, 2005).

24. For a rigorous analysis of the infamous scene, check out Alexandre O. Philippe's documentary, *78/52* (New York: IFC Films, 2017).

25. Boorstin, *Making Movies Work*, 139–43.

26. For a thorough immersion into Murch's creative process, read Walter Murch, *In the Blink of an Eye: A Perspective on Film Editing* (Los Angeles: Silman-James, 2001).

27. Andrey Tarkovsky, *Sculpting in Time* (Austin: University of Texas Press, 1986), 63–64.

28. Gottlieb, *Hitchcock on Hitchcock*, 255–56.

29. For a detailed overview of the entire process, see David Lewis Yewdall, *Practical Art of Motion Picture Sound* (Waltham, MA: Focal Press, 2012).

30. Mark Wilson, "How Ben Burtt Designed the Sounds of Star Wars," *Fast Company*, April 17, 2015, https://www.fastcodesign.com/3045177/how-ben-burtt-designed-the-sounds-of-star-wars.

31. Susan King, "Ben Burtt on the Sound of 'Raiders,' 'ET' and Spielberg's Inspiration," *Los Angeles Times*, October 2, 2012, http://herocomplex.latimes.com/movies/ben-burtt-on-the-sound -of-raiders-et-and-spielbergs-inspiration.

32. Gary Rydstrom, "Jurassic Park," on the Motion Picture Sound Editors website, copyright 2011, http://www.jasonryder.com/MPSE/education/jurassic.html.

33. The author of *The English Patient*, Michael Ondaatje, summons trade secrets from Murch in *The Conversations: Walter Murch and the Art of Editing Film* (New York: Alfred A. Knopf, 2004).

34. Academic studies of the power of soundtracks are rising, including the work of Kutter Callaway, *Scoring Transcendence: Contemporary Film Music as Religious Experience* (Waco: Baylor University Press, 2012).

35. Aaron Copland, "The Aims of Music for Films," *New York Times*, March 10, 1946, summarized in Pauline Reay, *Music in Film: Soundtracks and Synergy* (New York: Wallflower Press, 2004), 32.

36. To hear directly from composers like Hans Zimmer and John Williams as they talk about their craft, watch (and listen to) *Score: A Film Music Documentary* (Gravitas Ventures, 2017).

37. Matt Juul, "Why the Music of 'Jaws' Is Still Terrifying," *Boston Globe*, June 16, 2105, https://www.boston.com/culture/entertainment/2015/06/16/why-the-music-of-jaws-is-still-terrifying.

38. Jon Burlingame, "Women Film Composers Fight for an Even Score," *Variety*, August 24, 2016, http://variety.com/2016/music/spotlight/women-film-composers-1201843422/.

39. Steven Price explains his process of creating "The Sound of Action in Space" on the special features for the Blu-ray of *Gravity*.

Chapter 5: Where Form Meets Feeling

1. A. O. Scott, *Better Living through Criticism: How to Think about Art, Pleasure, Beauty, and Truth* (New York: Penguin Press, 2016), 17.

2. For an extended analysis of this phenomena, see Craig Detweiler, *Into the Dark: Seeing the Sacred in the Top Films of the 21st Century* (Grand Rapids: Baker Academic, 2008).

3. As of November 2017, *In the Mood for Love* is ranked at number 243 on the IMDb list of the top 250 films of all time, http://www.imdb.com/title/tt0118694.

4. Sergei Eisenstein, "The Cinematographic Principle and the Ideogram," in *Film Form: Essays in Film Theory*, trans. Jay Leyda (New York: Harcourt Brace Jovanovich, 1949), 28.

5. Griffith's breakthroughs are chronicled in the documentary *A Personal Journey with Martin Scorsese through American Movies* (DVD), directed by Martin Scorsese and Michael Henry Wilson (New York: Miramax, 2012).

6. Sergei Eisenstein, "Dickens, Griffith, and the Film Today," in *Film Form*, quoted in *Film Theory and Criticism: Introductory Readings*, ed. Leo Braudy and Marshall Cohen (New York: Oxford University Press, 1999), 426.

7. Eisenstein, "The Cinematographic Principle and the Ideogram," 29–30.

8. Gerald Mast and Bruce F. Kawin, *A Short History of the Movies*, 8th ed. (New York: Longman, 2003), 177–78.

9. Sergei Eisenstein, "A Dialectic Approach to Film Form," in *Film Form*, 62.

10. Eisenstein, "Dialectic Approach," 42.

11. Pioneering film theorist Rudolph Arnheim lamented the inevitable triumph of "the complete film" in *Film as Art* (Berkeley: University of California Press, 1957).

12. Sergei Eisenstein, Vsevolod Pudovkin, and Grigori Alexandrov, "Statement on Sound," in *Film Theory and Criticism*, ed. Leo Braudy and Marshall Cohen (New York: Oxford University Press, 2004), 361–62.

13. André Bazin, "The Evolution of the Language of Cinema," in *What Is Cinema?*, trans. Hugh Gray (Berkeley: University of California Press, 2005), 1:23.

14. André Bazin, "The Ontology of the Photographic Image," in *What Is Cinema?*, 1:10.

15. This point was noted by Bazin's gifted translator, Hugh Gray, in *What Is Cinema?*, 1:13.

16. Bazin, "Ontology of the Photographic Image," 15.

17. Bazin, "Evolution of the Language of Cinema," 38.

18. Bazin, "Evolution of the Language of Cinema," 36.

19. Bazin, "Evolution of the Language of Cinema," 34.

20. André Bazin, "The Myth of Total Cinema," in *What Is Cinema?*, 1:22.

21. Bazin, "Evolution of the Language of Cinema," 28.

22. Leo Braudy, *The World in a Frame: What We See in Films* (Chicago: University of Chicago Press, 1984), 105.

23. Braudy, *World in a Frame*, 104.

24. Braudy, *World in a Frame*, 105.

25. Martin Scorsese, in Martin Scorsese and Michael Henry Wilson, *A Personal Journey with Martin Scorsese through American Movies* (New York: MiramaxBooks/Hyperion, 1997), 33. In our discussion of how the western changed to reflect the changing shape of American culture, we are dependent on Scorsese's insightful comments.

26. Stanley Cavell, *Pursuits of Happiness: The Hollywood Comedy of Remarriage* (Cambridge, MA: Harvard University Press, 1981), 17.

27. Scorsese and Wilson, *Personal Journey*, 40.

28. Cf. Will Wright, *Six Guns and Society: A Structural Study of the Western* (Berkeley: University of California Press, 1975), 97.

29. Andrew Sarris, "Notes on the Auteur Theory," *Film Culture*, no. 28 (Winter 1962/63); and Sarris, *The American Cinema: Directors and Directions, 1929–1968* (Chicago: Da Capo, 1996), 29–33.

30. Pauline Kael, "Circles and Squares," *Film Quarterly* 16, no. 3 (Spring 1963): 12–26.

31. Sarris, *American Cinema*, 39.

32. We are indebted to Brian Henderson's insights from "Toward a Non-Bourgeois Camera Style," in Braudy and Cohen, *Film Theory and Criticism*.

33. At the 2018 Cannes Film Festival, Godard, now in his late eighties, screened his most recent film and was given a special achievement award by the festival jury. *Le livre d'image* (*The Image Book*) continued his personal critique of film in the twentieth century, more manifesto than entertainment.

34. On the website The Independents, www.godamongdirectors.com.

35. Christian Metz, *Film Language: A Semiotics of the Cinema*, trans. Michael Taylor (New York: Oxford University Press, 1974).

36. Molly Haskell, *From Reverence to Rape: The Treatment of Women in the Movies* (New York: Penguin Books, 1974).

37. Laura Mulvey, "Visual Pleasure and Narrative Cinema," *Screen* 16, no. 3 (1975): 6–18.

38. Among her many books and articles, see especially bell hooks, "The Oppositional Gaze," in *Black Looks: Race and Representation* (Boston: South End, 1992).

39. Megan Garber, "Call It the 'Bechdel-Wallace Test,'" *The Atlantic*, August 25, 2015, https://www.theatlantic.com/entertainment/archive/2015/08/call-it-the-bechdel-wallace-test/402259.

40. Jack G. Shaheen, *Reel Bad Arabs: How Hollywood Vilifies a People* (Northampton, MA: Olive Branch, 2014).

41. Craig Detweiler, "How Transformers and Michael Bay Shill for China (and Undercut Hong Kong)," Patheos, October 14, 2014, http://www.patheos.com/blogs/dochollywood/2014/10/how-transformers-and-michael-bay-shill-for-china-undercut-hong-kong.

42. Pauline Kael, "Trash, Art, and the Movies," *Harper's*, February 1969.

43. Michael Cavna, "How 'Wonder Woman' Director Patty Jenkins Cracked the Superhero-Movie Glass Ceiling," *Washington Post*, May 31, 2017, https://www.washingtonpost.com/news/comic-riffs/wp/2017/05/31/how-wonder-woman-director-patty-jenkins-cracked-the-superhero-movie-glass-ceiling.

44. Cavna, "'Wonder Woman' Director."

45. Trey Williams, "'Wonder Woman' Passes 'Mamma Mia!' as Highest-Grossing Film by Female Director," *MarketWatch*, June 24, 2017, https://www.marketwatch.com/story/wonder-woman-passes-mamma-mia-as-highest-grossing-film-by-female-director-2017-06-23.

46. Richard Brody, "The Hard-Won Wisdom of 'Wonder Woman,'" *New Yorker*, June 6, 2017, https://www.newyorker.com/culture/richard-brody/the-hard-won-wisdom-of-wonder-woman.

47. Ann Hornaday, "'Wonder Woman' Saves the Day, in More Ways Than One," *Washington Post*, May 31, 2017, https://www.washingtonpost.com/goingoutguide/movies/wonder-woman-saves-the-day-in-more-ways-than-one/2017/05/31/c20193c6-45ea-11e7-98cd-af64b4fe2dfc_story.html.

48. "Best Superhero Movies of All Time," Rotten Tomatoes, accessed May 10, 2018, http://editorial.rottentomatoes.com/guide/best-superhero-movies-of-all-time.

49. Andrew R. Chow, "Women-Only Screenings of 'Wonder Woman' Sell Out and Prompt Criticism," *New York Times*, May 28, 2017, https://www.nytimes.com/2017/05/28/movies/women-only-screenings-of-wonder-woman-sell-out-and-prompt-complaints.html.

50. Hadley Freeman, "James Cameron: The Downside of Being Attracted to Independent Women Is That They Don't Need You," *The Guardian*, August 25, 2017, https://www.theguardian.com/film/2017/aug/24/james-cameron-well-never-be-able-to-reproduce-the-shock-of-terminator-2.

51. Leon Watson, "Wonder Woman Star Gal Gadot Refuses to Make Sequel Until Producer Brett Ratner Ends Involvement," *The Telegraph*, November 12, 2017, http://www.telegraph.co.uk/news/2017/11/12/wonder-woman-stargal-gadot-refuses-make-sequel-untilbrett-ratner.

52. Casey Cipriani, "'Wonder Woman 2' Will Be the First Movie to Use New Sexual Harassment Guidelines and It's the Perfect Choice," Bustle, January 22, 2018, https://www.bustle.com/p/wonder-woman-2-will-be-the-first-movie-to-use-new-sexual-harassment-guidelines-its-the-perfect-choice-7977798.

Chapter 6: A Diverse Church Responds

1. Paul Woolf, "Turning toward Home," *Image: A Journal of the Arts & Religion* 20 (Summer 1998): 116.

2. John R. Rice, *What Is Wrong with the Movies?* (Grand Rapids: Zondervan, 1938), 3.

3. Bryan P. Stone, *Faith and Film: Theological Themes at the Cinema* (St. Louis: Chalice, 2000), 5.

4. Kevin Smith, quoted in Mick LaSalle, "Kevin Smith's Religious Experience," *San Francisco Sunday Examiner and Chronicle*, October 31, 1999, Datebook, 50.

5. Patrick Scully, quoted in Teresa Watanabe, "Chasing Catholicism," *Los Angeles Times*, November 10, 1999, sec. F, 1.

6. Cliff Rothman, "*Dogma* Opens in New York to Protesters' Jeers, Audience Cheers," *Los Angeles Times*, October 6, 1999, sec. F, 2, 4.

7. Charles Colson, "And the Winner Is: Death, Depravity and Dullness," *Breakpoint Commentary* #050301, March 1, 2005, http://freerepublic.com/focus/f-religion/1353564/posts.

8. Barbara Nicolosi, "The 'Passion' Oscar Snub: Revenge of the Blue States?," *Beliefnet*, http://www.beliefnet.com/story/160/story_16008.html.

9. Charles Colson, "Finding Good Movies," *Breakpoint Commentary* #71001, 1997; cf. Focus on the Family's Bob Smithouser, *Movie Nights: 25 Movies to Spark Spiritual Discussions with Your Teen* (Wheaton: Tyndale, 2002), 4: "The apostle Paul admonished Christians to *avoid* capture through 'hollow and deceptive philosophy.' To use a military model, there are two ways to avoid capture. One is to stay as far away from the enemy as possible. Another is to study the enemy's strategies from a safe distance, then engage that foe so adroitly that you can defend your homestead and also ensure escape. Families seeking wisdom in the latter should find this book extremely helpful."

10. Margaret Miles, *Seeing and Believing: Religion and Values in the Movies* (Boston: Beacon, 1996), 4.

11. Miles, *Seeing and Believing*, 15.

12. John C. Lyden, *Film as Religion: Myths, Morals, and Rituals* (New York: New York University Press, 2003), 32.

13. C. S. Lewis, *An Experiment in Criticism* (Cambridge: Cambridge University Press, 1961), 85.

14. Cf. William Romanowski and Jennifer L. Vander Heide, "Easier Said Than Done: On Reversing the Hermeneutical Flow in the Theology and Film Dialogue," *Journal of Communication and Religion* 30 (March 2007): 40–64.

15. Cf. T. S. Eliot, in his classic essay on reading literature, argued that "literary criticism [substitute "film criticism"] should be completed by criticism from a definite ethical and theological standpoint." But he also recognized that "whether it is literature or not can be determined only by literary standards." T. S. Eliot, "Religion and Literature," in *Religion and Modern Literature: Essays in Theory and Criticism*, ed. G. B. Tennyson and Edward E. Ericson Jr. (Grand Rapids: Eerdmans, 1975), 21.

16. Joel W. Martin and Conrad E. Ostwalt Jr., eds., *Screening the Sacred: Religion, Myth, and Ideology in Popular American Film* (Boulder, CO: Westview, 1995); Clive Marsh and Gaye Ortiz, eds., *Explorations in Theology and Film: Movies and Meaning* (Oxford: Blackwell, 1997).

17. Roy Anker, *Catching Light: Looking for God in the Movies* (Grand Rapids: Eerdmans, 2004).

18. Richard Blake, *Afterimage* (Chicago: Loyola University Press, 2000).

19. Robert K. Johnston, *Useless Beauty: Ecclesiastes through the Lens of Contemporary Film* (Grand Rapids: Baker Academic, 2004).

20. Nathaniel Dorsky, "Devotional Cinema," in *The Hidden God: Film and Faith*, ed. Mary Lea Bandy and Antonio Monda (New York: Museum of Modern Art, 2003), 261, 264.

21. Dorsky, "Devotional Cinema," 265.

22. See Robert K. Johnston and Catherine M. Barsotti, *Finding God in the Movies: 33 Films of Reel Faith* (Grand Rapids: Baker Books, 2004), 19–20.

23. Tony Campolo, foreword to Gareth Higgins, *How Movies Helped Save My Soul: Finding Spiritual Fingerprints in Culturally Significant Films* (Lake Mary, FL: Relevant Books, 2003), x–xi.

24. Clive Marsh, *Cinema and Sentiment: Film's Challenge to Theology* (Milton Keynes, UK: Paternoster, 2004), ix.

25. Marsh, *Cinema and Sentiment*, 35, 134.

26. John R. May, "Religion and Film: Recent Contributions to the Continuing Dialogue," *Critical Review of Books in Religion* 9 (1996): 117.

27. Scott Derrickson, quoted in Jeffrey Overstreet, *Through a Screen Darkly* (Ventura, CA: Regal Books, 2007), 1.

28. Overstreet, *Through a Screen Darkly*, 17–18.

29. Jonathan Brant, *Paul Tillich and the Possibility of Revelation through Film* (Oxford: Oxford University Press, 2012).

30. Private correspondence, used with permission.

31. Andrew Greeley, *God in Popular Culture* (Chicago: Thomas More, 1988), 250.

32. Richard McBrien, quoted in Vincent Miller, *Consuming Religion: Christian Faith and Practice in a Consumer Culture* (New York: Continuum, 2004), 189.

33. Greeley, *God in Popular Culture*, 250; cf. Albert J. Bergesen and Andrew M. Greeley, *God in the Movies* (New Brunswick, NJ: Transaction, 2000). Other Catholic theologians and film critics argue in similar ways. Richard Blake, for example, recognizes the need for the church "to broaden the question of religion and film from morality" (Richard Blake, "From Peepshow to Prayer: Toward a Spirituality of the Movies," *Journal of Religion and Film* 6, no. 2 [October 2002]). The religious dimension of film is not to be found either in the moviemaker's intention or in overtly religious content but in the observer-critic's experience (Richard Blake, "Secular Prophecy in an Age of Film," *Journal of Religious Thought* 27, no. 1 [Spring–Summer 1970]: 72).

34. Paul Schrader, *Transcendental Style in Film: Ozu, Bresson, Dreyer* (New York: Da Capo, 1988), 3. A new edition of the book with a new introduction has been published by the University of California Press (Berkeley, 2018).

35. Craig Detweiler, "Tree of Life: From Genesis to Revelation," Patheos, February 5, 2014, www.patheos.com/blogs/dochollywood/2014/02/tree-of-life-from-genesis-to-revelation.

36. For a discussion of "glossolalia" as an alternate film style to Schrader's, see Terry Lindvall, W. O. Williams, and Artie Terry, "Spectacular Transcendence: Abundant Means in the Cinematic Representation of African American Christianity," *Howard Journal of Communication* 7 (1996): 205–20.

37. An interesting case study in attempted "coercion" is the sequels to *The Matrix* where the profundity of the original gives way to viewer frustration and diminishing returns. What began on an Easter weekend inviting divine encounter ended up assaulting viewers with an overkill of images that left the viewer bored and disappointed.

38. H. Richard Niebuhr, *Christ and Culture* (New York: Harper & Row, 1951).

39. Cf. Glen Stassen, Diane Yeager, and John Yoder, *Authentic Transformation* (Nashville: Abingdon, 1996).

40. M. Basil Pennington, *Centering Prayer: Renewing an Ancient Christian Prayer Form* (Garden City, NY: Doubleday, 1980).

41. A more recent example is Josh Larsen, *Movies Are Prayers: How Films Voice Our Deepest Longings* (Downers Grove, IL: InterVarsity, 2017).

42. For a more complete discussion, see Robert K. Johnston, "Transformative Viewing: Penetrating the Story's Surface," in *Re-Viewing Theology and Film*, ed. Robert K. Johnston (Grand Rapids: Baker Academic, 2007).

43. Cf. Flannery O' Connor, "The Nature and Aim of Fiction," in Flannery O'Connor, *Mystery and Manners*, ed. Sally and Robert Fitzgerald (New York: Farrar, Straus & Giroux, 1969):

> The kind of vision the fiction writer needs to have, or to develop, in order to increase the meaning of his story is called anagogical vision, and that is the kind of vision that is able to see different levels of reality in one image or one situation. The medieval commentators on Scripture found three kinds of meaning in the literal level of the sacred text: one they called allegorical, in which one fact pointed to another; one they called tropological, or moral, which had to do with what should be done; and one they called anagogical, which had to do with the Divine life and our participation in it. Although this was a method applied to biblical exegesis, it was also an attitude toward all of creation, and a way of reading nature which included most possibilities, and I think it is this enlarged view of the human scene that the fiction writer has to cultivate if he is ever going to write stories that have any chance of becoming a permanent part of our literature. (72–73)

44. Cf. Northrop Frye, "Reconsidering Levels of Meaning," *Christianity and Literature* 54, no. 3 (Spring 2005): 397–421.

45. Cf. Johnston, *Useless Beauty*, where the encounter with such movies as *Monster's Ball* and *Magnolia* provides an evocation of beauty/Beauty that resonates personally, compels communal sympathy and action, and evokes a participation in the transcendent.

46. We want to thank Amanda Munroe for suggesting a similar methodology using "what."

47. Cf. Tony Wheeler, "Where Penguins Rule the Roost," *Los Angeles Times*, December 4, 2005, sec. L, 9. In this full-page feature on penguins in the travel section, the article's writer begins, "So if you've seen 'March of the Penguins' and now want to see those fabulous fowl, it's easier (and cheaper) than it has ever been."

48. Lennard J. Davis, "Penguins: A Poor Case for Intelligent Design, Family Values," *Chicago Tribune*, November 6, 2005, section 2, 3.

49. Davis, "Penguins."

50. The screenwriter for this movie, hired by Warner Brothers to replace the cartoonish original French narration, was Jordan Roberts, a friend of Craig's from their mutual church community. The love he writes about and which Morgan Freeman brings to life on the screen is something he also believes in and seeks to live out.

51. Karl Rahner, "Poetry and the Christian," in *Theological Investigations*, vol. 4 (London: Darton, Longman & Todd, 1967), 357–61.

Chapter 7: Discerning Mystery

1. For a fuller description of these events, see Terry Lindvall, *The Silents of God* (Lanham, MD: Scarecrow, 2001): 7–8, 44–78.

Parts of this chapter were first given as a plenary address to the Western section of the Society of Biblical Literature, Santa Clara, CA, March 25, 2012; as lectures at Dallas Theological Seminary, October 2014, and at Pepperdine University, January 2015. Readers are also directed to the following works by Johnston: "The Mystery Discerning Business," in *Don't Stop Believin': Pop Culture and Religion from Ben Hur to Zombies*, ed. Robert K. Johnston, Craig Detweiler, and Barry Taylor (Louisville: Westminster John Knox, 2012): 207–15; "Film as Parable: What Might This Mean?," in *Doing Theology for the Church: Essays in Honor of Klyne Snodgrass*, ed. Rebekah A. Eklund and John E. Phelan (Eugene, OR: Wipf & Stock, 2014), 19–32; "The Film Viewer and Natural Theology: God's 'Presence' at the Movies," in *Oxford Handbook of Natural Theology*, ed. Russell Re Manning (Oxford: Oxford University Press, 2013), chap. 38 (595–610); *God's Wider Presence: Reconsidering General Revelation* (Grand Rapids: Baker Academic, 2014), preface and chap. 3 (xii–xix, 42–66); "Can Watching a Movie Be a Spiritual Experience?," in *Religion and Popular Culture*, 3rd ed., ed. Jeffrey Mahan and Bruce Forbes (Berkeley: University of California Press, 2017), 373–89.

2. Lindvall, *Silents of God*, 44–78.

3. Lindvall, *Silents of God*, 56.

4. Klyne Snodgrass, *Stories with Intent: A Comprehensive Guide to the Parables of Jesus* (Grand Rapids: Eerdmans, 2008).

5. Snodgrass, *Stories with Intent*, 1.

6. Snodgrass, *Stories with Intent*, 8.

7. Paul Haggis, quoted in Sean Smith and David Ansen, "Prize Fighters; They Made the Most Moving, Provocative Films of the Year," *Newsweek*, February 6, 2006, 62.

8. See Peter Chattaway, "Stranger Than Fiction," *Christianity Today*, November 10, 2006, http://www.christianitytoday.com/movies/reviews/2006/strangerthanfiction.html.

9. *Stranger Than Fiction*, directed by Marc Forster, screenplay by Zach Helm (Culver City, CA: Sony Pictures Home Entertainment, 2007).

10. This section was originally published in a slightly different form in Johnston, "Can Watching a Movie Be a Spiritual Experience?," in *Religion and Popular Culture in America*, 3rd ed., ed. Bruce David Forbes and Jeffrey H. Mahan (Berkeley: University of California Press, 2017), 373–89.

11. The 84th Annual Academy Awards, February 26, 2012, ABC television.

12. To give but a sample: Joel Martin and Conrad Ostwald edited *Screening the Sacred* (Boulder, CO: Westview, 1995); Andrew Greeley and Albert Bergeson wrote *God in the Movies* (New Brunswick, NJ: Transaction, 2000); Ken Gire's popular study from 2000 was entitled *Reflections on the Movies: Hearing God in the Unlikeliest Places* (Colorado Springs: Chariot Victor, 2000); and Johnston's book *Reel Spirituality* also appeared first in 2000, followed by its second edition in 2006 (Grand Rapids: Baker Academic, 2000, 2006). Gareth Higgins's personal reflection entitled *How Movies Helped Save My Soul* (Lake Mary, FL: Relevant Books, 2003) came out in 2003; the study guide Catherine Barsotti and Rob Johnston wrote in 2004 was entitled *Finding God in the Movies* (Grand Rapids: Baker Books, 2004). Eric Christianson edited *Cinéma Divinité* with two colleagues in 2005 (London: SCM, 2005); Chris Deacy and Gaye Ortiz's book *Theology and Film* (Malden, MA: Blackwell, 2008) had as its subtitle "Challenging the Sacred/Secular Divide"; the subtitle of Craig Detweiler's *Into the Dark* (Grand Rapids: Baker Academic, 2008), published in the same year, was even more direct: "Seeing the Sacred in the Best Films of the 21st Century." In 2010, Roy Anker's book *Of Pilgrims and Fire* (Grand Rapids: Eerdmans, 2010) had as its subtitle "When God Shows Up at the Movies," which in 2017 he followed with *Beautiful Light: Religious Meaning in Film* (Grand Rapids: Eerdmans, 2017). And Kutter Callaway added *Scoring Transcendence: Contemporary Film Music as Religious Experience* (Waco: Baylor University Press, 2012).

13. T. S. Eliot, "Burnt Norton," *Four Quartets*, in *The Complete Poems and Plays, 1909–1950* (New York: Harcourt, Brace & World, 1971), 119.

14. Avery Dulles, "Revelation and Discovery," in *Theology and Discovery: Essays in Honor of Karl Rahner, S. J.*, ed. William J. Kelly (Milwaukee: Marquette University Press, 1980), 1–29.

15. The lecture has been published in two different forms: first in Robert McAfee Brown, *The Pseudonyms of God* (Philadelphia: Westminster, 1972), 96–103, and years later in Robert McAfee Brown, *Persuade Us to Rejoice: The Liberating Power of Fiction* (Louisville: Westminster John Knox, 1992).

16. Justin Martyr, *Second Apology* 13.

17. Brown, *Persuade Us*, 35.

18. For a fuller discussion of *American Beauty*, see Robert K. Johnston, "Beyond Futility: *American Beauty* and the Book of Ecclesiastes," in *The Gift of Story: Narrating Hope in a Postmodern World*, ed. Emily Griesinger and Mark Eaton (Waco: Baylor University Press, 2006), 85–96.

19. For a fuller discussion of the movie's relation to Ecclesiastes, see Robert K. Johnston, *Useless Beauty: Ecclesiastes through the Lens of Contemporary Film* (Grand Rapids: Baker Academic, 2004), 57–72.

20. For a fuller discussion of the Spirit's revelatory presence outside the believing community, see Robert K. Johnston, *God's Wider Presence: Reconsidering General Revelation* (Grand Rapids: Baker Academic, 2014), 67–119.

21. Thomas Weinandy, *Does God Suffer?* (South Bend, IN: University of Notre Dame Press, 2000), 32–34, quoted in Richard Mouw, *He Shines in All That's Fair* (Grand Rapids: Eerdmans, 2002), 89.

Chapter 8: Expanding Our Field of Vision

1. The author of the article goes on: "This recent group of tormented villains embodies a cultural war in an America anxious over its direction amid restive populations of women and people of color." Jeffrey Fleishman, "America's Anxious Times Made It a Banner Year for Villains and Bad Guys in Movies and TV," *Los Angeles Times*, December 27, 2017, http://www.latimes.com /entertainment/movies/la-ca-hollywood-villains-20171228-story.html.

2. Jolyon Mitchell, *Media Violence and Christian Ethics* (New York: Cambridge University Press, 2007), 11.

3. Mitchell, *Media Violence and Christian Ethics*, 11.

4. Harvey Cox, *When Jesus Came to Harvard: Making Moral Choices Today* (Boston: Houghton, Mifflin, 2004), 8, 25.

5. Kenneth Turan, "Time for an Adult Conversation about R's Failure," *Los Angeles Times*, October 2, 2000, sec. F, 1, 6.

6. Jack Valenti, "The Voluntary Movie Rating System," Motion Picture Association of America, February 22, 1997, quoted in Stan Williams, "Cinema's Divine Destiny" (unpublished manuscript), 56.

7. For a discussion of the Bible's treatment of sex and violence, see Anton Karl Kozlovic, "Religious Film Fears 2: Cinematic Sinfulness," *Quodlibet Journal* 5, no. 4 (October 2003); Brian Godawa, *Hollywood Worldviews: Watching Films with Wisdom and Discernment* (Downers Grove, IL: InterVarsity, 2002), 187–208.

8. One must hasten to add, however, that when a movie's "larger intention" rather than its "raw data" was used by review boards in an earlier era, Cecil B. DeMille became notorious for combining enough piety with his depictions of debauchery to put a thin religious gloss over otherwise salacious scenes. And the ratings were hardly better.

9. To give a famous (infamous?) example, *Midnight Cowboy* (1969) won the Oscar for Best Picture, despite being given an X rating (the earlier NC-17) by Valenti's Rating Board. After being judged to have artistic merit by winning an Oscar, the movie was re-rated by the MPAA and reassigned an R, even though not one frame was altered. Even the Rating Board could not stay only with the "raw data" in this case. Such inconsistency is simply confusing for all involved.

10. Cf. the comments of Janet Robinson, the chairwoman of the Ontario Film Review Board in Canada: "This is my opinion only, but here in Canada we are a little bit more lax on the sexual aspect of [entertainment products] and we're harder on violence. In the States, I think it's the direct opposite. If you show the least little bit of nudity in the States, the Bible Belt down in mid-America just has an absolute fit. Well, for heaven's sakes, we all have breasts, we all have sex, but we're not all violent up here." Quoted in Scott Colbourne, "Battle Heating Up over Gaming Content," *Globe and Mail*, July 27, 2005, R2. In Europe, similarly, there are an increasing number of movies that have transgressed traditional sexual taboo barriers with little public outrage or even interest.

11. Pope John Paul II, quoted in Michael Paulson, "US Catholic Bishops Taking On Death Penalty," *International Herald Tribune*, March 22, 2005, 7.

12. Jim Wallis, *America's Original Sin: Racism, White Privilege, and the Bridge to a New America* (Grand Rapids: Brazos, 2016).

13. Daniel Defoe, *Moll Flanders* (London, 1772), quoted in Steve Turner, *Imagine: A Vision for Christians in the Arts* (Downers Grove, IL: InterVarsity, 2001), 40.

14. Cardinal John Henry Newman, *The Idea of a University* (London: Longmans, Green, 1891), 229.

15. Ron offered these reflections as part of an assignment submitted to Rob Johnston in his Theology and Film class at Fuller Theological Seminary.

16. Cecilia Gonzalez-Andrieu, *Bridge to Wonder: Art as a Gospel of Beauty* (Waco: Baylor University Press, 2012), 23.

17. The notion of "indiscriminately celebrative" is borrowed from Gordon Lynch, *Understanding Theology and Popular Culture* (Oxford: Blackwell, 2005).

18. The phrase "ethical patience" is also from Gordon Lynch (*Understanding Theology and Popular Culture*, ix), who borrowed it from Michael Dyson.

19. This is to describe in general terms an approach that varies in degree and focus from one person to the next. See e.g., William D. Romanowski, *Eyes Wide Open: Looking for God in Popular Culture*, 2nd ed. (Grand Rapids: Brazos, 2007); Brian Godawa, *Hollywood Worldviews: Watching Films with Wisdom and Discernment* (Downers Grove, IL: InterVarsity, 2002); and Michael Medved, *Hollywood vs. America* (New York: HarperCollins, 1992).

20. Mitch Avila, "Responding Emotionally to Film," *Theology, News & Notes* 52, no. 2 (Spring 2005): 22–25.

21. Cf. Frank Burch Brown, *Good Taste, Bad Taste, and Christian Taste: Aesthetics in Religious Life* (New York: Oxford University Press, 2000), xi.

22. Dietrich Bonhoeffer, *Letters and Papers from Prison*, ed. Eberhard Bethge (New York: Macmillan, 1971), 198.

23. These rankings are fluid and constantly changing based on user ratings, but as of September 4, 2018, *The Wolf of Wall Street* is rated 78 percent fresh on Rotten Tomatoes and 8.2/10 on IMDb. Similarly, *The Big Short* has a rating of 88 percent on Rotten Tomatoes and 7.8/10 on IMDb.

24. Defoe, *Moll Flanders*.

25. Sam Adams, "Real Life Hasn't Punished Jordan Belfort. Why Should 'The Wolf of Wall Street'?" *IndieWire*, December 23, 2013, http://www.indiewire.com/2013/12/real-life-hasnt-punished -jordan-belfort-why-should-the-wolf-of-wall-street-127154.

26. Adams, "Real Life Hasn't Punished Jordan Belfort." In making these rather brash claims about the supposed lack of effect that movies have on viewers, one wonders if Adams has ever seen a film like *Requiem for a Dream*.

27. As chief film critic for *Christianity Today* at the time, Alissa Wilkinson was perhaps the most prominent Christian critic who gave the film high marks. "Let's be clear: *The Wolf of Wall Street* is a great and possibly terrific movie, one of the best Scorsese has made in a long while. . . . [Belfort's] in the wrong. That's for sure. But to walk away and not realize we're at least a little complicit, too, would be foolhardy." Wilkinson, "The Wolf of Wall Street: If You Google 'Off the Hook,' This Is Where You Land," *Christianity Today*, December 26, 2013, http://www.christianity today.com/ct/2013/december-web-only/wolf-of-wall-street.html?start=1.

28. Jeffery Overstreet, "Respect the Wolf of Wall Street (The Movie, Not the Man)," *Looking Closer with Jeffery Overstreet*, January 6, 2014, http://www.patheos.com/blogs/lookingcloser/2014 /01/respect-the-wolf-of-wall-street-the-movie-not-the-man.

29. Adams, "Real Life Hasn't Punished Jordan Belfort."

30. Wilkinson, "The Wolf of Wall Street."

31. David Edelstein, "The Wolf of Wall Street Is Thumpingly Insipid," *Vulture*, December 23, 2013, http://www.vulture.com/2013/12/movie-review-the-wolf-of-wall-street.html.

Chapter 9: Encountering the Other

1. Miroslav Volf, *Exclusion and Embrace: A Theological Exploration of Identity, Otherness, and Reconciliation* (Nashville: Abingdon, 1996), 17–21 (emphasis original). For contemporary examples of cultural "cleansings," one need look no further than the "Brexit" vote by the UK citizenry in 2016, which was at least partly the result of a desire to curb the flow of immigrants into the UK and deport "illegal aliens" (read: "unwelcome outsiders"). Similarly, Donald Trump built his entire presidential campaign on promises to erect a literal wall between the US and Mexico, to prevent "radical Islamic terrorism" from coming to the US by banning immigrants from predominantly Muslim countries, and to "Make America Great Again" by favoring the wealthy and privileged elite over and against the have-nots. His eventual election revealed the xenophobia and racism that had long existed just beneath the surface of US culture, and these inclinations were only magnified by the perceived threat of globalization and multiculturalism. This move to "cleanse" various nation-states from the perceived threat of the "other" is not isolated to the US, however. In 2017, Dutch populist Geert Wilders nearly secured the position of Prime Minister in the Netherlands, and much like Trump, Wilders built his campaign on an anti-immigration, anti-European Union platform. Some of his stated goals were "to close Dutch borders to immigrants from Muslim nations, shutter mosques and outlaw Islam's holy book, the Quran." Mike Corder, "Dutch Populist Wilders Warns of Backlash If He Is Frozen Out," *Associated Press*, February 12, 2017, https://www .yahoo.com/news/dutch-populist-wilders-warns-backlash-frozen-092121042.html.

2. Gaye Williams Ortiz, "World Cinema: Opportunities for Dialogue with Religion and Theology," in *Reframing Theology and Film: New Focus for an Emerging Discipline*, ed. Robert K. Johnston (Grand Rapids: Baker Academic, 2007), 84 (emphasis added).

3. Citing Julia Kristev's work, Volf notes: "Sometimes the dehumanization and consequent mistreatment of others are a projection of our own individual or collective hatred of ourselves;

we persecute others because we are uncomfortable with strangeness within ourselves." Volf, *Exclusion and Embrace*, 77–78.

4. Ortiz, "World Cinema," 85.

5. Ortiz, "World Cinema," 74.

6. Margaret R. Miles and Brent S. Plate, "Hospitable Vision: Some Notes on the Ethics of Seeing Film," *CrossCurrents* 54, no. 1 (2004): 22–31, here 25.

7. As Cecelia González-Andrieu has suggested, artists "routinely take the commonplace and defamiliarize it. Artists 'estrange' objects and complicate forms, making 'perception long and laborious.' By taking what is familiar and complicating it, the artist returns life to the everyday; artists 'make a stone feel stony' and arrest the fading of life into 'nothingness.'" González-Andrieu, *Bridge to Wonder: Art as a Gospel of Beauty* (Waco: Baylor University Press, 2012), 102.

8. We owe this insight to Sharon A. Suh, *Silver Screen Buddha: Buddhism in Asian and Western Film* (New York: Bloomsbury Academic, 2015), 85.

9. Suh, *Silver Screen Buddha*, 17.

10. Suh, *Silver Screen Buddha*, 23–24.

11. Suh, *Silver Screen Buddha*, 93.

12. Just imagine if Korean filmgoers understood a film like *Paul Blart: Mall Cop* (1 or 2!) in this way. It may very well expose them to certain Western sensibilities they would have otherwise not encountered (as it did with most viewers), but we would hardly say that their imagination had been expanded or that they had grown in their ability to enter empathetically into the world of the other.

13. Taitetsu Unno, *Shin Buddhism: Bits of Rubble Turn into Gold* (New York: Doubleday, 2001), 19, quoted in Suh, *Silver Screen Buddha*, 121.

14. Suh, *Silver Screen Buddha*, 131.

15. Mathew P. John, *Film as Cultural Artifact: Religious Criticism of World Cinema* (Minneapolis: Fortress, 2017).

16. Antonio D. Sison, *World Cinema, Theology, and the Human: Humanity in Deep Focus* (New York: Routledge, 2012).

17. Sison, *World Cinema, Theology, and the Human*, 2.

18. Volf, *Exclusion and Embrace*, 21 (emphasis removed).

19. Matt Ruskin is the writer and director of *Crown Heights* (2017). This quote is taken from an interview featured in Steven Zeitchik, "Tales of Injustice, Ripped from the Headlines," *Los Angeles Times*, February 5, 2017.

20. Interestingly (and perhaps tellingly), when American evangelicals do acknowledge racial or religious injustice, they perceive *themselves* to be the victims rather than the perpetrators of these injustices. A 2017 poll by the Public Religion Research Institute (PRRI) suggested that, in stark contrast to nearly every other subgroup (religious or otherwise), white evangelical Christians are more likely than their counterparts to say that people who are white, rather than people who are black, experience a great amount of discrimination in the US today, although it is difficult to separate this out from a similar trend that aligns with political party affiliations. What is easier to identify is that white evangelical Christians are the only major religious group in which a majority say Christians face more discrimination than Muslims. Daniel Cox and Robert P. Jones, "Majority of Americans Oppose Transgender Bathroom Restrictions," *Public Religion Research Institute*, March 10, 2017, http://www.prri.org/research/lgbt-transgender-bathroom-discrimination-religious-liberty.

21. "A new study and database crafted by Creative Artists Agency, however, is aiming to take some of the surprise out of box office performance, noting that across every budget level a film with a diverse cast outperforms a release not so diversified. Additionally, the data . . . demonstrates that the average opening weekend for a film that attracts a diverse audience, often the result of having a diverse cast, is nearly three times on average a film with non-diverse audiences." Tre'vell Anderson, "New CAA Study Says Diverse Casting Increases Box Office Potential across All Budgets," *Los Angeles Times*, June 21, 2017.

22. Part of the reason for this phenomenon is related to the particular kinds of movies that tend to premier at film festivals, which are often created, marketed, and consumed as an alternative to standard "Hollywood" fare. Consequently, as Cindy Wong notes in her book on film festival cultures, it is perhaps easier to identify what a "festival film" is not rather than what it is. But for our purposes, Wong's working definition will suffice. She identifies four basic characteristics of festival films: "their seriousness/minimalism in vision and sound; their open and demanding narrative structures; their intertextuality (including their use of 'stars'); and, finally, their subject matter, including controversy as well as freedom." Cindy Hing-Yuk Wong, *Film Festivals: Culture, People, and Power on the Global Screen* (Piscataway, NJ: Rutgers University Press, 2011), 68.

23. Amy Zimmerman, "Casey Affleck's Dark Secret: The Disturbing Allegations against the Oscar Hopeful," *Daily Beast*, November 11, 2016, http://www.thedailybeast.com/articles/2016/11/22/casey-affleck-s-dark-secret-the-disturbing-allegations-against-the-oscar-hopeful.html.

24. Zeitchik, "Tales of Injustice."

25. Reggie Rock Bythewood, quoted in Zeitchik, "Tales of Injustice."

26. Zeitchik, "Tales of Injustice."

27. Robert K. Johnston, "Retelling the Biblical Story of Noah: Jewish and Christian Perspectives," in *Noah as Antihero*, ed. Rhonda Burnette-Bletsch and Jon Morgan (New York: Routledge, 2017).

28. For an insightful analysis of such ideological dismissals of the film *Noah*, see Lisa Swain, "What Is God Saying? Navigating Scriptural Interpretation on Social Media" (PhD diss., Fielding Graduate University, 2018).

29. Brian Mattson, "Sympathy for the Devil," personal website, March 31, 2014, http://drbrian mattson.com/journal/2014/3/31/sympathy-for-the-devil (emphasis original).

30. Friedrich Schleiermacher, *Christmas Eve: A Dialogue on the Celebration of Christmas*, trans. W. Hastie (Edinburgh: T&T Clark, 1890), 10.

Chapter 10: The Trauma of Love in the Films of Christopher Nolan

1. These rankings are fluid and constantly changing based on user ratings. See "Top Rated Movies: Top 250 as Rated by IMDb Users," accessed May 28, 2017, http://www.imdb.com/chart/top.

2. See Box Office Mojo, accessed December 13, 2017, http://www.boxofficemojo.com/people/chart/?view=Director&id=christophernolan.htm.

3. According to Nolan, "The structure [of *Memento*] is intensely linear, but it runs backward." For this reason, we are using the language of a "fractured" narrative rather than "nonlinear." Christopher Nolan, "Rendez-vous with Christopher Nolan," Cannes Film Festival, May 12, 2018, https://www.festival-cannes.com/en/festival/event/rendez-vous-with-christopher-nolan.

4. Craig Detweiler, *Into the Dark: Seeing the Sacred in the Top Films of the 21st Century* (Grand Rapids: Baker Academic, 2008), 75.

5. Detweiler, *Into the Dark*, 62.

6. Detweiler, *Into the Dark*, 80.

7. David Bordwell, *Christopher Nolan: A Labyrinth of Linkages* (Madison, WI: Irvington Way Institute Press, 2013), 34, 37.

8. We owe this insight to Bordwell, *Christopher Nolan*.

9. "Medium shot/long shot, looking rightward/looking leftward, men in different rows/men in the same row; simple but reiterated differences assure immediate comprehension. Just as the repeated framings of their own act clarify the situation, so do these little polarities. Call it redundancy, if you like, but it's also precision and economy." Bordwell, *Christopher Nolan*, 24.

10. Bordwell, *Christopher Nolan*, 40–41.

11. Bordwell, *Christopher Nolan*, 44.

12. Note the similarities to Cornelius Plantinga's *Not the Way It's Supposed to Be: A Breviary of Sin* (Grand Rapids: Eerdmans, 1996).

13. Peter Buffett, "The Charitable-Industrial Complex," *New York Times*, July 26, 2013, http://www.nytimes.com/2013/07/27/opinion/the-charitable-industrial-complex.html.

14. Slavoj Žižek, *Trouble in Paradise: From the End of History to the End of Capitalism* (Brooklyn, NY: Melville House, 2014).

15. Žižek, *Trouble in Paradise*, 229.

16. Žižek, *Trouble in Paradise*, 229–30.

17. Žižek, *Trouble in Paradise*, 230.

18. Tyler O'Neil, "Dark Knight and Occupy Wall Street: The Humble Rise," *Hillsdale Natural Law Review* 21, July 2012, quoted in Žižek, *Trouble in Paradise*, 223.

19. "*This* is why the film deserves a close reading: the Event—the 'people's republic of Gotham City,' dictatorship of the proletariat on Manhattan—is *immanent* to the film; it is (to use the worn-out expression from the 1970s) its 'absent center.' This is why external critique of the film ('its depiction of the OWS reign is a ridiculous caricature') is not enough: the critique has to be immanent, it has to locate within the film itself a multitude of signs which point towards the authentic Event. . . . In short, pure ideology is not possible. Bane's authenticity *has* to leave a trace in the film's texture." Žižek, *Trouble in Paradise*, 231 (emphasis original).

20. Žižek, *Trouble in Paradise*, 234.

21. Merold Westphal, *Suspicion and Faith: The Religious Uses of Modern Atheism* (Grand Rapids: Eerdmans, 1993), 3.

22. Westphal, *Suspicion and Faith*, 84.

23. Craig Detweiler identified this aspect of Nolan's cinematic vision over a decade ago: "[*Memento*] is the ultimate cinematic portrait of original sin." Detweiler, *Into the Dark*, 62.

24. In this paragraph, we are indebted to Tommy Givens, who (through personal correspondence) served as a helpful dialogue partner in shaping our thoughts on Nolan's work and its connection to Paul's conception of sin.

25. Although he develops these themes in numerous places, we are interacting here primarily with John Caputo, *The Folly of God: A Theology of the Unconditional* (Salem, OR: Polebridge, 2016).

26. Miroslav Volf, "Human Flourishing," in *Renewing the Evangelical Mission*, ed. Richard Lints (Grand Rapids: Eerdmans, 2013), 13.

Epilogue

1. John Roger Stephens and Lonnie Rashid Lynn, "Glory," music from the motion picture *Selma* (New York: EMI Music Publishing, 2015).

2. Paul Schrader, "Canon Fodder," *Film Comment*, September/October 2006, http://paulschrader .org/articles/pdf/2006-FilmComment_Schrader.pdf.

3. To guard against this encroachment, after the O. J. Simpson project won, the Academy of Motion Picture Arts and Sciences barred multipart and limited series from the Best Documentary Feature category. Dave McNary, "Oscars: New Rules Bar Multi-Part Documentaries Like 'O.J.: . . . Made in America," *Variety*, April 7, 2017, https://variety.com/2017/film/news /oscars-new-rules-documentary-oj-made-in-america-barred-1202026406.

4. The full conversations with Scorsese and Schrader can be viewed, respectively, at Fuller Studio, "A Conversation on Faith and Film: Martin Scorsese," https://fullerstudio.fuller.edu /a-conversation-with-martin-scorsese-on-faith-and-film, and Fuller Studio, "Conversations with Paul Schrader," https://fullerstudio.fuller.edu/conversation-with-paul-schrader.

5. As an academic and a television producer (respectively), Kutter Callaway and Dean Batali consider the impact of our television watching in *Watching TV Religiously: Television and Theology in Dialogue* (Grand Rapids: Baker Academic, 2016).

select bibliography
of theology and film

Aichele, George, and Richard Walsh, eds. *Screening Scripture: Intertextual Connections between Scripture and Film*. Harrisburg, PA: Trinity Press International, 2002.

Anker, Roy M. *Beautiful Light: Religious Meaning in Film*. Grand Rapids: Eerdmans, 2017.

———. *Catching Light: Looking for God in the Movies*. Grand Rapids: Eerdmans, 2004.

———. *Of Pilgrims and Fire: When God Shows Up at the Movies*. Grand Rapids: Eerdmans, 2010.

Badowska, Eva, and Francesca Parmeggiani, eds. *Of Elephants and Toothaches: Ethics, Politics, and Religion in Krzysztof Kieslowski's "Decalogue."* New York: Fordham University Press, 2016.

Bandy, Mary Lea, and Antonio Monda, eds. *The Hidden God: Film and Faith*. New York: Museum of Modern Art, 2003.

Barsotti, Catherine M., and Robert K. Johnston. *Finding God in the Movies: 33 Films of Reel Faith*. Grand Rapids: Baker Books, 2004.

———. *God in the Movies: A Guide for Exploring Four Decades of Film*. Grand Rapids: Brazos, 2017.

Baugh, Lloyd. *Imaging the Divine: Jesus and Christ-Figures in Film*. Kansas City, MO: Sheed & Ward, 1997.

Bergesen, Albert J., and Andrew M. Greeley. *God in the Movies*. New Brunswick, NJ: Transaction, 2000.

Blake, Richard A. *AfterImage*. Chicago: Loyola University Press, 2000.

Blizek, William L., ed. *The Continuum Companion to Religion and Film*. New York: Continuum, 2009. (Also known as *The Bloomsbury Companion to Religion and Film*.)

Brant, Jonathan. *Paul Tillich and the Possibility of Revelation through Film*. Oxford: Oxford University Press, 2012.

Burnette-Bletsch, Rhonda, and Jon Morgan, eds. *Noah as Antihero*. New York: Routledge, 2017.

Buster, Bobette. *Do Story: How to Tell Your Story So the World Listens*. N.p.: The Do Book Co., 2013.

Callaway, Kutter. *Scoring Transcendence: Contemporary Film Music as Religious Experience*. Waco: Baylor University Press, 2013.

Christianson, Eric S., Peter Francis, and William R. Telford, eds. *Cinéma Divinité: Religion, Theology and the Bible in Film*. London: SCM, 2005.

Clarke, Anthony J., and Paul S. Fiddes, eds. *Flickering Images: Theology and Film in Dialogue*. Macon, GA: Smyth & Helwys, 2005.

Davidson, Elijah. *How to Talk to a Movie: Movie-Watching as a Spiritual Experience*. Eugene, OR: Cascade, 2017.

Deacy, Christopher. *Screen Christologies: Redemption and the Medium of Film*. Cardiff: University of Wales Press, 2001.

———. *Screening the Afterlife: Theology, Eschatology and Film*. London: Routledge, 2012.

Deacy, Christopher, and Gaye Williams Ortiz. *Theology and Film: Challenging the Sacred/Secular Divide*. Oxford: Blackwell, 2008.

Detweiler, Craig. *Into the Dark: Seeing the Sacred in the Top Films of the Twenty-First Century*. Grand Rapids: Baker Academic, 2008.

Downing, Crystal. *Salvation from Cinema: The Medium Is the Message*. New York: Routledge, 2015.

Felix-Jager, Steven. *Spirit of the Arts: Toward a Pneumatological Aesthetics of Renewal*. New York: Palgrave Macmillan, 2017.

Gire, Ken. *Reflections on the Movies: Hearing God in the Unlikeliest of Places*. Colorado Springs: Chariot Victor, 2000.

Hamner, M. Gail. *Imaging Religion in Film: The Politics of Nostalgia*. New York: Palgrave Macmillan, 2011.

Higgins, Gareth. *Cinematic States: Stories We Tell, the American Dreamlife, and How to Understand Everything*. Golden, CO: Burnside, 2013.

———. *How Movies Helped Save My Soul: Finding Spiritual Fingerprints in Culturally Significant Films*. Lake Mary, FL: Relevant Books, 2003.

Holloway, Ronald. *Beyond the Image: Approaches to the Religious Dimension in the Cinema*. Geneva: World Council of Churches, 1977.

hooks, bell. *Reel to Real: Race, Sex, and Class at the Movies*. London: Routledge, 1996.

Jewett, Robert. *Saint Paul at the Movies: The Apostle's Dialogue with American Culture*. Louisville: Westminster John Knox, 1993.

———. *Saint Paul Returns to the Movies: Triumph over Shame*. Grand Rapids: Eerdmans, 1999.

John, Mathew. *Film as Cultural Artifact*. Minneapolis: Fortress, 2017.

Johnston, Robert K. *The Christian at Play*. Grand Rapids: Eerdmans, 1983.

———. *God's Wider Presence: Reconsidering General Revelation*. Grand Rapids: Baker Academic, 2014.

———. *Reel Spirituality: Theology and Film in Dialogue*. Grand Rapids: Baker Academic, 2006.

———, ed. *Reframing Theology and Film*. Grand Rapids: Baker Academic, 2007.

———. *Useless Beauty: Ecclesiastes through the Lens of Contemporary Film*. Grand Rapids: Baker Academic, 2004.

Kickasola, Joseph G. *The Films of Krzystof Kieslowski: The Liminal Image*. New York: Bloomsbury Academic, 2004.

Knauss, Stefanie, and Alexander D. Ornella, eds. *Reconfigurations: Interdisciplinary Perspectives on Religion in a Post-Secular Society*. New Brunswick, NJ: Transaction, 2007.

Kreitzer, Larry J. *Gospel Images in Fiction and Film: On Reversing the Hermeneutical Flow*. London: Sheffield Academic, 2002.

———. *The New Testament in Fiction and Film: On Reversing the Hermeneutical Flow*. Sheffield, UK: JSOT Press, 1993.

———. *The Old Testament in Fiction and Film: On Reversing the Hermeneutical Flow*. Sheffield, UK: Sheffield Academic, 1994.

———. *Pauline Images in Fiction and Film: On Reversing the Hermeneutical Flow*. Sheffield, UK: Sheffield Academic, 1999.

Larsen, Josh. *Movies Are Prayers: How Films Voice Our Deepest Longings*. Downers Grove, IL: InterVarsity, 2017.

Lindvall, Terry. "Religion and Film, Part I: History and Criticism." *Communication Research Trends* 23, no. 4 (2004): 3–44.

———. "Religion and Film, Part II: Theology and Pedagogy." *Communication Research Trends* 24, no. 1 (2005): 3–43.

———. *The Silents of God: Selected Issues and Documents in Silent American Film and Religion, 1908–1925*. Lanham, MD: Scarecrow, 2001.

Loughlin, Gerard. *Alien Sex: The Body and Desire in Cinema and Theology*. Oxford: Blackwell, 2004.

Lyden, John C. *Film as Religion: Myths, Morals, and Rituals*. New York: New York University Press, 2003.

————, ed. *The Routledge Companion to Religion and Film*. London: Routledge, 2009.

Mahony, Cardinal Roger M. *Film Makers, Film Viewers: Their Challenges and Opportunities, A Pastoral Letter*. Boston: St. Paul Books & Media, 1992.

Malone, Peter, ed. *Through a Catholic Lens: Religious Perspectives on Nineteen Film Directors from around the World*. Lanham, MD: Rowman & Littlefield, 2007.

Malone, Peter, with Rose Pacatte. *Lights Camera . . . Faith! A Movie Lover's Guide to Scripture, A Movie Lectionary—Cycle A, Cycle B, Cycle C*. 3 vols. Boston: Pauline Books & Media, 2001–2003.

Marsh, Clive. *Cinema and Sentiment: Film's Challenge to Theology*. Bletchley, Milton Keynes, UK: Paternoster, 2004.

Marsh, Clive, and Gaye Ortiz, eds. *Explorations in Theology and Film: Movies and Meaning*. Oxford: Blackwell, 1997.

Martin, Joel W., and Conrad E. Ostwalt Jr. *Screening the Sacred: Religion, Myth, and Ideology in Popular American Film*. Boulder, CO: Westview, 1995.

May, John R., and Michael Bird, eds. *Religion in Film*. Knoxville: University of Tennessee Press, 1982.

McNulty, Edward. *Films and Faith: Forty Discussion Guides*. Topeka, KS: Viaticum, 1999.

————. *Praying the Movies: Daily Meditations from Classic Films*. Louisville: Geneva, 2001.

————. *Praying the Movies II: More Daily Meditations from Classic Films*. Louisville: Westminster John Knox, 2003.

Miles, Margaret. *Seeing and Believing: Religion and Values in the Movies*. Boston: Beacon, 1996.

Mitchell, Jolyon. *Media Violence and Christian Ethics*. Cambridge: Cambridge University Press, 2007.

————. "Theology and Film." In *The Modern Theologians: An Introduction to Christian Theology since 1918*, 3rd. ed., edited by David F. Ford and Rachel Muers, 736–59. Oxford: Blackwell, 2005.

Mitchell, Jolyon, and S. Brent Plate, eds. *The Religion and Film Reader*. New York: Routledge, 2007.

Overstreet, Jeffrey. *Through a Screen Darkly*. Ventura, CA: Regal Books, 2007.

Plate, S. Brent. *Religion and Film: Cinema and the Re-creation of the World*. 2nd ed. New York: Columbia University Press, 2017.

————, ed. *Representing Religion in World Cinema: Filmmaking, Mythmaking, Culture Making*. New York: Palgrave Macmillan, 2003.

—————, ed. *Re-viewing the Passion: Mel Gibson's Film and Its Critics.* New York: Palgrave Macmillan, 2004.

Ponder, Justin. *Art Cinema and Theology: The Word Was Made Film.* New York: Palgrave Macmillan, 2017.

Reinhartz, Adele. *Bible and Cinema: An Introduction.* London: Routledge, 2013.

—————. *Jesus of Hollywood.* New York: Oxford University Press, 2007.

—————. *Scripture on the Silver Screen.* Louisville: Westminster John Knox, 2003.

Rindge, Matthew S. *Profane Parables: Film and the American Dream.* Waco: Baylor University Press, 2016.

Satchel, Roslyn M. *What Movies Teach about Race: Exceptionalism, Erasure and Entitlement.* Lanham, MD: Lexington, 2016.

Schrader, Paul. *Transcendental Style in Film: Ozu, Bresson, Dreyer.* New York: Da Capo, 1988. Originally published: Berkeley: University of California Press, 1972. Republished with a new introduction: Berkeley: University of California Press, 2018.

Seay, Chris, and Greg Garrett. *The Gospel Reloaded: Exploring Spirituality and Faith in the Matrix.* Colorado Springs: Piñon, 2003.

Settle, Zachary, and Taylor Worley, eds. *Dreams, Doubt, and Dread: The Spiritual in Film.* Eugene, OR: Cascade, 2016.

Siegler, Elijah, ed. *Coen: Framing Religion in Amoral Order.* Waco: Baylor University Press, 2016.

Stone, Bryan P. *Faith and Film: Theological Themes at the Cinema.* St. Louis: Chalice, 2000.

Tarkovsky, Andrey. *Sculpting in Time: Reflections on the Cinema.* Translated by Kitty Hunter-Blair. Austin: University of Texas Press, 1986.

Vaux, Sarah Anson. *Finding Meaning at the Movies.* Nashville: Abingdon, 1999.

Wall, James M. *Church and Cinema: A Way of Viewing Film.* Grand Rapids: Eerdmans, 1971.

Walsh, Richard. *Finding St. Paul in Film.* New York: T&T Clark, 2005.

—————. *Reading the Gospels in the Dark: Portrayals of Jesus in Film.* Harrisburg, PA: Trinity Press International, 2003.

Watkins, Gregory J., ed. *Teaching Religion and Film.* New York: Oxford University Press, 2008.

Wright, Melanie J. *Religion and Film: An Introduction.* London: I. B. Tauris, 2007.

film index

general index

acting, 5, 69, 73–74, 95, 124
aesthetics, 14, 95, 187. *See also* art; beauty
African Americans, 4–5, 35, 40, 105–6, 194–95
ambiguity, 42, 96, 174
Anderson, Paul Thomas, 123–24, 201
Anderson, Wes, 71, 201
Anker, Roy, 120–21
Apostles' Creed, 35
appropriation
  cultural, 5
  of films, 114–15, 121–6
Aquinas, 2
Arbuckle, "Fatty," 29
archetype, 52, 139
Aristotle, 51–52, 56, 92, 96, 104
art(s), 10, 15–16, 51–52, 68–69, 72–74, 90–97,
    106–7
  art direction, 69–71
Assyrians, 149, 153
Atkinson, George, 34
atmosphere, 54–56, 63, 76, 85–90
Augustine, 148
Avila, Mitch, 167
avoidance of films, 114–19, 123–26, 183–85

Barsotti, Catherine, 18–19, 122
Barton, Bruce, 28–29
Bazin, André, 94–97, 100–103
beauty, 35, 64, 104, 132, 146–54, 162–67,
    174–77, 190. *See also* aesthetics
Bechdel-Wallace test, 106
Bible (books referenced)
  Genesis, 64, 71, 152, 158, 164, 223
  Judges, 158
  1 Samuel, 158
  2 Samuel, 158

1 Kings, 219
2 Kings, 158
2 Chronicles, 126, 152, 199
Esther, 54
Job, 5
Psalms, 5, 153
Proverbs, 40, 126, 151, 164, 168, 173, 177
Ecclesiastes, 121, 140, 150, 163, 169, 190–91
Song of Songs, 96, 158
Isaiah, 149, 151, 165
Ezekiel, 165
Micah, 182
Habakkuk, 5
Matthew, 164–66, 173, 183
Mark, 183
Luke, 18, 136, 164, 193
Acts, 126, 153
Romans, 126, 218, 223
1 Corinthians, 199, 222
2 Corinthians, 24
Galatians, 183
Philippians, 161, 165
1 John, 126
Revelation, 44, 121–24, 146, 149, 152–54,
    156
biblical interpretation, medieval, 127–31, 218,
    240n43
Blake, Richard, 121, 240n33
Bonhoeffer, Dietrich, 167
Booth, Herbert, 26, 231
Booth, William and Catherine, 26
Breen, Joseph, 31–32
Bridges, Jeff, 100
Brown, Michael, 195
Brown, Robert McAfee, 147–49
Bruce, David, 36

Buechner, Frederick, 54, 64
Burton, Richard, 22
Burton, Tim, 86

Cagney, James, 30
Callaway, Kutter, 19–22, 24, 121, 161–62, 184, 199
Calvin, John, 2, 148
Calvino, Italo, 50
Campolo, Tony, 122
capital punishment, 161
Capra, Frank, 144
Carlin, George, 117
Carrey, Jim, 140
Catholic League for Religious and Civil Rights, 116–17
Catholics, 30–32, 116, 124, 161
    International Catholic Film Office, 32
celebrity, 15, 173
censorship, 29–34, 114, 135, 161
Chaplin, Charlie, 27
characterization, 38, 55, 98, 204, 210. See also stereotypes
Cheadle, Don, 55
church confrontation with Hollywood, 27–33
cinematography, 68–70, 74–77, 95–96
Clapp, Rodney, 34
Coen, Joel and Ethan, 37, 100
Colbert, Claudia, 29
Colson, Charles, 118–19
communication, 11, 93, 137
Coppola, Francis Ford, 79–80, 84
Corliss, Richard, 35
Cox, Harvey, 156
creation, 35, 64, 74, 124, 132, 152–53, 164, 240n43
    re-creation and, 20, 54, 55, 89, 129, 181
    See also redemption
creativity, human, 51, 60, 70, 77, 94, 152–53
criticism
    auteur, 91, 100–103
    cultural, 91, 104–7
    film, 90–110, 115
    genre, 91, 97–100
    literary, 239n15
    thematic, 91, 107–10
    theological, 36
Cruise, Tom, 13

Damon, Matt, 1
Dante, 128
Davis, Bette, 96

Davis, Damon, 195
Davis, Geena, 13
Davis, Lennard, 130
Defoe, Daniel, 152
DeMille, Cecil B., 28–30, 243n8
Detweiler, Craig, 2, 14, 19–20, 37, 121, 124–25, 128, 204–5, 247n23
Dickson, William, 25
Dietrich, Marlene, 30
Disney (studio), 12, 20, 72, 86, 146. See also Pixar
Disney, Walt, 13
Dorsky, Nathaniel, 121
Dougherty, Dennis Joseph, 30
Douglas, Kirk, 113
Doyle, Christopher, 70
DVD, 34, 40, 142

Eastman, George, 25
Eastwood, Clint, 86, 99–100
Ebert, Roger, 52, 107, 234n9
Edison, Thomas, 25
editing, film, 78–82
Eisenstein, Sergei, 78–79, 91–94, 97, 102–4
Eliot, T. S., 144, 239n15
Elmer, Gregory, 23
empathy, 52, 74, 90, 157, 184
Episcopal Committee on Motion Pictures, 30–31
ethical patience, 166, 176, 243n18
euthanasia, 137
Evagrius, 150
evangelicals, 35, 117, 125, 193, 245n20
evil, 31, 42–44, 52, 55, 58, 97–99, 161–63, 167

Fairbanks, Douglas, 29
family, 21, 53–54, 60, 165
Fellini, Federico, 32–33
feminism, 3, 105, 108–9
film
    biblical interpretation and, 197
    Christian responses to, 113
        appropriation, 114–15, 121–22, 125
        avoidance, 114–17, 125
        caution, 114–15, 117–20, 125
        dialogue, 114–15, 120–21, 125
        divine encounter, 114–15, 123–25
    commercial viability of, 27, 195, 202
    editing, 78–82
    ethics and, 14, 114–15, 118–19, 155–77
    worldview of, 98, 107, 118
    financial crisis of 2008, 168–69

Martin, Catherine, 70
Martin, Joel, 120
Matties, Gordon, 37
May, John, 123–24
McBrien, Richard, 124
Medved, Michael, 33
#MeToo, 110
Miles, Margaret, 118–19, 184
millennium, turn of the, 3, 35, 123, 151, 201
Miller, George, 17–18, 62,
mise-en-scène, 94–97, 100, 209
Mitchell, Jolyon, 156
montage, 22, 78–80, 91–96, 114, 121
moral discourse, 155–77
Morissette, Alanis, 117
Mosjoukine, 78
Motion Picture Association of America, 33, 157
Motion Picture Producers and Distributors of
    America, 29
Mulvey, Laura, 105–6
Murray, Bill, 140
music in film, 4–5, 21–22, 81–88, 121, 210–11

narrative, 10, 13, 22, 35, 39–43
    fractured, 246n3
    lens, 49–65, 203–6
    theology, 234n6
    See also story
Native Americans, 15, 105, 160
Newman, John Henry, 163
Newman, Paul, 99
Newman, Robert, 52
Nicolosi, Barbara, 118–19
Niebuhr, H. Richard, 125–26
9/11, 11, 183, 229n6
Nolan, Christopher, 119, 201–24, 246n3
numinous, 225

O'Connor, Flannery, 128, 240n43
O'Connor, John Joseph, 116
openness, posture of, 33, 119, 148–51
Ortiz, Gaye, 120, 182–83
otherness, encounter with, 184–200
    cultural and religious, 184–92
    racial, 192–96
O'Toole, Peter, 22
Ottman, John, 84
Overstreet, Jeffrey, 37, 123

Pacatte, Rose, 2, 9, 37
parable, 41, 45, 53, 98, 129, 135–38, 140, 210

Parker, Nate, 37, 194
path of beauty, 35
Payne, Alexander, 14
Penn, Arthur, 99
Pennington, Basil, 127
Perry, Joseph, 26
Picasso, 167
Pickford, Mary, 27, 29
Pixar, 20, 72, 146, 235n7. See also Disney
    (studio)
pornography, 119, 170, 184
postmodernism, 57, 102–5, 205, 221
postsecular age, 39, 153
preaching, 18, 36, 114, 120, 162, 194
Preminger, Otto, 32
Prieto, Rodrigo, 74
Production Code, 30–33
production design, 70–72
production process, 69–88
Protestant theology, 124–26
purity, 23, 34, 80, 125, 162–66

Quigley, Martin, 30

Rahner, Karl, 133
ratings, film, 31–33, 157–61
Reay, Pauline, 85
redemption, 44, 64, 120. See also creation
Reed, Ron, 163
Reel Spirituality, 1–2, 23, 36, 162, 227
Renoir, Jean, 95–96, 101
revelation, 121–24, 146, 149, 152–53
Roberts, Jordan, 131, 241n50
Robinson, Edward G., 30
Robinson, Janet, 243n10
Robinson, Phil Alden, 122
Rock, Chris, 117
Rohmer, Eric, 17
Roth, Joe, 39
Ruskin, Matt, 192–95
Russell, Jane, 31–32

sacramentality, 80, 123–26
sadness, 114, 150
salvation. See redemption
Salvation Army, 26
Sandler, Adam, 140
Schindler, Oskar, 55
Schleiermacher, Friedrich, 200
Schrader, Paul, 56, 124–25, 226–27
Schuchardt, Read Mercer, 17